D0455147

Al’ America

Al' America

Travels Through America's Arab and Islamic Roots

JONATHAN CURIEL

NEW YORK
LONDON

Portions of Chapters 2, 8, and 11 originally appeared in the *San Francisco Chronicle*, used by permission.

Published in the United States by The New Press, New York, 2008
Distributed by W. W. Norton & Company, Inc., New York

LIBRARY OF CONGRESS CATALOGING-IN-PUBLICATION DATA
Curiel, Jonathan, 1960-
Al' America : travels through America's Arab and Islamic roots / Jonathan Curiel.
p. cm.
Includes bibliographical references and index.
ISBN 978-1-59558-352-9 (hc.)
1. United States—Civilization—Arab influences. 2. United States—Civilization—Islamic influences. 3. Civilization, Arab. 4. Civilization, Islamic. 5. Arab Americans. 6. Muslims—United States. I. Title.
E169.1.C853 2008
909'.0974927 dc22 2008024217

The New Press was established in 1990 as a not-for-profit alternative to the large, commercial publishing houses currently dominating the book publishing industry. The New Press operates in the public interest rather than for private gain, and is committed to publishing, in innovative ways, works of educational, cultural, and community value that are often deemed insufficiently profitable.

www.thenewpress.com

Composition by The INFLUX House
This book was set in Bembo

Printed in the United States of America

2 4 6 8 10 9 7 5 3 1

For Selma Curiel, who taught her son
to see the world in a different way.

Contents

Contents

PREFACE

The Irony of 9/11

Where the World Trade Center once stood were piles of steel and concrete and bones and disintegrated flesh. Putrid smoke filled the air as rescue crews fought their way to the site where, hours earlier, thousands of people had perished in an apocalyptic inferno witnessed live on national television. All the deaths that morning—the passengers who had been on the planes that smashed into the towers; the stock brokers, engineers, secretaries, and others who worked in the upper reaches of the skyscrapers; the desperate and panicked who jumped from their windows; and the firefighters caught unprepared as the buildings collapsed—seared into the minds of the millions watching the horror unfold minute by minute, second by second. Who on earth could have orchestrated the attacks? Who on earth would be so deranged?

Arabs. Muslims. Men named Atta, bin Laden, and al-Zawahiri.

The backlash began almost immediately. In Anaheim, California, an Iranian-American restaurateur, Mohammed Kasmaei, received a phone call saying, "You can't stay in the U.S."[1] In Fair Haven, Michigan, gas station owner Mazen Mislmanion endured epithets and vandals who shot up his windows.[2] In Dallas, convenience store owner Waqar Hasan—a Pakistani immigrant with a wife and four adolescent daughters—took a gun blast to his face. The killer, who first distracted Hasan by ordering two hamburgers, said he wanted revenge for 9/11. "I did it to retaliate against those who retaliated against us," said Mark Anthony Stroman. "I did what every American wanted to do but didn't."[3]

Instead of shooting Arabs and Muslims, many Americans voiced their revenge fantasies on web sites and Internet forums. In an e-mailed letter published on September 15, 2001, at WorldNetDaily.com—a conservative web site "dedicated to uncompromising journalism, seeking truth and justice"—a reader wrote that President Bush "can end this problem once and for all. Nuke every Islamic nation there is. . . . Nuke 'em and nuke 'em now."[4]

In the hours after 9/11, a similar message ("the Muslims are a bunch of savages that should be nuked off the face of the earth") was found at a more mainstream media site, http://abcnews.com, where this additional posting could be read: "The Islamic way of life, their nations, their culture, must be eradicated."[5]

Their culture. Arab culture. Muslim culture. Corrupt. Un-Godly. Un-American. Anti-American. Must be eradicated.

Beyond the sheer ludicrousness of such an idea is this question: What exactly is Arab and Muslim culture? Is it the promulgation of a unique kind of religious terrorism? Is it a confluence of backward practices that emphasize violence, misogyny, and (ultimately) the conversion of all non-Muslims? Judging by polls in the wake of 9/11, many Americans believe it is reducible to one or both categories. Of those Americans surveyed by the Gallup organization two weeks after the 2001 terrorist attacks, almost a third (32 percent) said that U.S. Arabs should undergo "special surveillance," while almost half (49 percent) said Arab Americans should be required to carry special identification.

Five years later, when the subject turned from "Arab Americans" to "Muslim Americans," Gallup's numbers remained the same: Almost four in ten (39 percent) admitted they were prejudiced against Muslims; almost a fourth (22 percent) said they didn't want a Muslim as a neighbor; almost a third said U.S. Muslims were sympathetic to al-Qaeda; and nearly four in ten (39 percent) said that Muslim Americans should be required to carry special identification.[6]

A 2007 *Newsweek* survey confirmed the malignancy of people's fears: Almost half of Americans surveyed (46 percent) said the United States lets in too many immigrants from Islamic countries; a similar number (41 percent) said they believed that Muslim culture glorifies suicide.[7]

This book is the story of that culture—not the culture of Americans' fears, but the culture of Americans' dreams. The culture that is connected to poetry and architecture and transcendent history. The culture that spawned Atta and bin Laden and al-Zawahiri, but also writer Kahlil Gibran, singer Kazim al-Sahir, and astronomer Abu al-Abbas Ahmad al-Farghani. The culture that over centuries—despite the separation of continents, and despite enmities that continues to plague relations between Arabs and America, and between Muslims and America—has embedded itself into the very soul of this country.

Some of America's most celebrated places—including the Alamo in San Antonio, the French Quarter of New Orleans, and the Citadel in Charleston, South Carolina—retain vestiges of Arab and Islamic culture. Some of America's most recognizable music—including the surf sounds of Dick Dale, and the rock and psychedelia of Jim Morrison and The Doors—is indebted to Arab music. Some of America's leading historical figures—including Elvis Presley and Ralph Waldo Emerson—relied on Arab or Muslim culture for intellectual sustenance. Even the origins of America—Columbus's discovery of the land we know as North America—is intimately connected to Arab and Muslim culture.

America loves irony, loves to laugh at narrative twists that reveal a hidden mystery or two. In sparking a backlash against Arabs and Muslims and their culture, the attacks of September 11, 2001, produced an irony that was decidedly unfunny. Unbeknownst to most Americans, the towers of the World Trade Center were ringed with pointed Muslim-style arches—a style that architect Minoru Yamasaki was proud to exhibit, albeit without fanfare or pretension. The most iconic image of Ground Zero—the photograph by Thomas E. Franklin that shows firemen raising the U.S. flag on the ruins of 9/11—was taken just feet from a ring of Muslim arches that survived the imbroglio.

What is Arab and Muslim culture? It is a multitude of cultures that is more than just religion, and more than Islam. Many Arabs are Christian and other religions, and a significant number of Muslims do not practice their faith. Oxford professor Tariq Ramadan estimates that only 15–20 percent of Muslims around the world actively follow their religion's precepts—that is, pray five times a day, attend Friday early-afternoon prayers (the most significant prayer session of the week for Muslims), perform the *hajj* to Mecca, donate to charity, abstain from alcohol, and follow the other commandments and prohibitions of traditional Islam.[8] In fact, nonpracticing Muslims—what we might call *secular Muslims*—may comprise the majority of the population in some Muslim countries.

Arab and Muslim culture has as many contradictions as other cultures, including that of the United States—a country founded on democratic ideals that enslaved blacks and decimated its native inhabitants. Since 9/11, it has been difficult for some people to see Arab and Muslim culture as anything other than terrorism and fundamentalism. (What if the world saw American culture as nothing more than George Bush, Washington politics, white separatists, and the legacy of slavery—thus ignoring jazz, baseball, Hollywood movies, Marilyn Monroe, Robert Frost, Frank Lloyd Wright, Bob Dylan, Alice Walker, Donald Trump, and everyone and everything else that Americans take pride in?) "Arab" and "Muslim" have become code words of alarm. Many of those I wanted to interview for this book refused to speak with me once they knew the subject matter. Through his publicist, former president George H. W. Bush—who in 1991 inaugurated a memorial garden in Washington, DC, that's dedicated to Gibran—rejected my request for a few minutes on the phone. I wanted to speak with Mr. Bush about Gibran's *The Prophet*, and the way that Mr. Bush helped shepherd the approval of Gibran's garden. Here's what Mr. Bush's assistant, Jim Appleby, told me via e-mail:

> Sir, First of all, thank you for your interest in President Bush's thoughts on *The Prophet*. However, President Bush does not, as a rule, comment on current world affairs. In addition, his extremely busy schedule simply does not allow him the time to participate in an interview or answer any questions at this time.

What does *The Prophet*, first published in 1923, have to do with "current world affairs"? In the aftermath of 9/11, Arab and Muslim culture has become politicized. Let's not be mistaken, though: Even before 2001, even in previous centuries without a "war on terror," Americans both demonized and lauded Arab and Muslim culture. In the past 500 years, no "golden period" existed when Americans completely embraced the culture. In 1852, for example, at the same time that Ralph Waldo Emerson was studying the poetry of Persian Muslims and incorporating it into his lectures and notebooks, lawyer Charles O'Conor—the son of Irish immigrants—was appearing in New York state court and arguing that Muslims had no right to be in America.[9] O'Conor, who would later run for the U.S. presidency, was defending slavery and the rights of two slave owners to transport their "property" to Texas when he said this to the court: "The free white race established this Republic. They made their Declaration of Independence, their Constitution, and their laws, for themselves. They did not intend to invite hither the Asiatic Mohammedan with his seraglio [harem] and his dozen wives."[10]

Al' America is not romanticized history. What it is, is history that confirms a continuous pattern of give-and-take between America and the Arab-Muslim world—a pattern that has incorporated wars, threats, misunderstandings, and, yes, acceptance. The collective history in these chapters had been hidden away before now—scattered in obscure academic tomes and dusty library books; or known in bits and pieces by an elite vanguard of academia; or simply ignored by professors, journalists, and cultural observers who were too busy focusing on the ideological (and military) divisions between East and West. The best-known champion of these divisions—at least among the lawmakers and neoconservatives who pushed for war in Iraq—is Samuel P. Huntington, whose 1996 bestseller, *The Clash of Civilizations and the Remaking of World Order,* posited a cultural clash between states and societies. According to this view, Islamic culture—with its emphasis on violence and absolutism—guarantees that Muslim countries will be a danger to America and the West for centuries to come. In fact, Islamic culture is antithetical to American and Western values and culture, Huntington concluded,[11] before implying that Arab and Muslim culture should never take root in the United States: "Some Americans have promoted multiculturalism at home. . . . Multiculturalism at home threatens the United States and the West. . . . A multicultural America is impossible because a non-Western America is not American."[12]

The backwardness of this statement is compounded by Huntington's use of the Alhambra—the 13th-century Spanish palace that Muslims built when they ruled the Iberian Peninsula—to represent what he says is the implicit fundamentalism of Islamic culture and civilization. The cover of *The Clash of Civilizations* features Alhambra arches that are covered with arabesques and Arabic calligraphy. Does Huntington know that one of America's best-known writers, Washington Irving, visited the Alhambra in the mid-19th century, fell in love with its history and architectural beauty, and then wrote and illustrated a book that subsequently inspired scores of Alhambra imitations in the United States? Islamic arches similar to those on the front of *The Clash of Civilizations* are now embedded in theaters and buildings around the United States—from New York to Los Angeles, including Evansville, Indiana, where a theater takes its name directly from the medieval Muslim fortress-palace. (In Arabic, *Alhambra* means "the red"—a reference to the red brick of the majestic building in Granada, Spain.)

Huntington's warning about a multicultural America comes too late. In the 21st century, the United States is composed of not just Judeo-Christian roots, but Muslim roots, too. Over the centuries, these roots have been badly disconnected from their original sources—so badly that visitors to the Alhambra in Evansville, Indiana, the Alamo in San Antonio, Texas, and the Citadel in Charleston, South Carolina, have no clue that these buildings are connected to Arab and Islamic culture. These links do not make the buildings religious, any more than Elvis Presley's love of Gibran's poetry makes the King of Rock 'n' Roll somehow Arabic. But the history in these pages will require a popular reassessment of America and its relation to Arab and Muslim culture. It's not "their" culture, but "ours." American culture. The culture of America.

Acknowledgments

A work such as *Al' America* requires the blessed assistance of scores of people. Without them, this book would not exist. Among those at the top are Kirsten Neuhaus, a super New York literary agent whose determination and steadfastness guided *Al' America* to a good home; Marc Favreau, The New Press's editorial director, who embraced *Al' America* with the enthusiasm it needed; Dr. Michael Hanssler and Dr. Angela Kuhnen of the Gerda Henkel Foundation, in Dusseldorf, Germany, whose generous financial support allowed me to travel around the United States and do reporting that was crucial to nearly every chapter; Paddy Coulter, who chose me to be a research fellow at England's Oxford University, where (supported by a grant from Gerda Henkel) I did work that inspired *Al' America;* Russell Smith, who brainstormed the book's *Al' America* title during a tête-à-tête at the Royal Oak in Oxford; and the other Oxford stalwarts—Debbie Pout, Jenny Darnley, and Gerald Dorey—who encouraged me.

In San Francisco, I relied on Thomas Centolella, a tremendous friend whose words of wisdom and humor were absolutely essential to writing this book; Zev Curiel-Friedman, the son I always wanted, whose listening to The Doors' music (at age 6) helped me realize that a connection might exist between the group's songs and Arab music; Jody Friedman, whose smarts and understanding have helped for years; Rebecca Curiel, the best writer in the family, whose way of seeing is always an inspiration; Gary Alessi and Shoshanah Curiel-Alessi; Justine Cudel, a great spirit who believed in *Al' America* from the start and was a friend when it counted the most; and Margie Conrad and Dana Tommasino (and their daughter Claire), whose laughter and worldview enlivened me at regular junctures.

At the *San Francisco Chronicle*, I owe thanks to numerous people for promoting the kind of world-affairs and arts journalism that provided the foundation for *Al' America:* former managing editors Robert Rosenthal, Jerry Roberts, and Jack Breibart; former deputy editor Narda Zacchino; former Insight editor James Finefrock; former foreign editors Mark Abel, Andrew Ross, and Gail Bensinger; executive Datebook editor David Wiegand; and assistant Metro editor Erik Ingram. I am also grateful to other former and current *Chronicle* colleagues, including the irreplaceable Paul Wilner, Elizabeth Fernandez, Debra Saunders, Kathleen Rhodes, Erin Allday, Scott Mattoon, Vicki Haddock, Judy Stone, Mike Kern, Leba Hertz, Jesse Hamlin, Rick Nobles, Ruthe Stein, Carla Meyer, Charles Burress, Dan McGrath, Mark Hedin, Mark Camps, Jeanne Carstensen, and Amr Emam (the *Chronicle*'s Daniel Pearl fellow). Others whose influence was essential to *Al' America:* Nettie Hendricks, whose love of arts and culture rubbed off on me in the best possible way, and to whom I am indebted for entering my life; Peter Dodd, the former head of the U.S. Fulbright program in Pakistan; Jamal Dajani, who is—every day—trying to bridge the gap between America and the Arab and Muslim world; the librarian at the San Francisco Public Library, who asked if I knew about Link+, the program that let me request books crucial to my research; and Cinqué Hicks and his copy-editing team, who fine-tuned *Al' America* into a more precise work.

Without the time of all the people I interviewed for *Al' America*, this book would be a shell of itself. I am especially grateful to Ray Manzarek for discussing the music of The Doors; Dick Dale for opening up about his Arab roots; and Ibrahima Seck, a University of Dakar professor who illuminated the connection between blues music and Muslim West Africa. Because art inspires other art, *Al' America* owes much to the musicians whose songs transported me during the reporting and writing of this book: Ali Farka Toure,

Habib Koité, Baaba Maal, Papa Amadou Fall and Cheikhou Coulibaly (aka Pape and Cheikh), Cheikh Lo, Nusrat Fateh Ali Khan, Axiom of Choice, Nick Drake, Afrissippi, Miles Davis, Bill Evans, and John Coltrane.

My mother, to whom this book is dedicated, would be proud of *Al' America*. Most of her life, she devoted herself to issues of peace and justice. For years, she worked for the Equal Employment Opportunity Commission. She was the one who first steered me toward journalism, religion, and the subject of the Middle East. One of her favorite movies was Frank Capra's *It's a Wonderful Life*, in which Jimmy Stewart comes to realize how much he has helped other people in his life. With *Al' America*, I came to realize just how much I rely on other people. No man (or woman) is an island, just as no country—not even the United States—can exist without leaning on other countries for support and inspiration.

Al' America

1

The Seeds of Islam in America: From Columbus to the Alamo

Two weeks earlier, he was sick from gout and a lack of sleep. The intense summer heat also made Christopher Columbus agonize about the welfare of his crew, who were in the seventh week of a grueling 3,000-mile journey across the Atlantic Ocean. Would their food and medical supplies run out? Would the sailors, strained and impatient as never before, consider mutinying? Columbus had been twice already to the land they called "the Indies," the first time with a translator who knew Arabic, but the Arabic interpreter, a Jewish Spaniard named Luis de Torres, was murdered when he stayed behind as a settler. Columbus knew the risks of his trips, but if he had any doubts about his latest venture, he kept them to himself—and as it happened, all reservations vanished that day of July 31, 1498, when an island of wide expanse appeared on the horizon. "A miracle," Columbus said, while the crewmen showed their gratitude by singing the "Salve Regina," an original Latin hymn ("Salve, Regina, Mater misericordiae, vita, dulcedo, et spes nostra, salve") that praises Jesus Christ and the Virgin Mary.[1]

Columbus was now in a generous mood. Two days later, sailing along the coast of the island known today as Trinidad, he marveled at the physical well-being of the young native people who had met his ship, saying in his journal that they were "all of very fine stature, tall and very graceful in their movements; their hair is very long and smooth, and they have their heads bound with certain worked scarves . . . which from a distance appear to be of silk and *almaizares*."[2]

Columbus was using Arabized Spanish when he referred to *almaizares*, a word incorporated into the language when Muslims ruled parts of Spain for 700 years. *Almaizares* means material from a Moorish scarf—that is, a scarf worn by Moors, the Muslims from North Africa who captured and governed much of the Spanish peninsula from 711 to 1492. Columbus's vocabulary was full of Arabized words, including one, *almirante*, that he relied on to sign his most important letters and documents. *Almirante* means "commander," and it stems from the Arabic *al-emir*,[3] which means "the commander." For Columbus, *almirante* was an honorific that signified his control of the high seas for Spain. His full title, given to him by Queen Isabella herself, was *Almirante del Mar Oceano*—"Commander of the Ocean Sea."

In theory, Columbus and Isabella were violently opposed to Arabs, Muslims, and their culture, but the influence of this culture had been so profound on Spain that it spread to the foundations of the country—so much so that it altered Spain's language, architecture, food, and even its ideas. Columbus's motivation for discovering America could even be tied to a Muslim: Abu al-Abbas Ahmad al-Farghani, the ninth-century astronomer whose theories about the Earth's diameter were a cornerstone of European understanding at the time of Columbus's journey. Without al-Farghani, Columbus may not have even attempted his initial voyage in 1492, according to Columbus's first biographer, his son Fernando. Columbus, who studied al-Farghani's calculations in their Latin translation, used the astronomer's Latinized name when he wrote, "I found myself in agreement with Alfraganus."[4]

Beyond al-Farghani, Columbus and other European explorers studied the work of the Arab geographer Abu Abdullah Muhammad al-Idrisi, whose maps set standards of accuracy in the late Middle Ages.[5] Al-Idrisi was the medieval equivalent of a MacArthur grant genius—a scholar who was given enormous amounts of money by the Christian king of Sicily, Roger II, to map out the world's lands and waterways. From 1145 to 1153, al-Idrisi lived in Sicily's capital, Palermo, where he oversaw a staff of assistants who helped him create *Al-Kitab al-Rujari* (*The Book of Roger*), which described—for the first time in one place—intricate details of Africa, Asia, Europe, and beyond, including the extent of differing climates and precise distances between cities of significance. Al-Idrisi had traveled widely before his commission from Roger II, who admired Arab culture so much that he spoke Arabic himself and dressed in robes adorned with stylized Arabic writing known as Kufic. The working partnership between al-Idrisi and Roger II reflected Sicily's history of ties to the Arab and Muslim world—for more than 200 years, Sicily was ruled over by Muslims, and trade between the European island and the Arab world flourished long before and after the end of Muslim rule there in 1072. During al-Idrisi's stay in Sicily, Arabic was still a lingua franca of the country, with official papers of the monarchy published in Arabic (along with Latin and Greek). This was a time in history when Arabs and Muslims were at the forefront of scholarship and exploration, and they enjoyed a cultural cultivation that was the envy of mainland Europe.

In Columbus's day in the late 15th century, cultural commingling between Arab and non-Arab was a common fact in Spain, even as the Christian part of the country waged war with its Muslim Spanish counterparts. In his financial dealings with Queen Isabella and King Ferdinand, Columbus may have talked tough about the need to expel the Muslims from every inch of Spanish territory, but he knew that without Arab knowledge, Spain's discovery of America—his discovery of America—could not have proceeded the way it did. In 1501, a year after his third journey to the Americas, Columbus specifically credited "Moors" (i.e., Muslims) among those who had aided him: "Every sea so far traversed have I sailed, I have conversed and exchanged ideas with learned men, churchmen and laymen, Latins and Greeks, Jews and Moors and many others of other religions."[6]

Throughout his maritime career, Columbus reaped the benefits of improvements that Arabs and Muslims had made to scientific and navigational aids—whether through the advanced cartography of al-Idrisi, the astronomical insights of al-Farghani, the streamlining of the mariner's compass (used for centuries before Columbus by Arabs navigating the Mediterranean and ocean waters), or the contouring of the caravel (the swift, lateen-rigged ships that comprised the *Nina* and *Pinta* of Columbus's first Atlantic voyage). Europeans adopted the caravel from the Arabic *qarib*, lateen-rigged boats used for centuries before their adaptation by European sailors. The triangular shape and angled setting of lateen-rigged boats allowed them to maneuver the winds more efficiently than the upright, square sails that large European ships had relied on before the caravel's advent. "The lateen sail is the special contribution of the Arabs to the development of the world's shipping," historian J.H. Parry noted in his book *The Establishment of European Hegemony*. Historian J.H. Kramers, in a 1931 essay titled "Geography and Commerce," went further, saying that European explorers like Columbus would not have made their way as swiftly without the legacy of Muslim astronomers and mathematicians, whose contributions were crucial to European understanding of geography. "Islamic geographical theory," Kramers wrote, "may claim a share in the discovery of the new world."[7]

Every year, the United States has an official holiday in honor of Columbus and the day (October 12, 1492) that he set foot on soil of the Americas—at San Salvador, in what is now the Bahamas. Columbus never made it to the land that's now the contiguous United States—though on his four voyages he came close, encountering the islands that include Cuba, Haiti and the Dominican Republic (which Columbus named Hispaniola), Puerto Rico, and Barbados. His ships also touched ground on South America and Latin America—ventures that would eventually lead to Spanish colonization of now-U. S. territory.

Americans are still debating Columbus's legacy, which includes widespread evidence that he mistreated native Americans.[8] As administrator of Hispaniola, Columbus oversaw the torture of native people and of Spaniards who crossed him or his brothers Bartolomeo and Diego, who helped govern Spain's islands. Spanish authorities eventually arrested Columbus for the dysfunctional way he ran Hispaniola, bringing him back to Cadiz in chains. He would win back the trust of the Spanish crown and sail again to the Americas, but in 1506—not yet at the age of 60 and in failing health—Columbus passed away. Columbus went to his grave thinking he had really discovered the eastern edge of India. So convinced was Columbus that he named the native people he encountered "Indians."[9]

Columbus could be a stubborn man who ignored evidence that contradicted his beliefs. Even his reliance on the Arab cosmographer al-Farghani was a mistake: Columbus misread al-Farghani's calculations, twisting them around to suit his notion that the distance between Spain and India's eastern flank was shorter than was generally thought. Columbus's recalculation made him (and Isabella and Ferdinand) believe that he would need just several weeks to complete his monumental first voyage. As it turned out, Columbus needed two months to reach America's southeastern edge.

More than 500 years later, Columbus is symbolic of many things—adventure, determination, vision, individual triumph, colonization, subjugation, slavery, oppression. Regardless of how they feel about Columbus personally, many Americans consider his voyage the starting point of their modern history. The seeds that Columbus planted were nurtured by a Spanish culture that, during the colonization of the Americas, continued to reflect the influence of Arab and Muslim traditions. Nowhere is this seen more dramatically than in New Orleans and San Antonio, both of which were under Spanish control before their formal envelopment by the United States.

To understand the story of Muslim culture and the Big Easy requires going back to 1762, when the French relinquished Louisiana to Spain. For the next 40 years (on and off), Spain ruled over the territory, all the while introducing Spanish customs and culture. French administrators were replaced with Spanish ones. Streets took on Spanish names rather than French. French bills and coins were (eventually) dropped for Spanish money, and Spanish became the official language of instruction in public schools. And in New Orleans—after two disastrous fires (the first in 1788, the next in 1794) destroyed most of the city's original French-style houses—Spanish-style houses became de rigueur.[10]

In the late 18th century, "Spanish style" meant a fusion of architectural norms, some of which Spain had adopted from centuries of Muslim influence in the Iberian Peninsula. Ironwork featuring elaborate, geometrical designs—intricate patterns emphasizing "arabesques" that symbolized God's (Allah's) perfection and beauty—was one of these norms. Spain's leaders had expelled the country's Muslims after the Inquisition, but the crown could not stamp out (nor did it want to) Islamic art forms that lingered on, in a nonreligious way, in industries such as metalwork. Even after Granada, Spain's last Muslim kingdom, fell in 1492, thousands of Muslims stayed in the country as *mudejares*—subordinated Muslims who continued to work in trades that maintained a Moorish identity—although in time, Spain's Christians adopted the trades and considered them their own. Arab and Muslim influence was noticeable in a range of Spanish arts, including literature, but ironwork was especially important, historian Martin Andrew Sharp Hume noted in his 1901 book *The Spanish People: Their Origin, Growth and Influence.* Referring to three cities in southern Spain where the Arab-Muslim impact was strongest—Almeria (which takes its name from the Arabic *al-Mariyat*), Murcia, and Seville—Hume wrote that "the Moorish influence on art and handicrafts in the formation of a new national Spanish style of decoration was infinitely greater than in literature. . . . The damascened and chased arms and metal work made by the Mudejares of Almeria, Murcia and Seville were in great request all over Spain."[11]

At the time of its acquisition of Louisiana in 1762, Spain's metalwork industry was still centered in southern (formerly Arab) Spain. After the 1788 and 1794 fires in New Orleans, the city's Spanish overseers relied on that metalwork industry to make the balcony irons that became such an integral part of the Crescent City. When he wrote a definitive guidebook to New Orleans's architecture in 1962, author Stanley Clisby Arthur pointed out homes in the Vieux Carré ("Old Square" in French) that embodied this Moorish character. One example was the building at 343 Royal Street, which was constructed in 1800. Arthur lavished praise on the home's swirling wrought-iron balconies, which he described as "among the finest examples of Spanish craftsmanship to be found in the Vieux Carré. . . . Like most of the early wrought-iron on the balconies of the Quartier, the design is Moresque [Arthur's way of saying "Moorish"] and doubtless the output of some Seville smithy."[12]

Arthur based his book *Old New Orleans* on French and Spanish housing records that went back to the 1700s. The building at 343 Royal Street, Arthur wrote, was constructed for Don Pablo Lanusse, the highest-ranking judge of the Cabildo, the Spanish City Council that governed New Orleans. Lanusse's home is still standing (its street-level storefront is now a high-end antiques store), but like all of the French Quarter houses with Moorish-looking balconies, 343 Royal Street does not advertise its origins to the public. No plaque on an outside wall says that the house was built in 1800, two years before Spain returned Louisiana to France (which then sold it to the United States as part of the Louisiana Purchase). No sign anywhere in the French Quarter elaborates on the 18th-century fires that destroyed most of the French-built architecture and led to the Moorish balconies. In fact, one of the guidebooks I checked before my visit to New Orleans, Frommer's *Portable New Orleans: A Full Post-Katrina Update*, did not even mention Spain's 40-year governance of New Orleans and the major architectural changes that occurred under Spanish administration.

As you walk around the French Quarter, the only public hint

of Spanish influence is the Cabildo (Spanish for "Town Hall"), which is now a museum, and the Spanish-looking plaques that grace some streets and tell tourists of the thoroughfares' old Spanish names. Barracks Street, for example, was called "Calle del Cuartel" (i.e., "Street of the Headquarters") during Spain's rule of New Orleans. Only when I saw these commemorative signs, and then marveled at the arabesque designs that dominate the balconies of the French Quarter, did I wonder whether there was a connection between the French Quarter and the Arab Quarters of Islamic Spain—a curiosity that led me to confirm that link, as well as another startling one: to the most famous building in Texas, The Alamo.

This landmark structure in San Antonio has been mythologized for more than 170 years, ever since an undermanned group of American soldiers bravely held off—for 13 harrowing days and nights—a thousand-strong army commanded by Antonio López de Santa Anna, Mexico's dictatorial president and military leader. In early 1836, Texas was a state of Mexico, albeit a disgruntled one that would soon declare independence from Santa Anna's government. Santa Anna's siege of the Alamo, which was then a key military outpost, led to the bloody deaths of nearly everyone inside, including Davy Crockett, one of America's most famous frontiersmen. The 13-day battle spawned layers of historical accounts—and modern-day movies such as John Wayne's *The Alamo*—that have cemented the building in the public imagination as a military garrison, which it was in 1836. But the Alamo was originally built in 1724 as one of a series of 18th-century Catholic missions in San Antonio—missions that were started by Spain, which had claimed San Antonio as part of its northernmost American territory. The Alamo's formal name is Mission San Antonio de Valero, and its formal style of architecture and design includes a Moorish element, as acknowledged in interpretive material at one of the Alamo's sister missions: Mission San Jose y San Miguel de Aguayo.

Located just five miles south of the Alamo, Mission San Jose is, among the five 18th-century San Antonio missions that survive to this day, "the Queen"—an honorific bestowed because of its size and majesty. Compared to the Alamo, Mission San Jose is a palace, with grounds and an assemblage of buildings that seem to go on forever. Unlike the Alamo, which the group the Daughters of the Republic of Texas runs today, Mission San Jose is overseen by the National Park Service. Where tourists at the Alamo are bombarded with information about the Alamo's role in Texas's war for independence, visitors to Mission San Jose get a big-picture perspective on everything about San Antonio's historic Spanish missions—including their architecture. At Mission San Jose's visitor center, behind a glass display that explains the architecture of all five surviving missions, is this statement: "The architecture of the structures reflected the architectural traditions of Spain, combining the styles of the Renaissance with Moorish design and craftsmanship."

At Mission San Jose, the Moorish design and craftsmanship becomes immediately apparent in paintings that recreate the mission's original 1782 opulence. One painting, part of a display that's located on the mission's outdoor walkway, shows the archways of the convent where the missionaries and lay assistants lived. The archways, featuring alternating red and white bands (called *voussoirs* in architectural language), are exact copies of archways from the Aljama Mosque, the grand Cordoban edifice first built in 784 by Spain's Muslim rulers. These red-and-white archways are a trademark of the Aljama, which was converted into a cathedral after the Reconquista and renamed *La Mezquita* (Spanish for "the mosque"). At Mission San Francisco de la Espada, the southernmost of San Antonio's historic missions, the chapel door is a Moorish horseshoe design straight from the Aljaferia Palace, an 11th-century Islamic fortress built in the northern Spanish city of Zaragoza. At Mission Nuestra Señora de la Concepción de Acuña—the mission closest to the Alamo—the dome would be at home in any number of Moorish mosques in medieval Spain. Spirals at the base of the dome, which resemble mini-minarets, are also rooted in the architectural style of Islamic Spain. (During Columbus's time, Spain's churches frequently borrowed from Muslim architecture, and Columbus himself admired Islamic buildings. During his initial voyage to America, Columbus saw a hill on the Cuban coast and said it resembled "a beautiful mosque.")[13]

What is Moorish about the Alamo? To start with, its front archway, according to historian and journalist Charles Fletcher Lummis, who in a 1908 magazine article referred to the Alamo's "beautifully carved Moorish doorway." Beyond these four words, Lummis didn't elaborate on the doorway, but he didn't have to: His article featured a large black-and-white close-up that accentuates the intricate, geometric floral pattern that dominates not just the door's archway but the rectangular overhang that frames the entire doorway. In architectural terms, this type of elaborate overhang is called an *alfiz*, and it was introduced to Spain in the eighth century via the Aljama Mosque.[14] During Spain's conquest of the Americas, which lasted 300 years, Spanish architects adopted the *alfiz* and other Moorish ideas into scores of churches, including sites in what are today Texas, Arizona, New Mexico, and Mexico. Especially in Mexico, churches that use some kind of Moorish design are ubiquitous—for instance, the Franciscan chapel in the village of Angahuan, which features an intricate *alfiz;* the former convent in Huejotzingo, whose crenellated roofline resembles that of a mosque ("Gothic-Mohammedan design" says one historian); or the Temple of Solitude Church in Tzintzuntzan, whose main doorway is trilobed and topped with a towering *alfiz*.[15] In the United States, Spanish-built churches with Moorish elements include Tucson's San Zavier del Bac, whose dome and roofline are mosque-like; La Parraquia in Santa Fe, New Mexico, a church resembling "a Moorish castle with crenellated towers" that was mostly rebuilt in 1869;[16] and the Mission San Carlos Borromeo de Carmelo in Carmel, California, whose Moorish features include its bell tower.

The Alamo would have had a dome and towers that were similar to its sister Spanish missions, but the Alamo's architectural plans were never carried out before those fateful 13 days in 1836. In the aftermath of the battle, the U. S. Army took over the Alamo, turned it into a military compound, and (in 1850) added the mound roof that now identifies the Alamo as much as the warfare that took place there.[17] During the 30 years that the Alamo was a military headquarters, it went through another major design change that would be hidden to historians for more than a century: Army personnel painted over the Moorish-looking frescoes that ringed the wall and ceiling of the Alamo's former sacristy. Featuring geometric patterns of flowers and pomegranates, the frescoes (which the military deemed "frilly")[18] are a missing link to the Alamo's Spanish-Moorish past. When Bruce Winders, the Alamo's official historian, saw the frescoes when they were first uncovered in 2000, he thought that at least a section of them resembled the geometric forms of Moorish art and architecture. When I interviewed him in 2007, Winders continued to believe that the frescoes are definitely rooted in Moorish culture. "Often," he told me, "what we think of as Spanish comes from that contact with the Moors."

Pomegranates were an important symbol of paradise to the Muslim rulers of Spain, who introduced the fruit to the country. The Muslim prophet Muhammad is reported to have said, "Eat the pomegranate, for it purges the system of envy and hatred." The Alhambra, Muslim Spain's most celebrated palace, features images of pomegranates on its walls. Granada, the city-state made famous by the Alhambra, is named for the pomegranate. When Granada, Arab Spain's last Muslim kingdom, finally fell in 1492 to Spain's conquering Christian armies, King Ferdinand and Queen Isabella ordered the pomegranate to be added to the Spanish flag. When Spain colonized the Americas, they brought pomegranate seeds with them and planted the fruit on American soil. A pomegranate motif can be seen in the chapels of San Antonio's other Spanish missions.

Since Christian traditions have also emphasized the pomegranate, particularly as a symbol of fertility, it is difficult to parse out exactly how much of the pomegranate symbolism in the Alamo is from Moorish influence and how much is purely Spanish. The intricate geometry of the frescoes suggests an obvious Moorish influence. Painted originally in red, orange, and green, the frescoes were only discovered by accident. The sacristy had not been used in decades, and workers were inside removing old flags when one looked up and noticed faint images on the upper reaches of the walls.[19] As it turned out, the whitewashing done by the military in the mid-1800s actually preserved the etchings from dirt and decay. The frescoes were probably painted soon after the Alamo was rebuilt in the mid-1700s; their discovery shows that even a building as well-known and studied as the Alamo can—centuries later—reveal new secrets.

When I toured the Alamo, the frescoes were one of many highlights of the sacristy, but they were not the biggest draw—not even close. The largest crowds gathered around the law book, journals, and other materials left behind by Davy Crockett, the coonskin-cap wearing icon of American valor and determination. Before visiting the Alamo, I had thought that Crockett and his fellow soldiers were almost entirely Anglo-Americans, but the Alamo's band of stalwart defenders included large numbers of Mexican Americans who opposed Santa Anna's governance, and at least one African American, who is listed on an Alamo plaque as "________, John a black Freedman." He is the only one of 189 people on the plaque without a last name.

It is a cliché of sorts, but I will say it anyway: Seeing a historical site firsthand reveals profound details that go missing from travel guides and history books. (Which is not always a good thing: In San Antonio, tourist shops sell all manner of tacky products emblazoned with the rallying cry "Remember the Alamo!"—a vow that once propelled American forces to capture Santa Anna and gain Texas's independence, but now beckons visitors to shell out Franklins for baseball caps, trucker hats, women's thongs, and the like.) In my guidebooks to New Orleans, nowhere is it mentioned that the French Quarter's courtyards are rooted in Spanish-Moorish culture—but they are. Like the ironwork on Spanish homes built in New Orleans, the courtyards were adapted over the centuries in which Europeans commingled with Spain's Arab-Muslim culture.

Open interior space has been an integral characteristic of Islamic architecture since the time of the prophet Muhammad. The world's first mosque—in Medina, Saudi Arabia, where Muhammad led prayer services[20]—featured a courtyard enclosed by outer walls made of mud brick. The holiest site in Islam, the Kaaba in Mecca, is in the courtyard of the Grand Mosque (the Masjid al-Haram). For their residences, Muslims in the Arabian Peninsula, North Africa, and then in Spain incorporated courtyards, which also became a hallmark of Muslim Spain's grandest buildings, including the Alhambra.[21] During Islamic rule in Spain, the most elaborate courtyards also featured fountains and gardens that were supposed to mirror paradise on earth and in heaven. Before and after Spain's Reconquista, the country's architecture adopted this emphasis on courtyard space, and when Spain began colonizing the Americas, this type of architecture followed.

"The Islamic legacy of open space can be seen in the multitude of sixteenth-century Hispano-American buildings with central courtyards and patios," notes historian R. Brooks Jeffery, in his essay "From Azulejos to Zaguanes: The Islamic Legacy in the Built Environment of Hispano-America." "Their application includes all scales and sizes, from houses and provincial mansions to convents and municipal royal palaces."[22]

In New Orleans's French Quarter, this design was applied in the late 18th-century houses built after the Vieux Carré's two disastrous fires. Notable French Quarter houses with courtyards include 710 Toulouse Street, whose outside walls are guarded by two crouching lions. This mansion was built in 1798 and became known in New Orleans as the "Court of the Two Lions"—a title that happens to parallel Court of the Lions, the Alhambra courtyard that features a phalanx of lions standing around a fountain. The French Quarter's "Court of the Two Lions" is popular with tourists and artists, who can be seen taking photos and drawing paintings throughout the day.

The French Quarter's first residential courtyards were a hit with the city's population. After Spain's colonial rule came to an end and Louisiana became part of the United States, New Orleans's architects continued to mimic the Spanish colonial style—including the use of courtyards, which is why Creole houses in the Quarter also have them. In his encyclopedic study *French Quarter Manual: An Architectural Guide to New Orleans' Vieux Carré*, architect and Tulane University professor Malcolm Heard says that the Quarter's Creole town houses are "a regularized version of the Spanish Colonial house." Heard adds that the "denser, more urban French Quarter ground plan we know today, common-wall structures and detached cottages intermingled with courtyards, began to emerge in the Spanish Colonial period."[23]

The French Quarter's historic connection to Muslim Spain does not mean that New Orleans's historic center should now be called "the Muslim Quarter." Likewise, San Antonio's historic connection to Muslim Spain does not mean that the Alamo and its parallel missions should now be called "those Muslim missions." At a basic level, though, the Islamic past of the French Quarter and of San Antonio's historic churches demands a reimagining of these cherished American icons. Of course, they were inherited by the United States when Louisiana and Texas became part of the union—the U.S. took the territories "as is"—but the links to Muslim architecture (and Arab and Muslim culture in general) continued even afterward.

In San Antonio, post-Spanish buildings that fall under the category of "Spanish Colonial Revival" (or, more accurately, "Moorish Revival" or "Islamic Revival") include the Old San Antonio Bank Building. Located on East Commerce Street a few minutes' walk from the Alamo, this two-story structure has an imposing minaret, crenellated roofline, and horseshoe arches—all odes to the time of

Muslim Spain. Built in 1886, the Old San Antonio Bank Building was designed by architect Cyrus Eidlitz, who would later become famous for the Times building that still anchors Manhattan's Times Square. A plaque on the Old San Antonio Bank Building, made by the Texas Historical Commission, acknowledges the former bank's "Moorish arches" but describes its minaret as a "corner tower" and says that the building's overall design is "Victorian"—a label that is completely misleading. (The Alamo's description of its frescoes is also misleading. On a sign meant for tourists in the sacristy, the pomegranate and floral images are labeled "Spanish frescoes.")

In New Orleans, Moorish Revival buildings include the Leon Fellman Building at 801 Canal Street, which employs horseshoe arches, and the Church of the Immaculate Conception at 130 Baronne Street, whose outside showcases horseshoe arches and two domed minarets, and whose inside showcases La Mezquita-like arches. (On its web site, the church takes pride in its Moorish reflection, saying that its original architect, Father John Cambiaso, "while living in Spain . . . became a great admirer of Moorish architecture. He therefore designed this church in the same graceful style.")[24]

As I walked around New Orleans, I saw other reflections of Arab and Muslim culture, from silly to profound. At the silly end was the turbaned fortune-teller named Zoltar, a cloth-and-plastic reproduction of an *Arabian Nights*-like seer, sitting in a booth on Canal Street, waiting for a passing tourist to deposit quarters in his coin slot. More silly (and almost offensive) was the burlesque bar on Decatur Street called the "Whirling Dervish," named after the mystical Islamic brotherhood that originated in Konya, Turkey. The bar's window featured a poster of a turbaned, bikini-clad, nipple-popping woman riding a horse-sized lobster. On the profound side, I saw Senegalese-Muslim merchants selling their wares in the French Market. These recent immigrants have settled in New Orleans to ply their trade, centuries after their ancestors were brought here in bloody chains and sold in such places as Congo Square, the historic New Orleans site that borders the French Quarter.

The new wave of Muslims in New Orleans includes Asim Naseer, a Pakistani American who moved to the Crescent City from New York in 2005. As it happened, Naseer saw the collapse of the World Trade Center towers on 9/11, then experienced Hurricane Katrina in New Orleans. Two major tragedies, and Naseer was on hand for both.

On September 11th, he was in his apartment in Jersey City, New Jersey, which he shared with his sister. Located on an upper floor, their flat had a clear view of the Lower Manhattan skyline. "I was sleeping the morning of 9/11," Naseer told me, "and my sister woke me up."

What Naseer saw horrified him, making him feel so uneasy that he considered moving away from the East Coast. In 2005, after finishing his computer science degree, he decided to live in New Orleans, prodded by two Pakistani American friends who encouraged him to join them. When Katrina hit, Naseer was in a building that protected him from the raging winds that would kill and injure thousands. Like other devout Muslims, Naseer believes that God plans things for a reason—that, somehow, Naseer was put into a witness role for both 9/11 and Hurricane Katrina. I'm sure Naseer would say that my meeting with him was also planned by God. How could it be a mere coincidence that he was my cab driver in my last minutes in Louisiana? (I asked my hotel receptionist—the one who said the city was still suffering a tourism drought in the wake of Katrina—to call me a taxi to take me to Louis Armstrong New Orleans International Airport, and I got Naseer.) On the way to the airport, Naseer told me he liked New Orleans, liked the fact that Muslims from different ethnicities and cultures—white, African American, Pakistani, Indian, and others—attended the same New Orleans mosques. In his native Pakistan, where he was born and raised, "people say, 'This mosque is Shia' and 'This mosque is Sunni,'" he told me. Naseer doesn't believe these divisions should be made, and in America they aren't—at least in New Orleans, where hundreds of Muslims attend mosque services on Fridays, the most important day of prayer in Islam. Naseer is affiliated with the Islamic Center of New Orleans, but there are at least seven other Muslim religious centers from which he can choose. In San Antonio, the situation is the same—a growing Muslim community that parallels a rise in the number of mosques. As in New Orleans, these mosques are all off the beaten path, so tourists who flock to both cities rarely see them or the thousands of Muslim Americans who now call these cities home.

In the Big Easy, the Islamic Center is located in a drab brick building on St. Claude Avenue near Pauger Street—just four blocks from the eastern edge of the French Quarter. Those blocks are a kind of buffer zone between ritzy, world-famous New Orleans and dressed-down, working-class New Orleans. For all intents and purposes, the Muslim religious presence in New Orleans is nonexistent to the city's legions of tourists.

The Big Easy's architectural connection to Muslim Spain is also obscured, but the passage of time can not erase its embodiment there, or in San Antonio. Both cities are a time capsule of the cultural détente that originated on the Iberian Peninsula more than a millennium ago. Even though Spain expelled its Muslims in 1609, and even though it prohibited them from traveling to the New World (any Muslim caught on a ship was subject to death), Arab and Islamic culture was still transported across the Atlantic. It took root here just as it had taken root in Cordoba, Cadiz, and other Spanish cities that Columbus traversed before he set off on his epic voyage to the shores of America.

2

Slavery and Islam: The Roots of American Blues Music

The year is unclear—it could be 1781 or 1787, or somewhere in between. The exact location is also a mystery. Is it the coast of Senegal? Sierra Leone? Gambia? What is not in doubt is that an African Muslim man is in chains on the coast of West Africa. He has been transported to a slave yard, from where he will be put on a ship and taken to a foreign country, most likely America. The slave is angry and confused, but he can do little. He has been captured. He is in a holding area. And within days, he will be sold for a couple of hundred dollars.

"He was a Mahometan, and could read and write Arabick," says a witness, whose account—with its antiquated references and spellings—is included in a 1794 work published in London.[1] The witness says the Muslim slave was "occasionally noisy; sometimes he would sing a melancholy song, then he would utter an earnest prayer, and then would observe a dead silence. This strange conduct, I was told, was from his strong feelings, on having been put, for the first time, in irons, the day before. As we passed, he cried aloud to us, and endeavoured to hold up his irons to our view, which he struck very expressively with his hand, the tear starting in his eye. He seemed, by his manner, to be demanding the cause of his confinement."

While this account is agonizing and heartbreaking to read, the witness preserved for posterity a realistic snapshot of a Muslim slave who—despite overwhelming conditions—maintained his religious regimen. The "melancholy song"? The witness had observed an Islamic recitation—probably the *adhan*, the Muslim call to prayer that, to a non-Muslim, can sound like a soulful and, yes, melancholy ballad. Chanted in Arabic ("*Allahu akbar . . . ash-hadu al-laa ilaha illa-llah* . . . God is supreme . . . I witness that there is no God but God. . . ."), the *adhan* is supposed to inspire Muslims to stop whatever they are doing and devote themselves to prayer. Like music, the adhan uses dramatic octaves, sweeping intonations, and calibrated shifts from major keys to minor ones and back again. Muslims often describe the *adhan* as one of Islam's most riveting rituals (traditionally, it is chanted from atop a mosque's minaret by a reciter called a *muezzin*), and even non-Muslims who hear it are struck by its power and musicality. The English poet Lord Byron, who heard the *adhan* countless times during his travels in Turkey and the Ottoman Europe, said about it in his 1813 work "The Giaour": "On a still evening, when the Muezzin has a fine voice, which is frequently the case, the effect is solemn and beautiful beyond all the bells of Christendom."[2]

"Beautiful" and "solemn" and, more likely, "strange"—that's how the *adhan* must have seemed in America during the slave trade. Upward of 20 percent of the slaves brought to America were Muslims from West Africa.[3] In the slave yards of Louisiana, on the plantations of Mississippi, and in the rice fields of Georgia, Muslim slaves continued to practice their religion and voice their belief in God. Some of them prayed in Arabic, chanted the *adhan*, and uttered the *iqamah*, a recitation that uses almost the exact same language as the *adhan* but is not chanted. Some of them continued to speak African languages that featured large swaths of Arabic. Some of them shouted out in plantation fields they were required to work from sunup to sundown. Decades later, these slaves' practices had evolved—parallel with different African singing traditions—into the shouts and hollers that begat blues music, according to historians and ethnomusicologists, who point to another crucial connection: Muslim slaves sang plaintive songs of their lives in Muslim

West Africa, and they played instruments like the banjo in a way that—similar to the *adhan*—bended notes in atypical major and minor scales.

The key factor, say ethnomusicologists, is that Arab musical and religious modulations had influenced West African culture for centuries before the onset of American slavery in the early 1600s. "The people who brought the blues to the United States were not Arabs, but they were Africans who had been linked with the Arab people for a long, long time," said Ibrahima Seck, a University of Dakar professor who is an expert on the connections between the blues and West Africa, in an interview for this book.

Islam spread to West Africa in the eighth century, when Arab traders from North Africa traveled south in a quest for greater commercial ties.[4] By the 11th century, Islam had taken firm root not just in West Africa's desert areas but in the coastal plains. The acceptance of Islam in Africa was reflected by two dynasties—the 14th-century Malian empire of Mansa Musa, who famously paraded to Mecca for the *hajj* with a caravan laden with thousands of pounds of gold; and the 11th-century rule of the Almoravids, who swept from Senegal northward all the way to Spain, where they ruled until the middle of the 12th century. Slavery between West Africa and the Arab north cemented the commercial and cultural ties between the regions, says Seck.

The only African scholar to lecture on the connection between the blues and West Africa (and someone who is such a fan of the music that he started the Bouki Blues Festival in his native Senegal), Seck says that "for at least for ten centuries, Africans had deported slaves to the Middle East, and Africans were deported to the Middle East, to North Africa, and to the south of Europe, especially to Spain. You had African people who had conquered North Africa and also Spain. We have all these historical links between Africa and the Arabs—they've been linked by trade for many centuries. You see mutual influences on each other. So it's not surprising that the blues sounds like Moorish music or Arab music."

America's slave trade lasted from 1619 to 1865, when the end of the Civil War brought the official end of the practice. In the years afterward, former slaves continued to work on Southern plantations, such as Hopson Plantation and Doherty Farms in the Mississippi Delta. It was in and around the Delta that the blues first began formally. In the Southern states of Mississippi and Louisiana, 60 percent of the slaves were from the former Senegambia region of West Africa—a Muslim-dominated area that, during the centuries of American slavery, "didn't just mean Senegal and Gambia, but south of Mauritania all the way to Sierra Leone to, in the east, Mali," says Seck. "These are the countries that we definitely need to go to in order to find the roots of the blues."

When filmmaker Martin Scorsese wanted to find the roots of the blues for his seven-part documentary series in 2003, he ventured to Mali, where his emissaries met Ali Farka Toure, whose twangy guitar-playing is so reminiscent of John Lee Hooker that Scorsese called Toure "the DNA of the blues." Toure, who was raised a devout Muslim, blended all his cultural elements into his music. If his songs sounded bluesy, he told me when I interviewed him outside of Timbuktu, it was because the music of African American blues singers was based on a collective memory of Africa that carried forth in slavery. "I am the root and trunk, and they are the branches and leaves," he told me, using an analogy that he used often with journalists. To another reporter, Toure once said, "There are no American blues. The word 'blues' is an American invention. This is a word that describes my tradition."

That tradition includes Islamic and Arabic singing styles that have inhabited Mali since before the time of Mansa Musa. Though Toure did not specifically cite the influence of Arab-Islamic culture on his music in his interview with me (or in those with other reporters), this influence can be heard in his songs' dissonant notes and guitar patterns in which he switches from major to minor keys, according to ethnomusicologist Gerhard Kubik. In his 1999 book *Africa and the Blues*, Kubik writes that "Arabic-Islamic singing techniques are a centuries-old heritage in Mali, and they persist in some of Ali Farka Toure's music. Many of the similarities actually perceived by listeners between his music and the blues are due to the fact that these techniques have been continued both in Mali and in the blues."[5]

Scorsese's documentary series, which was watched by millions, never mentioned the Arab-Islamic cultural connection to Toure's music, but it did highlight—for one of the few times before a broad audience—the blues' connections to West Africa. At the Delta Blues Museum in Clarksdale, Mississippi, the first display that visitors see showcases an African harp called a *kora* and photos of blues musician James "Super Chicken" Johnson visiting Senegal. John Lee Hooker Jr., a blues guitarist who followed his father into the business, tells me that "it's common sense" that the music stems from African Americans' preslavery period in Africa. When Hooker Jr., whose father was born and raised in Mississippi, visited Tunisia and Morocco to perform, "it was a very great experience because I knew that [Africa] is where they got us from," he tells me.

Besides the blues, the influence of Africa and Arab-Muslim culture can be heard in the Gullah language, which is spoken by the progeny of the Gullah people—slaves from West Africa who were brought in large numbers to Georgia and South Carolina to tend the rice harvests that became a crucial part of the South's slave economy. In 1949, Fisk University professor Lorenzo Dow Turner published his landmark work *Africanisms in the Gullah Dialect*, which shows that the South's Gullah language is infused with Arabic. Among the words stemming from Arabic are *sali* ("to pray"), *sadaka* ("almsgiving"), *anebi* ("a prophet"), *araba* ("Wednesday"), *alama* ("a sign"), *alansaro* ("three-o'clock prayer time"), *alkama* ("wheat, grain"), *alura* ("needle"), and *ala* ("God").[6]

Perhaps the most intriguing word is the Gullah for "ring dance," *saut*, which stems from an Arabized African word that Turner says means "to move around the Kaaba (the small stone building at

Mecca which is the chief object of the pilgrimage of Mohammedans) until exhausted."

Like the blues, the ring shout is an emotional and powerful musical form derived from African American slavery. Performed by the Gullah in the South during and after slavery times, the ring shout involves a group of people circling counterclockwise around a room. As Turner notes, that is the same direction used by Muslims performing their religious duties in Mecca. Ring shouts, which also involve call-and-response singing, hand-clapping, and percussion that intensified as the circling continued, were popular during slavery in the coastal areas of Georgia and South Carolina. "It's not surprising that the ring shout flourished in coastal areas where there are many other documented examples of African, including Afro-Arabic, survivals," notes author Art Rosenbaum in *Shout Because You're Free: The African American Ring Shout Tradition in Coastal Georgia*.[7] Though the ring shout has been historically associated with Christian spirituals, its connection to Islamic culture links it to another slave spiritual, the "Bell Done Ring." This tune was still being performed in the 1930s in the Georgia Sea Islands, when folklorist Lydia Parrish recorded it and noted its similarities to a West African song that had been recorded near Timbuktu. The Timbuktu work was "a war song" that ethnomusicologist Laura C. Bolton documented for her *African Music* collection. The musicians performing Bolton's song were Tuareg, Muslim nomads who are now concentrated in Mali, Libya, Algeria, and Mauritania. Parrish was stunned by the similarities between "Bell Done Ring" and the Tuareg war song, which she called "strikingly similar . . . even to the particularly reedy quality of tone," and then added, in language that is archaic by today's standards: "Our coastal Negroes appear to be musically more closely allied to the Tuaregs than to any other African tribe of whose songs I have been able to secure records. Record 86-B of the same [Bolton] series gives a lullaby song by a Tuareg woman which—except for the difference in language—might be sung by a grandmother anywhere along this coast."[8]

Bolton's series, which has been reissued on CD, features several Tuareg songs that seem to be the ones Parrish referred to in her 1942 book, but all of them are infused with what can be called Arabic-Islamic music patterns. When I interviewed Seck and played one song—a solo performance featuring a Tuareg man on *guimba*, a kind of West African guitar—Seck nodded his head and said, "Listen to the way he plays—the guitar is not perfectly tuned, like the blues singers do here, too."

"Here" is the United States, where Seck lived briefly in 2007 to do a research project in New Orleans. With Seck, I went to Congo Square, the historic outdoor space where, in the 1700s and 1800s, slaves used to congregate on Sundays and dance, shout, sing, and play music. Now part of Louis Armstrong Park, which (post-Katrina) is cordoned off by a high metal gate that keeps out visitors, Congo Square is eerily silent today[9]—a harsh contrast to its role as an incubator of African American music. In 1886, journalist and novelist George Washington Cable described a pre–Civil War Congo Square that had "gangs and gangs" of congregants, including those who were "wilder than gypsies; wilder than the Moors and Arabs whose strong blood and features one sees at a glance in so many of them."[10] In 1819, when British-American architect Benjamin Latrobe visited Congo Square, he was shocked by the cacophony of noise emanating from its perimeter, and by the instruments being played, including one he described as having strings, a calabash, and a "rude figure" of a sitting man atop the finger board. "No doubt," Latrobe wrote, the instrument "was imported from Africa."[11]

Instead of importing musical objects, though, African slaves often made them out of material they found—wood, string, and other objects. Long after slavery ended, poor Southern blacks still resorted to found objects to help make music. Around 1903, W. C. Handy saw a musician at a train station in Tutwiler, Mississippi, use a knife to play a song about hardship. Handy, whose parents were slaves, would go on to earn the moniker "Father of the Blues" for the way he formalized blues music over a 40-year career of writing songs and playing the cornet, but in that moment in Tutwiler, "the blues" hadn't been born yet.

"A lean, loose-jointed Negro had commenced plucking a guitar beside me while I slept," Handy wrote in his 1941 autobiography. "His clothes were rags; his feet peeped out of his shoes. His face had on it some of the sadness of the ages. As he played, he pressed a knife on the strings of the guitar. . . . The effect was unforgettable. His song, too, struck me instantly. . . . The singer repeated the line ("Goin' where the Southern cross' the Dog") three times, accompanying himself on the guitar with the weirdest music I had ever heard."

The song was about a nearby train station where different train lines intersected. As Handy noted, "Southern Negroes sang about everything. Trains. Steamboats, steam whistles, sledgehammers, fast women, mean bosses, stubborn mules—all became subjects for their songs. They accompany themselves on anything from which they can extract a musical sound or rhythmical effect, anything from a harmonica to a washboard. In this way, and from these materials, they set the mood for what we now call the blues."[12]

While washboards, in fact, became popular among later blues musicians such as Robert Brown (known as "Washboard Sam"), the technique that Handy witnessed—that of pressing the back of a knife blade on guitar strings—can be traced to Central and West Africa, where, as Kubik points out in *Africa and the Blues*, people play one-string zithers that way.[13] Handy assumed that the technique, now called "slide guitar," was borrowed from Hawaiian guitar playing, but it's more likely that the itinerant guitar player that Handy met in Tutwiler was manifesting his African roots. Kubik, a professor of ethnomusicology at the University of Mainz in Germany, has traveled to Africa many times for his research and has lived there, and his book is the most comprehensive on the subject of Africa's connection to blues music.

Kubik believes that many of today's blues singers unconsciously echo Arabic-Muslim music patterns in their songs. Using academic language to describe this habit, Kubik writes that "the vocal style of many blues singers using *melisma*, wavy intonation, and so forth is a heritage of that large region of West Africa that had been in contact with the Arabic-Islamic world of the Maghreb since the seventh and eighth centuries."[14] (*Melisma* is the use of many notes in one syllable; *wavy intonation* refers to a series of notes that veer from major to minor scale and back again, something that's common in both blues music and in the Muslim call to prayer, as well as in recitation of the Quran. The Maghreb is the Arab-Muslim region of North Africa.) Kubik summarizes his thesis this way: "Many traits that have been considered unusual, strange and difficult to interpret by earlier blues researchers can now be better understood as a thoroughly processed and transformed Arabic-Islamic stylistic component."[15]

African-Muslim slaves contributed to this component by playing instruments in an Arabic-Islamic song style. In fact, Kubik writes, Muslim slaves from Africa gravitated toward stringed instruments because in the Muslim regions of West Africa a long tradition exists of musical storytelling with stringed instruments. Drumming, which was common among slaves from the Congo and other non-Muslim regions of Africa, was banned by white slave owners, who felt threatened by its ability to let slaves communicate with each other and by the way it inspired large gatherings of slaves. Stringed instruments were generally allowed because slave owners considered them akin to European instruments such as the violin.

Focusing on the rural blues of the deep American South, Kubik says that this music is "stylistically an extension and merger" of two general "song-style traditions" from West Africa: an Arab-Islamic one that emphasizes "*melisma*, wavy intonation, pitch instabilities within a pentatonic (five-note) framework, and a declamatory voice production"; and a more ancient tradition of "pentatonic song composition, often associated with simple work rhythms in a regular meter, but with notable off-beat accents."[16]

Africa and the Blues contains a map that details those countries in West Africa where the blues originated. The core area—the part of Africa that Kubik says gave birth to the rural blues' most characteristic traits, including an emphasis on solo performing, stringed instruments, and words that seem to shake in the singer's vocal chords—are today and were at the time of American slavery heavily Muslim, including Mali and northern Nigeria.

Among the first people to publicly suggest a connection between the blues and Africa's Arab-Islamic traditions was Oxford scholar Paul Oliver, who in his 1970 book, *Savannah Syncopators: African Retention in the Blues*, described Muslim slaves in America, including Salih Bilali, a prominent slave hand on Georgia's Sapelo Island. Oliver, whose book divided African tribes into several that were primarily Muslim, was followed in 1972 by author John Storm Roberts, who wrote in his book *Black Music of Two Worlds* that the Muslim call to prayer's "relatively simple but long and highly decorated, very characteristic Arabic melodic approach found its way into much African music."[17] Roberts wrote that he could hear Arab musical patterns in the blues and jazz songs of Billie Holiday.

"I refer to the frequent bending of notes, reminiscent of Islamic African music," Roberts wrote. "The bending of notes is, as we have seen, of major importance in vocal blues, producing quartertones especially at the third and fifth and seventh of the scale. It has continued throughout jazz history, principally as a carryover from the blues. . . . It has been most common, of course, among singers. Billie Holiday used it with the greatest variety perhaps not only in the blues but in popular songs as well. As sung by her, a note may (in the words of Glenn Coutter) begin 'slightly under pitch, absolutely without vibrato, and gradually be forced up to dead center from where the vibrato shakes free, or it may trail off mournfully; or at final cadences, the note is a whole step above the written one and must be pressed slowly down to where it belongs.' Coincidence or not, all these features are found in Islamic African music."[18]

How much of a link exists between Muslim culture and American blues music is still being debated. Some scholars insist that there is no connection, and many of today's best-known blues musicians would say their music has little to do with Arab or Islamic culture. Because little documentation exists about the slave-time origins of blues, it's easy to argue about what can be linked to Africa and Muslim culture. Muslim and Arab culture have certainly been influences on other music around the world, including flamenco, which is rooted in seven centuries of Muslim rule in Spain, and European Renaissance music, which derived its lutes from the Arabic *oud* that Muslims brought to the Iberian Peninsula.[19]

What people now think of as blues music developed in the 1890s and early 1900s in Southern U.S. states such as Louisiana, Mississippi, and Alabama. Blues music was an outgrowth of all the different music that was then being performed in the South, from minstrels to street shows. Early blues performers didn't recognize the music's African or Muslim roots because, by then, the songs had more fully merged with white, European music and had lost their obvious connections to a continent that was 4,000 miles away. Also, by the turn of the 20th century, the progeny of America's Muslim slaves had generally been converted to Christianity, either by force or circumstance. Among Southern blacks in that period, there were few exponents of Islam. As more people research that period in history, though, they see plenty of signs that weren't obvious 100 years ago.

Cornelia Walker Bailey, a Georgia author whose great-great-great-great-grandfather was Bilali Muhammed of Sapelo Island, says that the African and Muslim roots of Southern U.S. traditions are often mistaken for something else. Bailey, who visited West Africa in 1989, lives on Sapelo Island, where many blacks can trace their ancestry to Bilali Muhammed. As Bailey describes in her memoir *God, Dr. Buzzard, and the Bolito Man*, Bilali was a Muslim slave born and raised in what is now the African nation of Guinea. An educated man, he spoke and wrote Arabic, carried a Quran and a prayer rug, and wore a fez that likely signified his religious devotion. Bilali had been trained in Africa to be a Muslim leader; on Sapelo Island, he was appointed by his slave master to be an overseer of other slaves.[20] Although Bilali's descendents adopted Christianity, they incorporated Muslim traditions that are still evident today.

Visitors to Sapelo Island are always struck by the fact that churches there face east. In fact, as a child, Bailey learned to say her prayers facing east—the same direction that her great-great-great-great-grandfather faced when he prayed toward Mecca—and says that the separation of men and women in her Sapelo Island church is "another Muslim tradition."[21] For his daily religious rituals, Bilali used a traditional Muslim prayer rug. He carried around traditional Muslim prayer beads. He wrote and read Arabic, and kept a journal that began with the *bismillah* ("In the name of God the merciful, the compassionate . . ."), an invocation that observant Muslims include on all their religious writings.[22] Bilali's grandchildren eventually adopted Christianity and changed their name to Bailey, but the name Bailey, in fact, is a reworking of the name Bilali, which became a popular Muslim name in Africa because one of Islam's first converts—and the religion's first *muezzin*—was a former Abyssinian slave named Bilal. (The Salih Bilali that Paul Oliver wrote about was another slave, not Bilali Muhammed, though the Bilalis knew each other.)[23] One historian believes that abolitionist Frederick Douglass, who changed his name from Frederick Bailey, may also have had Muslim roots.[24]

"History changes things," Bailey tells me. "Things become something different from what they started out as." A good example is the song "Little Sally Walker." It's been recorded by many blues artists, but it's also been recorded as "Little Sally Saucer" because the lyrics describe a girl "sittin' in a saucer." Frankie Quimby, a relative of Bailey's who also traces her roots to Bilali, says the song originated during slavery on the Georgia coast, written by songwriting slaves who took their slaveholder's last name, Walker, as their own. "I've seen [people] take the song and use different words," says Quimby, who sings slave songs with her husband in a group called the Georgia Sea Island Singers. "It was created by our ancestors as 'Little Sally Walker.' They were people on Sapelo Island with the last name."

Many Muslim slaves in the American South insisted on keeping their original names, even if their masters chose a Christian name for them. Salih Bilali, who was born in what today is Mali, was called "Tom" by his slave owners on St. Simon's Island, Georgia. Bilali Muhammed was referred to as "Ben Ali" by white biographers in the years after slavery.[25] Ayuba Suleiman Ibrahima Diallo, a Senegalese slave in Maryland in the early 1730s, was known as "Job Ben Solomon." Like Bilali Muhammed, Diallo publicly maintained his Muslim faith, but unlike Bilali—who was treated with respect by his owner—Diallo experienced degrading conditions. Frequently, as Diallo prayed in public, a white boy would mock him and throw dirt in his face. Diallo ran away, wound up in prison, and befriended a lawyer named Thomas Bluett, who was impressed by Diallo's "affable" nature and his ability to write Arabic. The publicity about Diallo's literacy and belief in Islam prompted a British philanthropist and abolitionist to arrange for his release, and within a year, Diallo had become one of the few American slaves who paid for his freedom and returned to his native West Africa. On the way, Diallo would write the Quran from memory, meet with Queen Caroline of England, and compose his biography with the help of Bluett. Published in English and titled *Some Memories of the Life of Job*, the biography documents Diallo's adherence to Islam, including his refusal to drink alcohol or eat pork, or to eat other meats unless they had been prepared by strict Muslim standards.[26]

Omar ibn Said, a Senegalese Muslim who spent five decades enslaved in South and North Carolina, wrote his own biography in Arabic.[27] In it, Said begins with the *bismillah*, writing "In the name of God, the merciful the gracious—God grant his blessing upon our Prophet Mohammed. . . ." Said maintained his observance of Ramadan during his first years as a slave, and spoke about performing the *hajj* to Mecca as a young man in West Africa, but he came to accept Christianity, according to Christian observers at the time. In his own research on Said, scholar Allan D. Austin, a specialist in antebellum American history, questions whether Said really converted to Christianity, suggesting that Said's apparent change of faith could have been a superficial way of appeasing his overseers. What is not in doubt is that Said is one of a select number of Muslim slaves whose biographical details—and image—were recorded in great detail while he was alive. A daguerreotype of Said, taken in the 1850s or 1860s when he would have been in his 80s, survives to this day. So do several of Said's Arabic manuscripts, one of which is displayed in the only American museum devoted to Islamic culture: the International Museum of Muslim Cultures in Jackson, Mississippi.

How the museum was established in Jackson—in the months before 9/11—is an incredible story in itself. In short, the museum's two Muslim American co-founders, Emad al-Turk and Okolo Rashid, live in the Jackson area and saw the need to create a place that paid tribute to the culture of Islam. The museum does that by detailing the contributions that Muslims made in Islamic Spain, Africa, the United States, and elsewhere. (Located on the second floor of Jackson's major downtown arts center, the museum was originally in a storefront that al-Turk and Rashid redesigned to resemble the Great Mosque of Cordoba, otherwise known as Aljama Mosque or "La Mezquita.") The museum's display on American slavery shows the types of iron masks, neck collars, and leg shackles that were used to punish slaves and restrict their movements. A bill of sale from 1844, from the hand of a J. W. Allison, is written in a casual manner: "I have on this day sold . . . [for] $535 . . . a man slave twenty four years of age." Next to that are images of slaves working in the cotton fields of the south, slaves in handcuffs, and then Omar ibn Said's autobiography. The cover page was written by Said's handlers, and reads, "The Life of Omar ben Saeed Called Morro, a Fullah Slave in Fayetville N.C. Owned by Governor

Owen, Written by Himself in 1831 to Old Paul." Rashid and al-Turk made a copy of an inside page, which reveals the distinctive Arabic script that Said could still write. Though Said would later lament that his knowledge of Arabic had dissipated, the Arabic from his autobiography is perfectly patterned, with Said even using vowel diacritics—marks above and below letters to indicate their specific pronunciation. (Modern Arabic leaves out these diacritics.) Said's autobiography, loaned to the museum by its owner, is the only surviving one written in Arabic by an American slave.

Other Muslim slaves in America, including Ibrahim Abd ar-Rahman, the princely son of an African king, wrote biographies in Arabic, but these biographies—cited in records of the day—have never been found. Abd ar-Rahman is the best-known of America's Muslim slaves—a man whose dramatic life story has inspired a serious academic profile (the book *Prince Among Slaves* by historian Terry Alford), a documentary film (based on Alford's book) that was broadcast on PBS, and countless articles, both in the United States and West Africa, where Abd ar-Rahman returned after being enslaved for 40 years. Born in Timbuktu, he was captured by a rival tribe in 1788, sold into bondage, and sent to Natchez, Mississippi, where around 1807, while selling potatoes on the streets of Natchez, he saw the only white American to have lived in his father's kingdom of Timbo (now a part of Guinea). John Coates Cox had become stranded in Timbo after leaving his ship and hurting his leg. Abd ar-Rahman's father, King Alman Abrahim, took in Cox for six months, then paid for Cox's trip back to America. In Natchez, when he realized who Abd ar-Rahman was, Cox immediately tried to buy his freedom, but Abd ar-Rahman's owner refused. Only in 1828, after his owner died and a newspaper editor took up his cause, did Abd ar-Rahman gain his release—a passage to West Africa that was preceded by a tour across the northern United States, during which time he met with President John Quincy Adams at the White House and raised money to get his children out of slavery.[28]

"There were a lot of Muslim slaves who came to America," says Guelel Kumba, a Muslim musician from Senegal who now lives in Mississippi. "I definitely know Abd ar-Rahman. He's a Fulani—I'm the same tribe."

Kumba, who resides in Oxford, Mississippi, a college town about five hours north of Natchez, laments the horrors of slavery. He knows about Mississippi's legacy—its role as an exploiter of slavery, where cotton plantations were run by generations of West African families, and its post-slavery status as the birthplace of the blues. If anybody symbolizes the passage of time and the possibilities of positive change, it's Kumba, who performs in a band called Afrissippi that features white and black musicians and plays bluesy songs mixing melodies and rhythms from West Africa and the American South. (On drums is Kinney Kimbrough, the son of iconic Mississippi blues singer Junior Kimbrough, whose guitar work is almost a facsimile of Ali Farka Toure's.) Kumba, who graces the cover of Afrissippi's first album by standing with his guitar in a Mississippi cotton field, believes there is a link between the blues and the Muslim call to prayer.

"It sounds like Fulani music," Kumba says of the call to prayer. "For sure, that area of West Africa was Muslim for a while. We are Muslims since the seventh century. I can say for sure that there is Arabic influence in West African music, but also, there is a lot of African influence in Arabic music. I know the blues is less originally African than [it is] Arabic or Islamic."

While Muslim slaves from West Africa were just one factor in the formation of American blues music, they were a factor, says Barry Danielian, a trumpeter who has performed with Paul Simon, Natalie Cole, and Tower of Power. Danielian, who is Muslim, says non-Muslims find this connection hard to believe because they do not know enough about Arabic or Muslim music. The call to prayer and other Muslim recitations, such as Sufi *zikr* chants, which entail loud chanting and even jumping up and down, have musicality to them, even if Westerners do not think of them as music, Danielian says.

"In my congregation," says Danielian, who lives in Jersey City, New Jersey, "when we get together, especially when the shaykhs [leaders] come and there are hundreds of people and we do the litanies, they're very musical. You hear what we as Americans would call soulfulness or blues. That's definitely in there."

In terms of popular culture, it is hard to find a single work—whether a novel, movie, song, or other art form—that covers the intersection of Muslim culture, music, and African slaves. *Daughters of the Dust*, Julie Dash's 1991 film about life on the Sea Islands of Georgia, features a Muslim man who portrays Bilali Muhammed, but a scene that shows him in prayer lasts just a few moments, and the movie received limited release. *Roots*, Alex Haley's novel that was made into a historic television series in the 1970s, features a main character (Kunte Kinte) who is Muslim.

The trading of African slaves created a diaspora unlike any other in human history, with at least 10 million Africans bought and sold into bondage in the Americas and elsewhere.[29] The pain felt by those slaves is evident in American blues music—a music that is often about cruel treatment, sad times, and a yearning to break free. Blues music is a unique American art form that travelled around the world and, in turn, influenced history. Without the blues, there would not be jazz, nor would there be the bluesy music of the Rolling Stones and the Beatles, whose early songs are basically Delta blues tributes.

Blues music, with its strong tempos and many lyrical references to relationships, has been described as "the devil's music" by those outside it. Many conservative Muslims think of blues music as decadent and indicative of permissive Western morals. But people such as Gerhard Kubik; Sylviane Diouf, author of *Servants of Allah: African Muslims Enslaved in the Americas*; and Moustafa Bayoumi, an associate professor of English at Brooklyn College, City University of New York, who has researched Muslim culture's connections to American music, are trying to correct the public record. Bayoumi wrote a paper several years ago that examines African Muslim history in the United States. In it, he argues that John Coltrane's best-known album, *A Love Supreme*, features Coltrane saying, "Allah supreme" in addition to the many refrains of "a love supreme."

"It's about uncovering a hidden past," says Bayoumi in an interview, asked about the spate of new scholarship on the subject of Islam and African Americans. "You can hear [influences of Muslim culture] in even the earliest days of American blues music. What you've gotten lately is an ethnomusicology that's trying to reconstruct that. These are deliberate attempts to rebuild a bridge, as it were."

Diouf, a scholar at New York's Schomburg Center for Research in Black Culture, is rebuilding that bridge by giving talks about the connections between Islam and the blues. She knows her audience might be skeptical, so to demonstrate the connection, she plays two recordings: The *adhan* and "Levee Camp Holler," an early type of blues song that first sprang up in the Mississippi Delta more than 100 years ago.

"Levee Camp Holler" is no ordinary song. It is the product of ex-slaves who worked moving earth all day in post–Civil War America. The version that Diouf uses in presentations has lyrics that, like the call to prayer, speak about a glorious God. But the song's melody and note changes are what most closely resemble one of Islam's best-known refrains. Like the call to prayer, "Levee Camp Holler" emphasizes words that seem to quiver and shake in the reciter's vocal chords. Dramatic changes in musical scales punctuate both "Levee Camp Holler" and the *adhan*, and a nasal intonation is evident in both.

"I did a talk a few years ago at Harvard where I played those two things, and the room absolutely exploded in clapping, because [the connection] was obvious," says Diouf. "People were saying, 'Wow. That's really audible. It's really there.' "

Today, people who visit Senegal, Mali, and other Muslim West African countries can hear these same elements not just in mosques but in the street, from musicians performing and even beggars uttering music-like prayers to passersby. "I don't know historically what the basis is (for the blues), but I do know that the Baye Fall (an Islamic brotherhood) in Senegal play songs that are very closely similar to what I've heard of American blues," Vieux Farka Toure, the only son of Ali Farka Toure to go into music, tells me. "The same would be true of a lot of the traditional songs for Muslim beggars in the street—they sound a lot like blues chants."

The blues emerged out of the horrors of slavery, which killed millions of Africans and transported those who survived into an unfamiliar world of cruelty and hardship, where their language, religion, and values were cut away for profit. Against all odds, these slaves did not completely capitulate, did not entirely relinquish the culture handed down to them in Africa by their forefathers. A few lucky ones managed to travel back home, but the rest were forced to remain where they were. In their lifetimes, they saw hints of an America that would one day embrace their culture and apologize for the suffering it had wrought. Abd ar-Rahman's 1828 meeting with President Adams and Secretary of State Henry Clay was one such hint. "They both received me very kindly," Abd ar-Rahman wrote to his children, adding that Clay "invited me to partake of the hospitalities of his house."[30] It would take another 100 years, though, before the culture of African Americans was looked at by most of their fellow citizens as anything beyond poor and pitiful. Blues music helped unite Americans, made them realize they had a new cultural tradition. Almost a century later, the blues remains a powerful force, and scholars from around the world are interpreting it anew for generations that want a better understanding of its unsettling past.

3

Emerson and Persian Poetry: The Transcendentalists Find Their Reflection in Southern Iran

Every day, somewhere in America, Ralph Waldo Emerson is quoted in public—not just by academics and poets, of which Emerson was both, but by those who Sly Stone might call "everyday people." In ABC-TV's "One Life to Live" soap opera, the character played by actress Erika Slezak—a woman named Viki who endured stroke, breast cancer, and heart disease—cited Emerson as she sat with friends for Thanksgiving dinner, saying, "For each new morning with its light,/For rest and shelter of the night,/For health and food,/For love and friends,/For everything thy goodness sends."[1] Trying to sell more sink faucets, power drills, and potting soil, Orchard Supply Hardware showcased Emerson in its TV campaign for a big no-sales-tax sale. Orchard's tagline was "Every advantage has its tax—Ralph Waldo Emerson."[2] In an antiwar rant against George W. Bush, political activist and former CIA analyst Ray McGovern—after questioning the president's intelligence—cited Emerson's oft-used saying, "A foolish consistency is the hobgoblin of little minds."[3]

Emerson is America's historic yogi—a Harvard-educated wise man who was of his time and beyond it, whose wisdom is now embraced by both liberals and conservatives, working class and upper class, pop-culture hipsters and postdocs in pedagogical philosophy. Apt to be labeled everything from "The father of transcendentalism" to "America's first public intellectual" to "The poet who hung out with Thoreau and Whitman," Emerson embodies the best of American virtues and values. In the mid-1800s, he was a moral crusader who opposed slavery. He was a dissident theologian who tried to reform the stodgy precepts of his religious elders. He was a charismatic activist who urged people to be self-reliant—not in an egregious, materialistic way, but in a way that fostered self-awareness and respect for nature. Emerson was also an internationalist—someone genuinely concerned not just with foreign affairs but the historic connections between people of different continents. These are Emerson's lasting gifts to America—the depth behind the quotes that still inspire people and sustain the livelihoods of soap opera writers, ad execs, and political pundits.

"Every advantage has its tax"? That is taken from his 1841 essay "Compensation," in which Emerson argues forcefully that beauty and truth can't be bought—that no shortcuts exist to gain the grace and respect of others (and God), that the moral principles of life, what Emerson calls "character," apply to people everywhere, whether they live in post-Puritan New England or (as Emerson cites as a contrast) Muslim Turkey.[4] To stress this point of shared humanity, Emerson writes that "the proverbs of all nations" contain the same elements of "absolute truth."[5]

"A foolish consistency is the hobgoblin of little minds"? That is taken from the 1841 essay "Self-Reliance," in which Emerson argues that people have to be nonconformist—not just with society's expectations but their own expectations.[6] Relying on outside sources for true inspiration or approval—from religious figures, from scholars, or even from your own family—is a tragic mistake. Dare to break free of your own (outdated) thinking and a fear of contradicting yourself, and you will have reclaimed your soul, he says. Do not scour "the lustre of the firmament of bards and sages"[7] or travel halfway around the world—to places like Thebes, Palmyra (Syria), or Rome[8]—when the answers are in your very being. To emphasize this point, Emerson cites Imam Ali, the son-in-law of the Muslim prophet Muhammad, whom Shi'ites believe was Muhammad's rightful heir: "The Caliph Ali," Emerson writes, said, "Thy lot or portion of life is seeking after thee; therefore be at rest from seeking after it."[9]

That Emerson quote on *One Life to Live?* It is unclear exactly where that passage is from (I could find no essay, sermon, or book anywhere that contained the recitation), but Emerson talked about Thanksgiving—and giving thanks—countless times in his writings, including his 1841 essay "Friendship," in which he says, "I awoke this morning with devout thanksgiving for my friends, the old and the new. Shall I not call God the Beautiful, who daily showeth himself so to me in his gifts?"[10] That same collection of essays, which are among Emerson's most esteemed work, features an essay titled "Love" that—in its very first words—quotes from the Quran: "I was as a gem concealed;/Me my burning ray revealed."[11]

Emerson was not a Muslim. He was a Unitarian minister, from a long line of ministers, who devoted himself to Scripture. But when Emerson resigned as pastor from Boston's Second Church in 1832, he embarked on a spiritual odyssey that would see him embrace the literary and religious traditions of the East, including Islam, and including Sufi-Muslim poetry from Persia. To read much of Emerson's most vaunted work is to see multiple references to Persian-Muslim culture, sprinkled like gold dust in his books, essays, and notebooks. The Persian poets Hafiz and Saadi became Emerson's spiritual twins—men from other centuries whose own sense of the divine mirrored Emerson's and earned them Emerson's unbridled devotion. Until almost the day he died, Emerson championed Hafiz, Saadi, and the universalism of disparate religions, including Islam. In 1865, for instance, Emerson wrote the preface for the American edition of Saadi's *Gulistan* ("Rose Garden"), in which Emerson lauded Saadi and agonized that more Americans weren't familiar with Persian, Arab, and "Eastern" poets.[12]

"The slowness to import these books into our libraries—mainly owing, no doubt, to the forbidding difficulty of the original languages—is due also in part to some repulsion in the genius of races," Emerson wrote, before adding: "When once the works of these poets are made accessible, they must draw the curiosity of good readers. It is provincial to ignore them. . . . We wish that the present republication may add to the genius of Saadi a new audience in America."[13]

The genius of *Gulistan* is its insight into human behavior, the playful and entertaining way it tells stories of fortune and misfortune, its word choices, its layered (and hidden) meanings, and its reassuring sense that the world—that God—always provides, even if there are trials and tribulations that (in the end) snag those who deserve to be snagged. Written in the year 1258, when the Mongols had overrun the Persian empire and sacked Baghdad, *Gulistan* is a road map to living well in a world where rulers and the ruled are tempted by excess. How should kings treat their enemies? Is it good to borrow money from friends? How much should people eat without getting fat? Can a teenager of feeble education get straightened out before it's too late? It's all in the *Gulistan*, in the form of anecdotes, parables, allegories, metaphors, and witticisms that are as timeless as they are provocative. Emerson called *Gulistan* a kind of bible.

"A man without hope speaketh boldly; as the cat, when driven to dispair, seizeth the dog," reads a couplet from the opening story of *Gulistan*.[14]

In a later tale, a Sufi dervish visits Baghdad, where a corrupt and violent governor named Hojaj Yousuf summons him:

> *A Durwesh, who never prayed in vain, made his appearance at Bagdad. Hojaj Yousuf sent for him and said, "Offer up prayer for me." He said, "O God take away his life." Hojaj asked, "For God's sake what kind of prayer is this?" He answered, "It is a salutary wish for yourself and for all Moslems. O thou powerful wretch, who oppressest the weak, how long will this violence*

> *continue? Of what use is thy government? It is better that thou shouldst die, because thou art an oppressor of mankind."*[15]

This is what happens in Saadi's *Gulistan*—righteous dervishes speak their minds to kings without fear of punishment. Sufism, the mystical branch of Islam that stresses an infinite love for God and the courage to make correct moral choices, occupies a prominent place in the book. Saadi was a high-ranking Sufi who devoted his book to God, writing a rhapsodic preface that, like the words in the body of the work, are poetic and reverential, as in "The rain of his infinite mercy refresheth all places,"[16] and "By His power, the juice of the cane is converted into delicious honey."[17]

In Sufi poetry, sweet tastes like honey and transportive drink like wine become potent symbols of the divine. In *Gulistan* and other Sufi works, they can be taken literally, but usually they are substitutes for spiritual sweetness and intoxication. In *Gulistan*, this is evident in a story about a young man who sees a beautiful girl on the street and becomes apoplectic with desire. Typical of Saadi, the story has an unforeseen twist.

"I cast my eyes on a beautiful girl," the narrator says, recalling the incident of his youth.

> It was in the autumn, when the heat dried up all moisture from the mouth, and the sultry wind made the marrow boil in the bones, so that, being unable to support the sun's powerful beams, I was obliged to take shelter under the shade of a wall, in hopes that some one would relieve me from the distressing heat of summer, and quench my thirst with a draught of water. Suddenly, from the shade of the portico of a house, I beheld a female form, whose beauty it is impossible for the tongue of eloquence to describe; inasmuch that it seemed as if the dawn was rising in the obscurity of night, or as if the water of immortality was issuing from the land of darkness. She held in her hand a cup of snow

> water, into which she sprinkled sugar and mixed it with the juice of the grape. I know not whether what I perceived was the fragrance of rosewater, or that she had infused into it a few drops from the blossom of her cheek. In short, I received the cup from her beauteous hand, and drinking the contents, found myself restored to new life. The thirst of my heart is not such that I can be allayed with a drop of pure water; the streams of whole rivers would not satisfy it. How happy is that fortunate person whose eyes every morning may behold such a countenance! He who is intoxicated with wine, will be sober again in the course of the night; but he who is intoxicated by the cup bearer, will not recover his sense until the Day of Judgment.[18]

In his preface to *Gulistan*, Emerson lauds Saadi for his "wit, practical sense, and just moral sentiments,"[19] and compares the Persian poet to Benjamin Franklin for the way that Saadi "has the instinct to teach, and from every occurrence must draw the moral."[20] Emerson began seriously reading Persian poetry in the early 1840s, discovering the poets via translations in German, which he read fluently. So taken was he with Saadi (who, like Emerson, was a poet and a religious scholar) that, in 1842, he published a poem called "Saadi" in the pages of the transcendentalist periodical *The Dial*.[21] The poem is a tribute to a poet to whom God had given the gift of music and lyricism. The Saadi of this poem faces obstacles in his path, just like the real Saadi did. Born and raised in the southern Iranian city of Shiraz, the original poet left as a teenager to study in Baghdad, not to return to Shiraz for more than 40 years; during this time, he embraced Sufism, performed the *hajj* to Mecca as many as 14 times,[22] and traveled around the Middle East, Asia, and Africa. At one point, he was captured by Crusaders in Syria who forced him into a work detail, but Saadi managed to flee, and on his return to Shiraz he found a patron who supported his poetry. *Saadi* means "fortunate" in Persian, Emerson noted, and his poem "Saadi" describes a poet blessed by Allah, who sends him "the good of truth."

The Quran captivated Emerson, and his reading of the Muslim holy book in the early 1840s coincided with his immersion in Persian poetry.[23] By 1850, the Quran and Persian poetry would intersect in Emerson's "Representative Men," a work about history's inspirational figures in which Emerson notes that

> The Koran makes a distinct class of those who are by nature good, and whose goodness has an influence on others, and pronounces this class to be the aim of creation: the other classes are admitted to the feast of being, only as following in the train of this. And the Persian poet exclaims to a soul of this kind, "Go boldly forth, and feast on being's banquet; Thou art the called, the rest admitted with thee."[24]

Transcendentalism was about self-transcendence—about connecting to higher principles without a constant drumbeat of authoritarian prescription—and Emerson believed these ideals were evident in Saadi, Hafiz, and Sufism. In 1845, Emerson read an English translation of a medieval Persian book called *The Practical Philosophy of the Muhammadan People*, whose original title (*Akhlak-i-Jalaly*) Emerson thought should be translated as "Transcendental Ethics."[25] In his journals, Emerson quoted from this book 50 times,[26] with one biographer saying that Emerson "tended to do more of his Islamic browsing there than in the Koran itself."[27] Sayings from *The Practical Philosophy of the Muhammadan People* showed up in what many critics consider Emerson's greatest work, the 1860 essay collection *The Conduct of Life*. In it, Emerson pleaded for a new spiritual awakening in America on the eve of the Civil War, writing that

> The religion which is to guide and fulfill the present and coming ages, whatever else it be, must be intellectual. The scientific mind must have a faith which is science. "There are two things," said Mahomet, "which I abhor, the learned in his infidelities,

> and the fool in his devotions." Our times are impatient of both, and specially of the last. Let us have nothing now which is not its own evidence.[28]

Later on in *The Conduct of Life*, Emerson writes, "The Persians have thrown into a sentence: 'Fooled thou must be, though wisest of the wise: then be the fool of virtue, not of vice.'"[29]

Both passages are indebted to *The Practical Philosophy of the Muhammadan People*—the sort of borrowing that prompted Emerson biographer Robert D. Richardson Jr. to say that "Islam had a major impact on Emerson, especially but not exclusively through Sufi poetry."[30]

Among the founding members of America's transcendentalist movement, Emerson was the one who most consciously gravitated toward Islam and Sufi poetry, but the movement's other major figures—including Thoreau—also followed suit, even if they did nothing more than dip their toes into the fountains of Sufism and its literature. In a crucial section about breaking free of convention, Thoreau cited Saadi and *Gulistan* in his seminal work *Walden*.[31] In it, Thoreau suggests that more people should follow the lead of the *azad*s in *Gulistan*—"religious independents" who, like cypress trees, flourish in all seasons. Two years before *Walden* was published in 1854, Thoreau wrote a long journal entry in which he described Saadi as his soul mate—he carried around Saadi in his very being, and by default, Saadi was alive and well in 19th-century America.[32] Thoreau referred to Saadi as "Sadi," using one of the many Anglicized versions ("Seyd" is another) of the poet's name.

"The entertaining a single thought of a certain elevation makes all men of one religion," Thoreau wrote.

> It is always some base alloy that creates the distinction of sects—thought greets thought over the wildest gulfs of time with unerring free-masonry. I know for instance that Sadi entertained once identically the same thought that I do—and thereafter I

> can find no essential difference between Sadi and myself. He is not Persian—he is not ancient—he is not strange to me. By the identity of his thought with mine he still survives. It makes no odds what atoms serve us. Sadi possessed no greater privacy or individuality than is thrown open to me. He had no more interior and exterior and sacred self than can come naked into my thought this moment. Truth and a true man is something essentially public not private. If Sadi were to come back to claim a personal identity with the historical Sadi he would find there were too many of us—he could not get a skin that would contain us all. . . . By living the life of a man is made common property. By sympathy with Sadi I have embowelled him. In his thoughts, I have a sample of him, a slice from his core.[33]

Thoreau read *Gulistan* because of Emerson.[34] Before their falling out in 1848 over Thoreau's first book, *A Week on the Concord and Merrimack Rivers* (a commercial flop that he subsidized after Emerson's encouragement), the two were close friends. Walden Pond, where Thoreau lived between 1845 and 1847, was on Emerson's Massachusetts property, and Thoreau moved into Emerson's house immediately after his subsistence-living experiment at Walden was over. (Emerson was in Europe on a lecture tour.) Because of Emerson, Thoreau also took interest in Hafiz, which lead Thoreau to cite the Persian poet in his first book. Islam also was of interest to Thoreau, but not nearly in the way that it was to Emerson. For Thoreau, the Muslim faith was simply a subject of reference, as in his essay "Walking," in which he complained bitterly about Americans' lethargy in the 1850s. "It's remarkable how few events or crises there are in our histories, how little exercised we have been in our minds, how few experiences we have had," Thoreau wrote. "It would be well if all our lives were a divine tragedy even, instead of this trivial comedy or farce. Dante, Bunyan, and others appear to have been exercised in their minds more than we: they were subjected to a kind of culture such as our district schools and colleges do not contemplate. Even Mahomet, though many may scream at his name, had a good deal more to live for, aye, and to die for, than they have commonly."[35]

What was happening in the 1850s that Americans would "scream" at the name of the Muslim prophet? For Americans who read the *New York Times*, there was a steady stream of news from around the world that described an Islamic barbarism unrivaled by any other religion. If it wasn't the murder of American missionaries in Turkish-controlled Syria, or the killing of an English teacher in Turkish-controlled Jerusalem ("Another Mussulman Outage," the paper headlined), it was a Muslim riot in Bombay, India, that injured a woman ("Mussulman Riot at Bombay"), a deadly Wahhabi takeover of Islam's most revered mosques in Mecca and Medina ("The Holy Places Desolate"), or the indiscretions of the Ottoman Empire's Grand Sultan, whose multiple relationships with women were characterized in this way in a big 1853 feature story: "The Padishah never marries. While his royalty is considered a statelier thing than that of other potentates, his domestic morality brings him down to the level of the animals—begging the animals' pardon for saying so."[36] The same story said that the sultans' sons "are instructed in all the maxims of religious obedience as well as despotic authority," while the *Times* report on the Wahhabi's 1851 insurrection said that the Quran had a "primitive simplicity."[37] Beyond these reports were the *Times*'s blatant anti-Muslim references in stories that had nothing to do with Islam. The lead story in its August 3, 1858, edition was a stinging critique of President James Buchanan that went: "No doubt can any longer exist as to the line of personal policy which the President has marked out for himself, and is pursuing—a line almost as narrow and dangerous as the single hair from the beard of Mahomet, on which the faithful are bridged over to Paradise and its waiting joys."[38]

In 1850s America, Islam was publicly disparaged for two main reasons: (1) Americans knew little about the religion, which is evident by the way that Muslims were called either "Mahometans," which implied that they were adherents of the prophet Muhammad (not of God), or "Mussulmans," which made them seem like "musclemen" (i.e., muscle-bound brutes). For example, Webster's 1856 *American Dictionary of the English Language*, which described a "Mussulman" as a "Mohammedan, or follower of Mohammed," also listed three descriptive words that could be used for Muslims: Mussulmanic, Mussulmanish, and Mussulmanly ("in the manner of Mussulmans").[39] (2) Most of what Americans knew about Islam was filtered through the lens of war, especially war involving the Ottoman Empire, which—despite its rapid eclipse—was still viewed as a menacing threat by Christian countries, and still had nominal control over the Holy Land and its sacred Christian (and Jewish) sites.

Washington Irving, America's best-known writer in the early- to mid-1800s, was among those who interpreted Islam in both illuminating and problematic ways. Irving, whose literary reputation was sealed with "The Legend of Sleepy Hollow" and "Rip Van Winkle," wrote a two-volume book about Muhammad and Islam that described the Muslim prophet as a "voluptuary," meaning that he was fixated on sex and luxurious items. Published in 1850, *Mahomet and His Successors* featured this passage:

> In some respects he was a voluptuary. "There are two things in this world," he would say, "which delight me, women and perfumes. These two things rejoice my eyes, and render me more fervent in my devotion." From his extreme cleanliness, and the use of perfumes and of sweet-scented oil for his hair, probably arose that sweetness and fragrance of person, which his disciples considered innate and miraculous. His passion for the sex had an influence over all his affairs. It is said that when in the presence of a beautiful female, he was continually smoothing his brow and adjusting his hair, as if anxious to appear to advantage.[40]

Still, *Mahomet and His Successors* took an approach to Islam that—

compared to the vicious attacks happening from other sources—was relatively well-balanced. For instance, Irving said that Islam retains such high ideals as respecting strangers and feeding the poor without consideration of compensation. He also endowed Mohammad with many positive characteristics, including "intellectual qualities [that] were undoubtedly of an extraordinary kind."[41]

Mahomet and His Successors, which provided Thoreau with much of his information about Islam,[42] was a hit with many American literary critics. A periodical called the *United States Magazine and Democratic Review* said that "it is scarcely necessary to add, that the romantic story of the founders of the Moslem faith, is here told with a perspicuity and grace which has seldom been equaled."[43] The review's description of a "romantic story" pinpoints the reverence that some Americans had for Islam's history and its followers. At least at a literary level, Americans could find inspiring aspects of Arab and Muslim culture. Irving's book was the continuation of nearly a century of writing that tried to make parallels between America and the Arab and Muslim world. In 1779, Benjamin Franklin—who was familiar with Saadi's poetry—published "An Arabian Tale," a short story about a retired Arab magician named Albumazar who gets advice from a tall genie about the vagaries of evil. The story, one analyst said, helped Franklin come to terms with his own doubts about God's existence.[44]

In 1797, novelist Royall Tyler published *The Algerine Captive*, which centers on a New England Calvinist who is captured and enslaved by Algerians. Despite the central character's trying conditions, he finds that Islam and Christianity have much in common, and he pronounces

> Neither their Alcoran nor their priests excite them to plunder, enslave or torment. The former expressly recommends charity, justice and mercy towards their fellow men. I would not bring the sacred volume of our faith in any comparative view with the Alcoran of Mahomet; but I cannot help noticing it as extraordi-

> nary that the Mahometan should abominate the Christian on account of his faith, and the Christian detest the Mussulman for his creed when the Koran of the former acknowledges the divinity of the Christian Messiah, and the Bible of the latter commands us to love our enemies. If each would follow the obvious dictates of his own scripture, he would cease to hate, abominate and destroy the other.[45]

Tyler's novel was published at a time of dramatic tension between America and North Africa (which was ostensibly part of the Ottoman Empire). Between 1785 and 1796, Algerian vessels captured more than 10 American ships and 100 American crewmen, keeping some of the Americans hostage for a decade. A treaty ended the piracy attacks by Algeria, but the terms required annual payments—bribes, basically—to guarantee that U.S. schooners would be safe in Mediterranean waters. Continued American disputes with the so-called Barbary States led to two wars—the first from 1801 to 1805, the final one in 1815—that cemented America's sense that Muslims were contemptible.[46] (In the first Barbary War, a U.S. military unit led by William Eaton and Presley O'Bannon made a dramatic attack on the stronghold of Derna, Libya, which convinced Tripoli's leader to negotiate an end to the war. In thanks to the troops, the rightful heir to the Tripoli throne, Hamet Karamanli, gave O'Bannon a Mameluke scimitar that became a model for the U.S. Marines that is still used today. The expression "to the shores of Tripoli" remains part of the official Marines hymn.)[47]

Three years after the second Barbary War, a Boston editor wrote a fictional work about a spy for the Otttoman Empire, Ali Bey, who travels in disguise to the United States and surveys the Boston area to see how Americans can be converted to Islam. Bey visits Boston's highest hill and plots the spread of Islam: he imagines that Muslim missionaries can establish an Islamic college in Boston and that Islam will soon "cleanse" and "renovate" American men, help American women become better wives, and "improve the morals of the city." "I counted from this height," the Bey character writes, "nearly twenty spires or cupolas rising from as many churches—but alas not one minaret, not one mosque—nor a single monument of the true faith!"[48]

W. F. Thompson, who translated *The Practical Philosophy of the Muhammadan People* that Emerson so admired, hoped that this 1839 work would tamp down the West's fear-mongering. At the very least, Thompson wanted Westerners to get an encyclopedic, somewhat glossy, yet somewhat warted perspective of a people they had vilified for centuries. Thompson, a lawyer living in British-controlled India, translated the book from a major 15th-century Persian text that had been compiled by a Persian philosopher named Jaladeddin Davani.[49]

Islam, Thompson's book said, had borrowed heavily from the teachings of Plato, Aristotle, and other Greek philosophers who anchor the Western canon of ethics. It encouraged its adherents to be charitable to strangers, avoid violent conflicts, and to inculcate virtuousness in themselves and others. To remain pure of soul and be magnanimous, the book says, Muslims are asked to "take no note of honor or disrepute, pay no regard to affluence or adversity; but remain entirely unaffected by praise or censure, by wealth or want."[50] This applies especially to Muslim rulers, who are commanded to distribute benefits to all men, even those who are not resolutely faithful to Islam, because "to elevate any one above his equals without pre-eminent desert is to be unjust to them."[51] An Islamic leader should "lay the foundation of all his undertakings in courtesy and kindness, never in violence and anger."[52] If war is a necessity, a Muslim ruler "is not to despise a lowly enemy." Echoing today's Geneva Conventions, Muslims in war were required "as long as it is practicable to take prisoners alive"—and even "after victory, it is not even lawful to kill them."[53] In times of peace and war, Muslims are asked to turn the other cheek if antagonized ("requite a good act and let a bad one pass")[54] and to exhibit righteousness, patience, and a lifelong interest in books and knowledge. Humor is also an important virtue. "Good humor," according to Thompson's translation, is "the soul's submission, by voluntary process, to any thing that may arise."[55] Giving alms was also essential to being a good Muslim. "The really liberal man is he who gives away his money, not from any design, but because liberality is a noble quality, the delight of which he seeks after."[56]

It is no wonder that Emerson—a man who disdained ostentatiousness and identified so closely with Muslim Persian poets—would embrace this Muslim-Persian text with such fervor and quote from it in his journals and essays.

A prominent journal published in England and America, the *Foreign Quarterly Review*, said that Thompson's translation should be required reading. If previous generations of Westerners had been privy to detailed information on Islam and taken a serious interest in the Muslim world, said the journal, they might have rescinded their demands for war against the Ottoman Empire, and they might have seen Muslims as more than just religious adversaries. "We have been told, for centuries, that Mahommedism opposed literature and learning; that the Turks were the most stupid of Mahommedans; that their sacred tenets were averse to improvement and to good government, and that, therefore, the Turks should be driven out of Europe, and the Greeks substituted in their place. So insisted the PUBLIC!" read the journal's 1840 review of Thompson's book. "Could the public have been persuaded that the unhappy Mahommedans do sometimes write and think, they would not have urged a crusade against Turkey."[57]

The same 1840 edition carried an article about America that mentioned the country's "tendency to adopt the prejudices of older nations." This review cited Emerson and his call for Americans to divorce themselves from historic hatreds. By 1858, Emerson would deliver a public homage to Persian poetry, in the form of an essay published in the *Atlantic*. In it, Emerson predicted that Persian poetry would skyrocket in the esteem of Americans—a prediction that should have credited himself for his role in spotlighting this poetry. From German to English, Emerson translated more than 60 Persian poems, as well as more than 600 individual lines of Persian poetry, focusing particular attention on Saadi and Hafiz.[58]

Like Saadi, Hafiz was from Shiraz, a city that teemed with colleges during Europe's Dark Ages; also like Saadi, he was a devout Muslim who embraced Sufism. Hafiz's name (sometimes spelled "Hafez" in English) means someone who has memorized the Quran. In his poetry, Hafiz couched his religion in ecstatic words of love and desire—allegorical terms that fundamentalists in 14th-century Persia deemed un-Islamic and for which they had him punished. Here is Hafiz as Emerson quoted in his *Atlantic* essay: "I will be drunk and down with wine; Treasures we find in a ruined house,"[59] as well as this defiant stanza from another of the poet's works:

I will not mourn my woeful banishment,
He that has hungered for his lady's face
Shall, when she cometh, know a great content.
The Zealot seeks a heavenly dwelling-place,
Huris to welcome him in Paradise;
Here at the tavern gate my heaven lies,
I need no welcome but my lady's grace.[60]

Hafiz celebrated Islam, but also left behind question marks about the religion, says Fatemeh Keshavarz, an Iranian-born professor of Persian language and comparative literature at Washington University in St. Louis. "He takes a very critical perspective," Keshavarz tells me. "For example, he says, 'If you sin as a human being, it's not your fault—it's your nature, but just be polite and say, "It was my fault."' Hafiz and Saadi are both thinkers—obviously they are not accepting everything wholeheartedly. They're not accepting the whole package [of Islam] without questioning it."

Which is yet another reason that Emerson was drawn to these poets. Like him, Hafiz and Saadi questioned a religion to which they still felt strongly attached. Emerson's relationship with Persian poetry changed him. Reading Saadi and Hafiz, and translating them into English, caused his own poetry to become more like theirs. Here is the opening to a Hafez poem that Emerson translated:

Butler, fetch the ruby wine
Which with sudden greatness fills us.

Here is the opening to Emerson's poem "Bacchus":

Bring me wine, but wine which never grew
In the belly of the grape.

Emerson biographer Robert D. Richardson Jr. says that "Persian poetry was a new homeland for Emerson. It gave him the form, the imagery, and the tone for a poetry of ecstasy, a poetry to express his strong emotional non-Apollonian side, a poetry that did justice to the sweetness of life lived in the senses as well as to the spiritual enjoyments to which such a life corresponded."[61]

Other transcendentalists who were taken with Persian poetry included abolitionist William Rounseville Alger, who published a book of *Poetry of the Orient* that Emerson endorsed; abolitionist Moncure Daniel Conway, whose *Sacred Anthology (Oriental): A Book of Ethical Scriptures* emphasized the poetry of Omar Khayyam; and writer Amos Bronson Alcott, who said in his book *Table-Talk* that authors who try to work their prose to perfection are inspired by "the beautiful Persian apologue: If not the rose they have been near the rose, and left its fragrance near the rose."[62]

None of them went as far as Emerson did in reaching out to Persian-Islamic culture. Although he never traveled to Shiraz, Emerson did set foot in the Muslim world, visiting Egypt in 1873 with his daughter Ellen.[63] In the 1830s, Emerson inspired himself to write by inhabiting "a sort of alter ego" named Osman. The Osman persona helped Emerson to write the last passages of his 1836 work "Nature." Richardson speculates that "the name of Emerson's daemon apparently derives from the Turkish form of Othman, transliterated as Osman. Othman or Osman was the founder of the Ottoman Empire in the thirteenth century."[64]

Whatever its exact origin, "Osman" is another example of the way the transcendentalists sought refuge in the Muslim world in highly unlikely ways, especially at a time when anti-Muslim prejudice was such a vocal part of American culture. Emerson was certainly aware of Americans' distaste for Islam, but—typical of Emerson—he did not care. Thoreau was the same way. With the passage of time, the details of their rebelliousness have faded away for many Americans. What is left—especially with Emerson—are the quips and sayings that get truncated from his long body of work. Divorced from their original context, they become bumper-sticker slogans that are molded to fit the occasion. People take of Emerson what they want, leaving behind the long journey that was his life. More than 100 years after Emerson's death, that life still seems remarkable. He was both of his time and ahead of his time, a mystic who encountered sorrow and fame and—like the Persian Sufis he felt kinship with—transcended them as best he could.

4

P.T. Barnum and the Taj Mahal: The Spread of Muslim Art from One Continent to Another

He was a visionary entrepreneur, a man who knew what people would pay for, but Phineas Taylor Barnum never said, "There's a sucker born every minute." Like other popular myths about well-known figures, this one was fed by hazy memories and conflated accounts of history. During his lifetime, Barnum—"the greatest showman on earth"—did mislead people for profit, most famously in 1842, when he exhibited the "Fejee Mermaid," a dead creature he claimed was half fish, half woman. (It was actually three animal parts sewn together: the tail of a large fish; the shoulders, arms, and breasts of an orangutan; and the head of a baboon.)[1]

The U.S. mermaid tour made Barnum rich and confirmed his belief that paying customers would walk away content if they were amused or at least titillated. The tour also propelled Barnum's first overseas venture: an 1844–1845 trip to England, Ireland, Scotland, France, Belgium, and Spain that showcased "General Tom Thumb," a 25-inch boy who Barnum taught to dance, sing, quip, and mimic such famous people as Hercules and Napoleon.[2] A "fresh-faced little person" (i.e., a dwarf in Barnum's day), Tom Thumb—whose real name was Charles Sherwood Stratton—made Barnum one of America's first millionaires. With those riches, Barnum constructed a mansion in Bridgeport, Connecticut, that was modeled after the Royal Pavilion in Brighton, England, which Barnum visited multiple times during his European sojourn.

"Tom Thumb basically paid for that house," Frederick Fleischer, customer service manager at the Barnum Museum in Bridgeport, told me when I visited the museum.

Barnum's Bridgeport villa had a name that, in today's environment of war and diplomatic posturing, is stunning: Iranistan. The building's architecture was also breathtaking: Minarets crowded the roofline, which was topped by multiple, mosque-like domes; the main entrance had a horseshoe arch straight out of Islamic Spain; and fronting the edifice were more than 15 archways lobed in a fashion borrowed from Muslim architecture. Finished in 1848, Iranistan was the first building of its kind in the United States—and one of the most spectacular ever constructed as a personal home.

As with all of Barnum's endeavors, Iranistan aroused widespread curiosity, was ultimately applauded by both critics and the general public (people from New York and beyond made regular visits to the three-story mansion)—and was also soundly ridiculed, in this case because of its name and the building's "Oriental" aesthetic.

"When the name 'Iranistan' was announced," Barnum wrote in his 1855 autobiography, "a waggish New York editor syllabled it, I-ran-i-stan, and gave as the interpretation, that 'I ran a long time before I could stan!'"[3]

Around the same time, a Brooklyn playwright and critic, William Knight Northall, described the villa as "queer, large, dazzling, splendid, mean, conveniently-inconvenient, incongruous piles that will not admit of description." But Northall then proceeded to describe it, using scurrilous language to say it resembled a mish-mash of Barnum's previous acts and attractions, including a black former slave named Joyce Heth, two obese children, several Africans, and a parade of seven-foot people. "You fancy you can trace in (Iranistan's) composite construction," Northall wrote, "a little of Joyce Heth, a sprinkling of Tom Thumb, a large clot of the two fat boys, the tail of the anaconda, a dash of the spotted nigger, and a monstrous slice of the two last giants."[4]

"Contemptible," said another Iranistan critic, Andrew Jackson

Downing, who wrote at the time, "So far as an admiration of foreign style in architecture arises from the mere love of novelty, it is poor and contemptible. . . . A villa in the style of a Persian palace (of which there is an example lately erected in Connecticut), with its Oriental domes and minarets, equally unmeaning and unsuited to our life and climate, is an example of [this]."[5]

Barnum didn't care what people thought—at least not openly. Without sensationalism (which for Barnum must have been difficult), he tried to convey the true meaning of Iranistan to the public, as in an 1848 pamphlet that said the mansion was "of the Byzantine, Moorish, and Turkish styles of architecture," and featured "minarets of the most elegant appearance."[6] As for its name, Barnum said it could be translated as "Eastern Country Place" or "more poetically, 'Oriental Villa.' "[7]

Among those who lauded Iranistan was *Gleason's Pictorial Drawing Room Companion*, a Boston weekly newspaper that, in 1851, called the building "magnificent" and "splendid," and noted that its ceiling "is of rich arabesque mouldings of white and gold."[8] The periodical also said the building's name was a combination of Persian (the "Iran" part) and Hindi (the "stan" part—"as in Hindostan," wrote the anonymous writer)—a half-correct, half-misleading interpretation that jumbled the building's true origins. Iranistan was inspired by Brighton's Royal Pavilion, whose architecture was inspired by Muslim-Mughal monuments in India built in the 16th and 17th centuries. The Taj Mahal—a majestic Islamic edifice constructed as a tomb for Mughal ruler Shah Jehan and his wife Mumtaz Mahal—was the most illustrious example of these Muslim-Mughal monuments. Other monuments that inspired British architects included the mausoleum of Hyder Ali Khan, who ruled over the southern Indian kingdom of Mysore in the 18th century, and the mausoleum of Sultan Parvez, the son of one of India's greatest rulers, Nuruddin Salim Jehangir.

When the Royal Pavilion was built in the early 19th century, the Mughal style of architecture was the most fashionable style in

Britain, fueled by England's cultural romanticizing of India, where the British had had a presence since 1600. Mughal gardens, Mughal buildings, and Mughal design patterns were adopted throughout British society, most notably by the Prince of Wales, George Augustus Frederick, who ordered that the Royal Pavilion's riding stables be built in Mughal style in 1803, and then ordered the main palace be rebuilt in Mughal style between 1815 and 1822. The result was a kind of fantasy complex—a palace with more minarets than an average mosque, with domes that were more pronounced than those of the Taj Mahal or Hyder Ali Khan's mausoleum.

The Royal Pavilion was both applauded and mocked by a public that debated whether a sultan's palace was appropriate for British royalty, and in the end, the only voice that counted—Queen Victoria—decided the pavilion was unsuitable for England's noblest bloodline. Buckingham Palace sold the structure in 1849 to the City of Brighton, where it is now the city's most valuable tourist attraction.

Iranistan met a decidedly less satisfying fate. In 1857, nine years after it was constructed, the villa burned to the ground after a worker accidentally sparked a fire on the roof. Today, the only way to see Iranistan's once-splendid grandeur is through reproductions of lithographs or by visiting Bridgeport's Barnum Museum, which has an exact model of the building, as well as furniture and other items that survived the inferno. The museum has also recreated Iranistan's stunning library room, where Barnum studied and surrounded himself with reminders of Muslim-Mughal India. In the recreated room, the walls are covered with dreamy, almost-life-sized scenes of India during the time of Shah Jehan and Jehangir. In the images, turbaned men walk and sit amid ornate, mosque-like buildings that evoke the Taj Mahal. Matching the Islamic motif, the room's windows all have crenellated ridges that mimic the crenellations found on mosque roofs. Painted in gold leaf, the windows also have lobed arches that were intrinsic to religious buildings in Mughal India.

In a separate section of the museum lies an object that also apparently came from Iranistan: A hookah (water pipe) with Arabic writing on it—writing that appears to feature the Arabic word for God, Allah.[9] Barnum was an inveterate smoker of cigars. Did he smoke with the pipe and wonder what the Arabic writing stood for? How often did he luxuriate in Iranistan with a hookah that embodied his interest in Mughal India? (Beyond displaying the water pipe, the museum has no details on its background, and the museum's director did not respond to my repeated inquiries about the object.) What's clear is that Barnum had a lifelong interest in the Arab and Muslim world—and that he both admired it and (as with all other things about Barnum) saw it as a place to capitalize for profit.

In the years after building Iranistan, for example, Barnum recruited for his New York museum (which was really more a Broadway production than a "museum") a 7-foot-11 man whom he called the "Arabian Giant." Also known as the "Palestine Giant," the man—Routh Goshen—was one of Barnum's top bills in 1863. In a *New York Times* advertisement from November 26 of that year, Barnum listed Goshen as "an enormous living giant" who was "born in Jerusalem, 27 years old, one of the most splendid men ever seen."[10] In a similar ad in 1872, Barnum touted Goshen as "the Great Arabian Giant, and the largest human being ever on exhibition."[11] Goshen may not have even been of Arab descent (various reports list his real background as British), but Barnum didn't care—he knew that listing Goshen as "Arabian" would generate more interest in his New York museum, where freaks and foreigners were displayed for visitors to see and speak with. Today, a man like Barnum would (deservedly) be picketed for showcasing dwarves, giants, bearded women, Siamese twins, Arabian giants, Afghan and Syrian tribesmen, Polynesian and albino families, and super-sized children for spectacle and profit, but in Barnum's time, his museum—and his subsequent circus ventures, which spawned the spectacle that still bears his name (Ringling Bros. and Barnum

& Bailey)—were mostly embraced by a curious public that had few other outlets to see and experience the otherworldly.

By contrast, Barnum had the money and the status to travel the globe, meet kings and queens (as he did in England and France with Tom Thumb), befriend the famous (including Abraham Lincoln), and ask anyone he met for favors. During its existence, Iranistan became a status symbol to impress those whom Barnum did not yet know, including one of Europe's most beloved opera singers, Sweden's Jenny Lind.

In 1849, Lind was such a commanding figure that, in Vienna, she received 25 curtain calls; in Stuttgart, Germany, adoring fans visited her hotel and tore her bedsheets for keepsakes; and in London, Queen Victoria tossed flowers to her on stage.[12] Four American promoters had vied to bring Lind to the United States when Barnum also had the idea to tour her across the country. Why would Barnum turn his sights from dwarves and giants to an opera star whose music he had personally never heard? He wanted to redeem himself—to prove to Americans (and himself) that he was a man of high culture. "He wanted to be heralded as more than an entrepreneur of freaks and oddities," wrote biographer Irving Wallace in his 1967 work, *The Fabulous Showman*. "He wanted to be known as impresario of an artistic attraction. . . . In his mind, Jenny Lind represented culture. She might also make money for him, but that was not the point. Even if she failed, he would succeed in gaining prestige."[13]

Unfortunately for Barnum, his reputation for "freaks and oddities" preceded him to Europe, where a rival promoter, Henry Wikoff, told Lind that Barnum was "a mere showman" who would "put her in a box and exhibit her through the country at twenty-five cents a head."[14] But Barnum had two things in his favor: His offer to Lind was more lucrative than others she had seen (he guaranteed her $1,000 a night—a hefty sum that's equivalent to $25,000 a night today[15]), and his offer was relayed to her on stationery that featured an image of Iranistan. Lind saw Iranistan and immediately decided to negotiate with Barnum's European representative, John Hall Wilton, which led her to sign with Barnum for a tour that took her to America in 1850 and 1851.

One day, during a break from her concert schedule, Lind walked the grounds of Iranistan with Barnum and admitted her initial reluctance to join him in partnership—and her subsequent change of mind.

"Do you know, Mr. Barnum," she told him, "that if you had not built Iranistan, I should never have come to America for you?"

Shocked, Barnum asked her to elaborate.

"I had received several applications to visit the United States, but I did not much like the appearance of the applicants, not did I relish the idea of crossing 3,000 miles of ocean; so I declined them all," she said. "But the first letter which Mr. Wilton, your agent, addressed me, was written upon a sheet headed with a beautiful engraving of Iranistan. It attracted my attention. I said to myself, a gentleman who has been so successful in his business as to be able to build and reside in such a palace cannot be a mere 'adventurer.' So I wrote to your agent, and consented to an interview, which I should have declined, if I had not seen the picture of Iranistan!"

Barnum's reply: "That, then, fully pays me for building it, for I intend and expect to make more by this musical enterprise than Iranistan cost me."[16]

In 1848, Iranistan cost Barnum $150,000 (which is millions of dollars by today's standards). Barnum's series of Lind concerts, which lasted nine months, netted him $535,000, so his pledge to Lind became true, and Barnum's Mughal palace paid dividends he could only have imagined when he first thought of building it six years earlier.[17] So important was Iranistan to Barnum's well-being—financially, emotionally, and as the embodiment of his worldliness and sophistication—that he credits it effusively in his autobiography. Visitors to the Barnum Museum in Bridgeport can see a surviving copy of the Iranistan stationery that Barnum used in his heyday. The museum's copy, from 1849, has an image of Iranistan at the top, under which are these words:

> IRANISTAN AN ORIENTAL VILLA
> Bridgeport, Connecticut
> The County Residence of P. T. Barnum

In the United States of 1849, "Oriental" was an all-encompassing term that could mean everything from Japanese and Chinese to Indian and Muslim. If an observant Muslim had visited Iranistan when it stood in Bridgeport, he or she would have blushed—not because of the mansion's opulence, but because of its semi-naked statues. Classical busts of women guarded the main entrance like goddesses sent from the time of Bacchus.[18] Barnum, who drank alcohol with regularity (before quitting abruptly a few years after Iranistan was built), stocked the villa with wine and hard liquor and emblazoned Iranistan's carriages with a coat of arms that featured the phrase, "Love God, and Be Merry!" Because the estate was 17 acres, Barnum had the space to be merry in privacy, but he constructed Iranistan as a public edifice—he practically encouraged people to gaze, and he chose its location in Bridgeport because it was yards away from the railway line that connected Connecticut to Manhattan. At one point, Barnum paid for a man in the turbaned dress of Mughal India to plow Iranistan's fields with a large elephant—an act he hoped would inspire train passengers traveling past the estate to visit his New York museum.[19] "I thought," Barnum would say later, "that a pile of buildings of a novel order might indirectly serve as an advertisement of my museum."[20]

It seemed that Barnum had thought of everything—except the possibility of a calamitous fire. After Iranistan burned to the ground, Barnum admitted that the house only had insurance to cover $28,000 worth of damage. Rather than create a second Iranistan, Barnum eventually built another mansion in Bridgeport, this one in a more austere, quasi-Victorian style. Today, the only vestiges of Iranistan are in the Barnum Museum in downtown Bridgeport, and on a street that pays homage to the building and cuts through Barnum's old neighborhood. The street's name: Iranistan Avenue.

At the intersection where Barnum's mansion had once been, I took out my camera and took pictures of the "Iranistan Avenue" sign, then made note of the corner store across the way, called Danny's. Like Barnum's Iranistan, the merchant had a scantily clad woman in front, but this was no statue—just a Budweiser poster that showed her smiling in a swimsuit alongside an interested man. Women and liquor—that was the one constant from Barnum's time to the present day. At least I thought it was. But as I walked down Fairfield Avenue, I came across another constant: Islamic culture. Two blocks from the old Iranistan is a new Muslim house of worship—the Al Aziz Islamic Center, which features this saying near its front door: "With Allah's Name, The Merciful Benefactor, The Merciful Redeemer." In Islam, these words open every major religious work or recitation. Repeating them ("*Bismillahir-Rahmanir-Rahim*" in Arabic) acknowledges God's will and control over all things on earth.

Similar words are found at the Taj Mahal, where Quranic inscriptions are a major motif designed to inspire visitors about the benevolence of a God that allowed the Mughal empire and created Paradise, not just on earth but in the afterlife—especially in the afterlife, whose gardens, fountains, and majesty the Taj Mahal tries to encapsulate. The Taj Mahal has 22 Quranic verses—in both Arabic and Persian, which was the official language of the court—on its walls, main gate, and other outward spaces. Visitors entering the complex see this verse, which is from Sura 89, "The Dawn" (*al-Fajr*):

But O thou soul at peace,
Return thou unto thy Lord, well-pleased, and well-pleasing unto Him.

Enter thou among my servants,
And enter thou My Paradise.[21]

The Taj Mahal complex feels like paradise because of its perfect proportions—a garden of cypress trees surrounding a reflecting pool leads visitors to the white marble mausoleum that melds pointed archways, soaring minarets, *chhatris* (domed pavilions), intricate *muqarnas* (stalactite vaulting), floriated inlays, calligraphy, and a majestic dome topped with the symbol of ascendant Islam: a crescent moon. While its design borrows from India's Hindu heritage (most notably in the *chhatris*), the Taj Mahal owes its life to Persian aesthetics. Under India's Mughal rulers—descendants of Turkic Muslims from Central Asia who intermarried with Persians from what is now Iran—Persian was the language of the court (*Taj Mahal* means "the Crown Palace" in Persian), and Persian architecture was the template from which to build anything of importance. One precursor of the Taj Mahal was the Emam Mosque in Esfahan, Iran, which was built two decades before the Taj Mahal was completed in Agra, India. The domes of the two monuments have a "close resemblance," according to historian Henri Stierlin, who writes that "the Taj Mahal reflects a purely Persian style."[22]

It also reflects an Islamic one, from the calligraphy and crescent moon, to the fact that Shah Jehan and Mumtaz Mahal were buried with their heads toward Mecca, to the fact that the Taj complex has an adjoining mosque meant to emphasize the mausoleum's religious character.

The Taj Mahal's Persian and Muslim roots are altogether forgotten in popular renderings in the United States—whether in an Indian restaurant menu that spotlights the monument's silhouette, or Donald Trump's Atlantic City casino-hotel complex, which turned one of the world's great structures into an orgiastic fantasy of gambling, drinking, cavorting, and other indiscreet pleasures. In early-19th-century Britain, however, when Brighton's Royal Pavilion realized the form it has today, the Taj Mahal's religious history was well understood. By the turn of the century, such design books as *Oriental Scenery* (whose drawings showcased New Delhi's Friday Mosque), *Twelve Views of Places in the Kingdom of Mysore* (which showcased India's Mughal mausoleums), and *Select Views of India, Drawn on the Spot, 1780–1783* (which featured some of the first published images of the Taj Mahal) were popular with British architects and designers. When the Prince of Wales was considering what style of architecture to incorporate into the royal grounds in Brighton, sketches of Mughal India by Thomas and William Daniell, from their *Oriental Scenery* work, were drawing big crowds at London's prestigious Royal Academy.

"These books, their many other prints, and the paintings exhibited at the Royal Academy," noted art historian Carl J. Weinhardt Jr., "had a cumulative effect that was extraordinary."[23] The effect snowballed when the Prince of Wales gave his go-ahead to build Brighton's stables in a Mughal style—a decision that Weinhardt says gave "royal recognition and approbation" to the form.[24] Historian John Dinkel says that the prince's decision "introduced the romantic and unfamiliar outlines of Muslim India" to British society.[25]

By extension, it also introduced the outlines to America after Barnum visited the Royal Pavilion and was captivated by what he saw. "It was the only specimen of Oriental architecture in England," Barnum noted in his autobiography, "and the style had not been introduced into America. I concluded to adopt it."[26]

Whether he realized it or not, "Iranistan" was an appropriate name for a mansion that ultimately owed its aesthetics to Persian culture. (Barnum also adopted some of the Chinese interior designs favored in the Royal Pavilion.) Barnum had at least one thing in common with Shah Jehan: Both spent whatever it required (Jehan almost bankrupted his treasury) to build their masterpieces. Barnum told his architect and builders to "spare neither time nor expense in erecting a comfortable, convenient, and tasteful residence."[27]

Typical of Barnum's showmanship, he threw a major housewarming party for Iranistan when it was finally completed in

November of 1848. More than 900 people attended, "including the poor," Barnum noted.[28] Throughout 1848 and 1849, Barnum spent most of his days at Iranistan with his wife, Charity, and their three young daughters, Caroline (who would be married on Iranistan's grounds), Helen, and Pauline. When he wrote his autobiography in 1855, Barnum said those two years were "among the happiest of my life. I had enough to do in the management of my business, and yet I seemed to have plenty of leisure hours to pass with my family and friends in my beautiful home of Iranistan."[29]

What began as a money-making tour of Europe with Tom Thumb ended with a home in Bridgeport that was unlike any other in America. For Barnum, being an architectural trailblazer fit in with his sense of bravado and daringness. Had Iranistan, the villa with the Persian name, survived the 1857 fire and the ravages of time, it would be a landmark as big as anything Barnum left behind. Instead, the only shadows of its memory left are the remnants at the Barnum Museum and a thoroughfare with a name that once stood for grandeur, and for one man's larger-than-life connection to India's Muslim-Moghul empire.

Even "Iranistan Avenue" is disconnected from its Persian origins:

"People in Bridgeport don't pronounce it 'Iran-i-stan'," Fleischer told me. "They pronounce it 'Arn-i-stan.' "

Arnistan? As in "land of Arns"?

"You have to be kidding me?" I thought as I stood in the lobby of the Barnum Museum. "This is some sort of joke, right? How could it *not* be pronounced 'IRAN-istan'?"

I didn't say anything, though. Instead, I bought a postcard of Iranistan's recreated library, said good-bye to Fleischer, and marveled at the fact that P. T. Barnum, the world's greatest showman, had given life to a building with Persian and Muslim elements that was (briefly) the most noteworthy house in America.

5

Language and Names: The Arabic Origins of "Giraffe" and "Coffee"—and What About "Mecca, U. S.A."?

Take this three-part quiz to test your knowledge of English and the United States:

(1) Which of the following words came into English directly or indirectly through Arabic? (Check the appropriate box)

❒ Alcohol	❒ Chess	❒ Lemon	❒ Saffron
❒ Alcove	❒ Decipher	❒ Lute	❒ Sahara
❒ Algebra	❒ Elixir	❒ Magazine	❒ Syrup
❒ Apricot	❒ Gauze	❒ Mummy	❒ Talisman
❒ Assassin	❒ Harem	❒ Orange	❒ Zenith

(2) Which of the following famous American utterances features at least one word that entered English from Arabic? (Check the appropriate box)

❒ "Hey! Mr. tambourine man, play a song for me.
I'm not sleepy and there ain't no place I'm going to."
—Bob Dylan, 1964

❒ "In the United States today, we have more than our share of the nattering nabobs of negativism."
—Spiro Agnew, Nixon's vice president, 1970

- ❒ "Like taking candy from a baby."
  —*Seinfeld* lawyer Jackie Chiles telling Kramer he's set to win big money, 1996

(3) Which of the following are really towns or cities in the United States? (Check the appropriate box)

- ❒ Aladdin, Wyoming
- ❒ Arabia, Nebraska
- ❒ Bagdad, California
- ❒ Cairo, Illinois
- ❒ Koran, Louisiana
- ❒ Mahomet, Illinois
- ❒ Mecca, California
- ❒ Mecca, Indiana
- ❒ Palestine, Texas
- ❒ Sultan, Washington

Before the answers are revealed, let's consider this fact: In the Top 10 list of languages that have contributed the most words to English, Arabic is No. 6.[1] This placing has held steady over the past 100 years, despite (or because of) wars, geographic upheavals, and shifting patterns of trade and immigration. In 1892, for example, the *Stanford Dictionary of Anglicized Words and Phrases* found that Arabic was the seventh-most important language for originating words in English.[2] Only Latin (No. 1), followed by French, Italian, Spanish, Greek, and "Hindoo" were more important. In 1994, Arabic was sixth, behind French (No. 1), then Japanese, Spanish, Italian, and Latin, according to *The Arabic Contributions to the English Language: An Historical Dictionary.*[3] Scholars debate exactly how many words that Arabic has fed into English. Garland Cannon, professor emeritus of English at Texas A&M University, and author of *The Arabic Contributions to the English Language*, accounts for 2,338 words or phrases that stem at least partly from Arabic. In their 1996 study, *Arabic Contributions to the English Vocabulary*, James Peters and Habeeb Salloum said that more than 6,500 English words or their derivatives originated with Arabic or were transmitted to English via Arabic.[4] The first serious study of the subject, Walt Taylor's *Arabic Words in English* (1933), said that "there are about a thousand main words of Arabic origin in English, and many thousand derivatives from those words."[5]

Most of these words are so obscure—or have fallen so far out of use—that only etymologists and lexicographers (and perhaps the most rabid contestants on *Jeopardy!*) would recognize them. "Nabk"? It's a noun that means "a thorny shrub, a Christ's thorn."[6] "Musnud"? It's a noun that means "a cushioned seat, especially an Indian prince's throne."[7] "Jorobado"? It's the name of a fish with a humpback.[8] "Jorobado" passed from Arabic into Spanish, from where it was adopted into English. (You'll find the word in older fiction and nonfiction, often used to describe people with a physical malformation, as in the 1843 book *The Zincali: Or, An Account of the Gypsies of Spain*, in which the author describes an unattractive man by writing, "The other [man] was neither tall nor red-faced, nor had he hair about his mouth, and, indeed, he had very little upon his head. He was very diminutive, and looked like a jorobado.")[9]

At the opposite end are words that have not only survived the centuries but are just as common today as they were at the time of their initial crossover into English. Hundreds and hundreds of these words anchor the language, from A to Z—including the words "admiral" (adapted into English about the year 1205), "bazaar" (1340), "cipher" (1399), "drub" (the verb, not the noun; 1634), "endive" (circa 1375), "fanfare" (circa 1625), "giraffe" (1594), "hazard" (1300), "imam" (circa 1625), "jasmine" (1562), "kabob" (circa 1675), "lackey" (1529), "monsoon" (1584), "nadir" (1391), "ogee" (an architectural term, 1428), "pia mater" (an important medical term referring to brain matter; circa 1425), "quran" (circa 1875), "racket" (1500), "sequin" (1613), "tariff" (1591), "usnea" (a type of lichen that grows around the world; 1597), "vizier" (1562), "wadi" (circa 1825), "xebec" (an 18th-century ship now popular with model ship-builders; 1756), "yashmak" (a kind of veil mentioned in Thackeray's *Vanity Fair* and now cited regularly in news reports about the dress of Muslim women; 1844), and "zero" (1604).[10]

Among frequently used words in English that stem from Arabic, the most popular include all 20 words from this chapter's first question (alcohol, alcove, algebra, apricot, assassin, chess, decipher, elixir, gauze, harem, lemon, lute, magazine, mummy, orange, saffron, Sahara, syrup, talisman, and zenith), words from each of the three sentences in the second question (tambourine, nabob, and candy), and the following words: adobe, alameda, albacore, albatross, alchemy, alfalfa, almanac, amalgam, amber, arabesque, artichoke, average, barrio, caliber, camphor, check, chemist, chiffon, coffee, cotton, crimson, cumin, ghoul, hashish, henna, hummus, masquerade, mattress, mecca, mocha, safflower, sesame, sherbet, sherry, soda, sofa, spinach, sugar, tangerine, tarot, traffic, and tuba.[11]

For many of these words the crucial connection is Spain—the country where, under the Moors, Arabic was a lingua franca, and where more than 3,000 Arabic words entered the Spanish language, from which they spread into French, Latin, and English. Take the name of the famous prison in San Francisco Bay, Alcatraz. The word stems from the Arabic word *al-ghattas*, which means "the white-tailed sea eagle," according to Cannon's *The Arabic Contributions to the English Language*. From *al-ghattas*, the Portuguese and Spanish adopted the word *alcatras*, which they used to describe a range of sea birds, including pelicans. The Spanish and Portuguese would name any island inhabited by pelicans and other birds Isla de Alcatraces. The word was first used in English, according to the *Oxford English Dictionary*, in 1564, when English slave trader Sir John Hawkins sailed into Portuguese territory and noted that an island was called Alcatrarsa, and that sea birds were called alcatrarses.[12] In 1775, Spanish explorer Juan Manuel de Ayala gave the San Francisco island the name Isla de los Alcatraces—in English, Alcatraz Island.

The word *alcohol* entered Spanish from the Arabic word *al-kuhul*, meaning "the powdered antimony," of a kind that Arab scientists perfected during the Muslim ascension in the sciences. From Spain, says Cannon, the word was adapted into medieval Latin, from which it spread to English.[13] "Alfalfa" is from the Arabic word *al-fasfasah* ("the alfalfa"), which entered into Spanish with a slight change in spelling.[14] Often, a word bypassed Spanish and went straight from Arabic to Latin, such as "algebra," which is a translation of the Arabic *al-jabr* ("the algebra"). The Arabic word refers to a famous mathematics book, *Kitab al-Jabr wa-l-iMuqabala* ("The Book of Restitution and Comparison"), which was written by the ninth-century Muslim mathematician Muhammad ibn Musa al-Khwarizmi—a holy figure in the history of mathematics whose name begat the word "algorithm."[15]

In Arabic, the prefix *al* is a definite article that means "the"—an important clue to the scores of English words that ultimately derive from Arabic. These "*al* words," which include "alcove" (from *al-qubbah*),[16] "alchemy" (from *al-kimiya*),[17] and "almanac" (from *al-manakh*),[18] are the most obvious sign that Arabic is one of English's mother tongues. Still, many Arabic words in English are like sixth-generation Americans—they're related to distant ancestors overseas, but those ancestors are so different from their progeny that it hardly seems possible they're part of the same family tree. Take the word "broker." According to Cannon, the word is from the Arabic *al-buruq*, which means "gift or gratuity."[19] During Arab rule of Spain, *al-buruq* spread to Spanish in the form of *alboroque*, which then likely spread to southeastern France, where the word became *abrocador*. From there, it spread to northern France as the word *broquier*, meaning to "tap a cask," and from there, it became *broucour*. Thanks to Norman rule over England in 1066, which begat a cross-culturalization between English and French, *broucour* spawned the word "broker," which—in the United States—has come to mean someone who makes gobs of money from the stock exchange. The New York Stock Exchange is a long way from Arab-ruled Cordoba, but words have ensured that the connection (as surreal as it seems) remains alive.

More surrealism: The chess expression "checkmate" derives from Arabic and Persian. In *The Arabic Contributions to the English Language*, Cannon says that the original expression is *shah mat*, which means "the king is dead!"—*shah* being Persian for "king," *mat* being Arabic for "dead." A thousand years ago, Muslim chess players yelled that after successfully cornering their opponents' king pieces. (Persian crept into Arabic after Arabs captured Persia in the seventh century.) The *Oxford English Dictionary* says that the phrase entered English circuitously—first into Spanish and Portuguese as *xaque mate*, where it morphed into *xaquimate* and *jaque y mate*, then into Italian as *scaccomatto*, before it reached French as *eschec mat* and *eschec et mat*. From there it entered medieval English as *chek mat*. In 1374, say Cannon and the *Oxford English Dictionary*, Chaucer introduced the phrase into English, where it has remained a favorite expression of chess players to this day.[20] "Islam" and "chess" may seem oxymoronic given that, in the past 30 years, Iran and Afghanistan have banned chess on occasion, saying that the game is un-Islamic and induces its participants into gambling. In the medieval Muslim world, however, Islamic leaders more than tolerated chess, despite the orthodoxy of their countries' mullahs. "While the religious law-givers in Islam were anything but enthusiastic regarding the 'graven images,' the caliphs loved chess," write Salloum and Peters in *Arabic Contributions to the English Vocabulary*. "Many kept a chess master on staff. Muslim chess masters were the first to subject chess to scientific study and the first to write on chess theory. Wherever Islam went, from Spain to Indonesia, chess went too."[21]

And so did traders and soldiers from non-Islamic countries, who crossed the borders of Muslim lands and returned home with booty whose names were Arabic in origin. Sherry, the fortified (and highly alcoholic) Spanish wine, takes its name from the country's southern town of Jerez de la Frontera, which takes its name from the Arabic Sharish. After the Reconquista, according to a folktale from *Arabic Contributions to the English Vocabulary*, English mercenaries who fought beside Christian Spaniards took home sherry, introducing the prized liquor to Britain.[22] (Not only is sherry's name Arabic in origin, but the wine owes its punch to Arabs, since it was Spain's Arab rulers who introduced distillation to the country's southern region.)

Other Arab city names that have transmogrified into English words include Tangier, the Moroccan city whose famous orange fruit (*tanjah* in Arabic) became our "tangerine";[23] Mocha, the Yemenese city (*mukha* in Arabic) that became a color and a kind of coffee;[24] and Mecca, Islam's holiest city, which became a noun that means a place at the center of something important.[25]

Italy and Sicily are where some Arabic words settled before continuing onward to England. Muslims controlled Sicily in the ninth and tenth centuries, and medieval Italy—particularly Venice—maintained a lively trade with the Muslim world for centuries. That's why an Arabic word like *qalib* ("mold for casting metal"), Cannon says, became *calibro* in Italian before morphing into *caliber* in French, and then into English, where it is also "caliber."[26] In this case, says Cannon, Arabic was simply a transit language for the original Greek word, *kalapous*. In another example of how Arabic was a conduit of different words from different languages, Cannon says, the Dravidian word for candy ("khanda") likely spawned the Arabic word *qandi*, which in Italian became *zucchero candi* (sugar candy), which morphed into the English word that brings joy to every child's face.[27] Fun words, sad words, words denoting death and drugs, words that signify our daily habits and occupations, words representing things we love—they've all come into English via Arabic.

In his 1933 book, Walton estimated that Arabic gave English about 260 words that could be considered to be in everyday use.[28] In their 1996 work, Salloum and Peters doubled the total, saying, "There are, perhaps, over 500 words which impregnate our everyday speech."[29] Cannon wasn't specific, but his totals for "everyday words" had to be higher, since he included so many derivatives of words that partly connect to Arabic. For example, English gets its word "coffee" from the Arabic word *qahwah*. The French and English word for a coffee house is "café," which Cannon includes in his word total. Whether that unfairly boosts the number of Arabic contributions to English is debatable, but what's not is that Arabic is still contributing words to English—and that most of the recent entries fall under the category of "war and violence."

Here is a sample of Arabic words that have become prominent in English over the past 25 years: Fatwa. Jihad. Sharia. Intifada. All of them come direct from Arabic, and all of them carry a negative connotation for many Americans—especially for those who don't know Arabic. In Arabic, *jihad* means "personal struggle" or "exerting effort." In America, the word is now synonymous with "holy war," which in Arabic is not *jihad* but *al-harb al-muqaddas* (a term never found in the Quran). Unlike in earlier times, when the written word was everything, language in the 21st century means the mass media, which is dominated by television and its emphasis on dramatic images. Arabic is usually heard and seen by Americans against a backdrop of war and terrorism, or of the threat of war and terrorism. In this environment, even the Arabic word for God, *Allah*, becomes a negative word in American eyes, as does the Arabic refrain for "God is great," *Allahu akbar.* Yet in the midst of what could politely be called a "down period" in Arabic-to-English borrowings, there are still examples of Arabic words that have crept into English-language pop culture in neutral or positive ways. In fact, the Arabic word for "great," *akbar,* has been adapted into George Lucas's Star Wars franchise, in the form of Admiral Ackbar, a heroic character and military commander whose success in space helps Luke Skywalker and the Rebel Alliance repel Darth Vader's Galactic Empire. Featured in *Return of the Jedi*, Ackbar is just one of many characters and settings in the Star Wars universe that have an Arabic background. Luke Skywalker's home planet, Tatooine, takes its name from the Tunisian city of Tataouine (al-Tataouine in Arabic). Darth Vader's home planet is Mustafar, a slight variation of Mustafa, an Arabic name that means "the chosen one" (and is one of 99 names for the Muslim prophet Muhammad). *Attack of the Clones* showcases Queen Jamillia, whose name is a slight variation of *jamilla*, an Arabic word for "beautiful." And *Revenge of the Sith* features Senator Meena Tills, whose first name means "heaven" in Arabic.

These names are no accident. George Lucas shot the first Star Wars film in Tunisia, and he continued to return to this Muslim country of stunning vistas and otherworldly locations, where a moderate form of Islam is practiced and where French is as widely spoken as Arabic (because of France's history of colonization there). The scene in the first Star Wars film in which Luke Skywalker stands and looks at two moons? Actor Mark Hamill was standing in a dried-up lake named Chott el-Jerid, which is a part of the Sahara desert that cuts through Tunisia's southern half.[30] The Tunisian man who first convinced Lucas of Tunisia's allure, Tarak Ben Ammar, says the director's love affair with the country convinced Stephen Spielberg to film *Raiders of the Lost Ark* there. "Star Wars brought great power," Ben Ammar told the *Financial Times*, "and then George says, 'Stephen Spielberg wants to make this desert film but is scared of Arab countries.'"[31]

That Tunisia disabused Spielberg of his phobia is understandable, given the North African country's position as a stable, progressive—and historic—entry point for Islam and its culture. The religion reached Tunisia in the late seventh century, and Tunis soon established itself alongside Cairo as an important Muslim city. Ez-Zitouna, a madrassa and mosque in Tunis, is one of the oldest continually run institutions in the Muslim world (and Islam's oldest university, according to the institution's claims).[32] Tunisia became a safe haven for Muslims (and Jews) who were expelled during Spain's Reconquista, and it was Tunisia where one of Islam's most important scholars, Ibn Khaldoun, was born and raised. Called "the father of sociology"[33] and "the father of economics"[34] for his pioneering work on the theories of history, evolution, and economics, Ibn Khaldoun wrote a 1337 book called *Al-Muqaddimah*

("The Introduction") that was translated into Latin and studied throughout Europe. Among the things Ibn Khaldoun postulated—almost 500 years before Darwin—was man's evolution from animals: "The animal kingdom was developed, its species multiplied," he wrote, "and in the gradual process of Creation, it ended in man & arising from the world of the monkeys."[35]

Ibn Khaldoun wrote widely about many subjects, including astronomy and the positions of the stars,[36] which in his time were denoted with Arabic names. They still are—which may be another reason why Lucas chose to embed Arabic names within his Star Wars franchise. More than 150 stars gained their names from Arabic,[37] including the second brightest star in the constellation Canis Major,[38] Adhara, whose original Arabic name is *Al-Adhara* ("the maidens"). According to the Islamic Crescents' Observation Project, other stars with Arabic names include Albali (Al-Bali, "The Swallower"); Alchibah (Al-Khibah, "The Tent"); Algedi (Al-Jady, "The Goat"); Algebar (Al-Jabbar, "The Giant"); Algol (Al-Ghul, "The Ghoul"); Algorab (Al-Ghurab, "The Raven"); Alnair (Al-Nayyir, "The Bright One"); Alnilam (An-Nidham, "The String of Pearls"); Alya (Al-Alyah, "The Fatty Tail of a Sheep"); Arrakis (Ar-Raqis, "The Dancer"); Deneb (Dhanab ad-Dajajah, "Tail of the Hen"); Eltanin (At-Tinnin, "The Great Serpent"); Gomeisa (Al-Ghumaisa, "The Bleary-Eyed One"); Keid (Al-Qaid; "The Broken Egg Shells"); Meissa (Al-Maisan, "The Shining One"); Murzim (Al-Murzin, "The Roarer"); Phact (Al-Fakhitah, "The Dove"); Rasalgethi (Ra'is al-Jathi, "Head of the Kneeling One"); Sadachbia (S'ad al-Akhbiyah, "Lucky Star of the Tents"); Sirrah (Surrat al-Faras, "Navel of the Steed"); and Zubeneshemali (Az-Zuban ash-Shamali, "The Northern Claw").

The Arab world begat the Wyoming town of Aladdin, which is tucked away in the northeast corner of the state, away from most everything except a nearby highway. Fifteen people live in Aladdin, which was founded in the late 1800s and takes its name from the famous character in *The Thousand and One Nights*, the collection of folktales also known as *The Arabian Nights*. (In Arabic, Aladdin's name is spelled Ala al-din, which means "excellence of faith.") Bagdad, California, is a town in the Mojave Desert. When it was founded a century ago, townspeople thought of other parts of the world that were hot and arid and yet still thrived. Presto: Baghdad, Iraq.[39]

Most of the American towns with Arabic names (and, yes, every town in Question 3 is a real town) are small and off the beaten path. Arabia, Nebraska, is in the far upper reaches of the state. Like other railroad towns from the 1800s, it was named by the railroad itself.[40] An auditor for a Nebraska railroad picked the name because he thought the soil in the area was similar to the sandy soil of the Arabian Desert.[41] At the opposite end of the state, in the extreme southern part, is the village of Abdal, an Arabic name meaning "a good or religious person."[42]

More than 100 years ago, especially among American Christians, the Arab world was seen as a place of biblical importance. Whatever prejudices they may have had about Islam, Americans looked to the deserts and cities of Arabia, Iraq, and Egypt for names they thought signified hope, strength, perseverance, and history. Memphis, Tennessee, took its name from a historically important city along the Nile River. Cairo, Illinois, took its name from Egypt's capital. Mecca, Indiana, took its name from the birthplace of Islam. And Medina, Ohio, took its name from the second holiest city in Islam, where the prophet Muhammad established the world's first mosque and where he is buried. Elijah Boardman, who fought in the American Revolutionary War and then became a U.S. Senator in Connecticut, gave Medina, Ohio, its name—after first calling the town Mecca.

Here's how William Henry Perrin, J.H. Battle, and Weston Arthur Goodspeed describe the origins of Medina, Ohio, in their 1881 book, *History of Medina County and Ohio:* "It was originally called Mecca, and is so marked on the early maps of the state, from the Arabian city famous in history as the birthplace of Mahomet.

Some years later, it was changed to its present name of Medina, being the seventh place on the globe bearing that name. The others [include] Medina, a town of Arabia Deserts, celebrated as the burial-place of Mahomet. . . ."[43]

In 1800s America, Mahomet was the standard name for the prophet Muhammad. And so it was that the town of Mahomet, Illinois, took its name from the prophet of Islam. It is the only place in the United States named after Muhammad, to my knowledge. The Illinois town (or village, as it is also considered) was bestowed with the name "Mahomet" in 1871, after it was first called Middletown.[44]

The language that all Americans use is full of words that originated in the Arabian Peninsula. Take a word like "giraffe," which is rooted in the Arabic word *zarafa*. "Giraffe" was first recorded in English in 1594 when, according to the *Oxford English Dictionary*, English author Thomas Blundevil wrote, "This beast is called of the Arabians, Gyraffa."[45] It was in Oxford that the first book about English's connection to Arabic, Walt Taylor's *Arabic Words in English*, was published. The only two other books on the subject that I know of, *The Arabic Contributions to the English Language: An Historical Dictionary* and *Arabic Contributions to the English Vocabulary*, were also published outside the United States. All three are available in university libraries, but their relative obscurity may explain why the English-Arabic connection is little known in mainstream America. If the connection were better known, people would realize that every time they say the word "guitar" (from Arabic *qitar*),[46] or "lute" (from Arabic *al-ud*),[47] or "magazine" (from Arabic *makhzan*),[48] or "crimson" (from Arabic *qirmizi*),[49] or "cotton" (from Arabic *qutun*)[50] or "barrio" (from Arabic *barri*, meaning "of the open country"),[51] they are using words that stem from Arabic by way of Spain. Even the name "California" is traceable to Arabized Spain. In his 1510 novel *Las sergas de Esplandian* ("The Adventures of Esplandian"), Spanish novelist Garci Rodriguez de Montalvo describes an island in the Indies that is ruled by a Queen named Calafia. De

Montalvo fought in Spain's Reconquista and wrote his novel at the time of Columbus's discovery of the Indies. In his work, de Montalvo puts Queen Calafia in the country of California, from where she joins with pagans who are fighting for control of Constantinople. In their book *Lands of Promise and Despair: Chronicles of Early California, 1535–1846*, authors Rose Marie Beebe and Robert M. Senkewicz say that de Montalvo created the Queen's name and her fiefdom from the Arabic word *khalifa*.[52]

"The names Calafia and California were rooted in the Arabic word *khalifa*, which enters English as 'caliph,'" write Beebe and Senkewicz. "The use of the word is clearly meant to call to mind the reconquista. In the novel, California is consistently associated with gold and wealth." De Montalvo's novel, according to many accounts, inspired Spanish explorers to name the land they discovered on America's West Coast "California," because they first thought the land mass was a large island.[53]

Five centuries after de Montalvo's work, American writers are also playing with geography by adapting the Persian suffix *-stan* for everything from caricatures to serious prose. In the wake of 9/11, *The New Yorker* devoted a cover to "New Yorkistan," showing a map that divvied up the city into different fiefdoms, including "Taxistan" and "Fuhgeddabouditstan." Writers for *The Onion* have warned their readers about "Nukehavistan" and "Ethniclashistan." In 2006, New York author Gary Shteyngart published the novel *Absurdistan*, about a large Russian man whose adventures across Russia, Europe, and the United States are (not surprisingly) a bit absurd. And in 2007, conservative blogger Matt Hurley took Democrats to task for their political maneuverings, at one point referring to "Protecting Incumbistan."

The *-stan* motif is the latest entry in a long procession of word loans that involve the Muslim world. One of the first Arabic words in English, according to both Taylor and Cannon, was "cumin," which they say entered the language about the year 897. The *Oxford English Dictionary* acknowledges that Arabic could be an originator of that word in English, but says there is no certainty. On one word they all agree that Arabic had a primary role: "alchemy." This word, which entered the English language around 1362, has come to mean the remixing of different substances into a new and improved one. That is what Arabic has done to English—alchemy at its best.

6

Arabs and the Ice-Cream Cone: The Joy of Eating (and Drinking), from Damascus to St. Louis, Missouri

On display were the Liberty Bell,[1] the log cabin where Abraham Lincoln was born,[2] and statues of Andrew Jackson, James Madison, Benjamin Franklin, and Thomas Jefferson.[3] U. S. flags were everywhere.[4] This was America at its proudest—an America that, at the turn of the 20th century, was a full-fledged nation with a strong military, an expansionist outlook, and an optimism that was unparalleled in recent history. What better place to show this off than St. Louis, the city where Ulysses S. Grant had once lived before rejoining the Army and directing the successful defeat of the Confederacy. That's why St. Louis was draped in such haute Americana in 1904, why Washington had spared no expense in converting the city into the site of a World's Fair that would have no equal.

Ostensibly, the fair was to celebrate the 100-year anniversary of the Louisiana Purchase, which doubled the territory of the United States, but the exposition went far beyond putting candles on an old land deal. As much as anything, it was a coming-out party to show that America was at the center of the world. Representatives of 53 foreign countries converged on St. Louis to pay tribute in 1904.[5] "It has caused," said the president of the Louisiana Purchase Exposition, waxing hyperbolic, "a gathering here of all the nations of the earth."[6]

From the Arab and Muslim world came Egypt, Morocco, Persia, and Turkey, which still had nominal control over much of the

Middle East, including Jerusalem. Arabs and Muslims from all these areas arrived in St. Louis for a spectacle that was officially known as the Louisiana Purchase Exposition. Ambassadors and consuls general were among the visitors (Persia's official representative, Dikran Khan Kelekian, has his telephone number listed in the fair program),[7] but the majority of Arabs and Muslims there were entertainers and hawkers—people dressed in traditional garb who put on shows or sold wares to the millions of Americans who came through the turnstiles. To accentuate the authenticity of these Arabs and Muslims, herds of camels were brought to St. Louis, and a facsimile of a sacred Islamic building, the Dome of the Rock, was built in the center of the exposition. In this version of the Dome of the Rock, St. Louis organizers thought they had actually reconstructed a mosque—"The Mosque of Omar," they called the building.[8] This faux mosque, which anchored the fair's Jerusalem section (and was close to the popular Ferris wheel), was one of the first models of an Islamic place of worship ever built on American soil. Just south of the mosque was another faux structure with an Islamic motif: The Taj Mahal, whose reconstructed entrance fronted the fair's "Mysterious Asia" section.[9] There and all along "The Pike," which was the fair's main boulevard for entertainment, Arabs and Muslims danced, juggled, rode camels, swallowed swords, displayed their native foods, and otherwise posed for pictures. Other people considered unusual or exotic were also showcased along the thoroughfares, including geishas from Japan, dog eaters from the Philippines, and pygmies from central Africa. (The Native American leader known as Geronimo signed autographs during a leave granted him by the U.S. government, which was then holding him prisoner.) The 1904 exposition—which also featured pig and mule exhibits, Vatican treasures, jewels from Britain's Queen Victoria, and the latest displays of technological ingenuity—was part Disneyland, part circus, part Smithsonian, and part *National Geographic* magazine come to life—an event that organizers instantly labeled "the greatest World's Fair in the world's history."[10]

Into this milieu stepped two natives of Syria, Ernest Hamwi and Abe Doumar, who hoped to make big money peddling items to fairgoers. Whenever he sat at his booth or walked near the Mosque of Omar to sell souvenirs, Doumar wore Arab robes. His prize possession was holy water from the Jordan River, which he offered to people in small, conical-shaped containers for 50 cents.[11] As it happened, Doumar worked alongside Hamwi and other Syrians who were selling *zalabia*—flat, gridlike pastries that were popular in their native land. Americans at the fair had likely never heard of *zalabia*, unless they were ardent followers of Middle Eastern culture and knew, for example, that *Arabian Nights* translator Sir Richard Burton snacked on *zalabia* during his years in Damascus.[12] One day, an ice-cream salesman next to Doumar ran out of plates. Doumar had an instant epiphany: Why not roll the *zalabia* into conical shapes and put the ice cream in there? What happened next reverberates to this day: Fairgoers discovered they loved the new combination. A treat was born.

"My dad could see the idea of putting them together," Ray Doumar, Abe's son, tells me from Florida, where he is a lawyer. "That's how the ice-cream cone was born. The one booth ran out of plates and couldn't serve the ice cream. So my dad could see the idea of wrapping it and making it into a cone."

So, who deserves credit for inventing the ice-cream cone that day in St. Louis—Doumar for thinking up the idea, or Hamwi, for actually providing the *zalabia* that turned into the cone? The debate hasn't been settled in the century since the fair. Others who have taken credit for the St. Louis matchmaking are David Avayou, a Turkish immigrant, and Charles Menches, an ice-cream vendor at the fair who claimed that it was he—not Hamwi—who rolled up a *zalabia* wafer into the first cone.[13] At least one expert says that it doesn't matter who gets credit—what is more important is that people know that the cone was popularized at the 1904 fair, and that it derives from the Arab world.

"What historians will generally say is that the cream cone definitely became a part of the American landscape at the 1904 St. Louis World's Fair," Suzanne Corbett, culinary historian with the National Park Service in St. Louis, told the *Chicago Tribune* for its story on the cone's 100th anniversary. "There seems to be one common thread: The ice cream cone was based on a Middle Eastern–style cone."[14]

That style can be seen today in Norfolk, Virginia, where Abe Doumar's relations are still in the ice-cream business. In fact, Doumar's Cones & Barbecue (the restaurant's motto: "Since 1904 Great Cones & Barbecue") uses Abe Doumar's first cone-making machine, which he created a year after the St. Louis Fair. The machine makes cones the old-fashioned way: by baking flat, *zalabia*-like waffles, which are then rolled by hand into an ice-cream cone. Some customers come into the eatery just to see Albert Doumar (Abe's nephew) and Thaddeus Doumar (Albert's son, and Abe's grand nephew) make the tasty cylinders. When tour groups visit, Albert Doumar tells them the story of the St. Louis Fair—how Abe Doumar realized right away that the *zalabia* cone would be a hit, how Abe Doumar made a *zalabia* machine that he used for the rest of the exposition (the fair lasted from April 30 to December 1, 1904), and how Abe Doumar was so excited about his new creation that he went into the ice-cream business as soon as the fair ended, opening scores of ice-cream stands, including one in Coney Island, New York. After Abe Doumar died in the 1940s, his family donated his machine from the St. Louis Fair to the Smithsonian, which keeps it in its historical archives.

What visitors to Doumar's Cones & Barbecue never hear is the story behind the story—the tale of Abe Doumar's immigration to America and of his family's deep roots in Syria and Lebanon. In the 1800s, Doumars were craftsmen in Syria. Buildings from that period that still stand in Damascus likely have the Doumar touch. "The Doumar family were stone cutters—they built arches," Thaddeus Doumar tells me.[15] "The Doumars were a Lebanese family but they located to Damascus for business reasons." The Doumars were

Christians in a predominantly Muslim country, but that didn't stop them from thriving in Damascus, where there is a long history of the Christian faith. Churches dot the city, and before the advent of Islam, Damascus's most prominent religious building was a church devoted to John the Baptist. (The mosque that replaced the church has a shrine to John the Baptist that supposedly contains his head—one reason why Pope John Paul visited the mosque in 2001.) Still, at the turn of the 20th century, Abe Doumar decided he had to leave Damascus after a Muslim man there charged him with a crime. In the family retelling of the story, the exact crime is unknown. "He left the Turkish empire when he was accused of a crime by a Muslim, which means it didn't matter whether he was guilty of it or not," Thaddeus Doumar tells me. "So, he basically had to leave."

So, without the legal threat to Abe Doumar in Syria, the ice-cream cone may never have been born that day in St. Louis. Undoubtedly, the cone would have surfaced eventually, and there are claimants who say they invented it before 1904. An Italian immigrant in New York, Italo Marchiony, said he was the cone's originator, because of a patent he received in 1903 for an edible ice-cream cup. Historians dismiss Marchiony's claim because his cup looked nothing like a vertical cone with a pointy bottom. In her book *Everybody Loves Ice Cream: The Whole Scoop on America's Favorite Treat*, Shannon Jackson Arnold says that Marchiony should take a back seat to both Doumar and Hamwi.[16] The *zalabia*-turned-cone was so important because, for the first time in history, it made ice cream transportable. Instead of eating it from a plate or saucer, people could now walk around with ice cream and enjoy it at their leisure.

The large numbers of people who attended the fair probably contributed to the cone's quick adoption into American culture. In contrast, another consumable with Arab origins took years before it became a favorite of American palates. Coffee originated in the Arabian Peninsula in the 1400s, from where it found its way to Europe 200 years later—but not before it took a wild route that started with Sufi Muslims in Yemen,[17] went north across the desert to Mecca (where the world's first coffeehouse was born), then across the Red Sea to Cairo before crossing the Mediterranean to Constantinople. By the time coffee drinking became fashionable in Paris, London, and Boston in the late 1600s, the Pope had reputedly blessed the beverage as permissible for Christians, ignoring the protests of priests who said the caffeinated drink was the product of Muslim devils,[18] and Captain John Smith (of Jamestown fame) had, fortunately for Americans, encountered its aroma as a captive of the Ottomans.

First, the Sufis. In medieval Arabia, these mystics of Islam were a firm part of the population, with different branches called *tariqas* that rallied around individual sheikhs. The Shadhiliyya, whose founder was a 13th-century North African named Abu al-Hasan al-Shadhili, was a *tariqa* described as "one of the most moderate in tone."[19] An advocate for the poor during his lifetime, al-Shadhili once wrote to a disciple that "the pillar of kings is arms and military defenders, while the pillar of the poor is the finding of sufficiency with God and the patient bearing of the courses of His decrees."[20] In Egypt, Yemen, and other areas where the Shadhiliyya thrived, they emphasized leading "socially normal and economically productive lives,"[21] and participation in *zikrs*—devotional ceremonies that involve chanting about God for long periods of time. *Zikrs* frequently took place in the evening, which required Sufis to be alert at all hours of the night. This is why, around the year 1400, Shadhili Sufis in Yemen began consuming coffee—to get more pep for their religious ceremonies. Coffee grew in regions around the Red Sea (particularly in Ethiopia), but in Yemen, coffee berries at the time of the *tariqas* assumed a more prominent role. The Shadhili and other *tariqas* relied on coffee, which prompted other Yemenis to imbibe the lively drink. "The spread of coffee from Sufi devotional use into secular consumption was a natural one," write Bennett Alan Weinberg and Bonnie K. Bealer in their book, *The World of Caffeine: The Science and Culture of the World's Most Popular Drug.* "Though the members of the Sufi orders were ecstatic devotees, most were of the laity, and their nightlong sessions were attended by men from many trades and occupations. . . . When morning came, they returned to their homes and their work, bringing the memory of caffeine's energizing effects with them and sharing the knowledge of coffee drinking with their fellows. Thus, from the example of Sufi conclaves, the coffeehouse was born."[22]

Not in Yemen, though—in Mecca, which has the distinction of both having the world's first coffeehouse (around 1500)[23] and being the first place where coffeehouses were banned (1511).While Sufis embraced coffee as a natural stimulant, some Muslim leaders said its consumption was un-Islamic—that coffee altered human consciousness, and that coffeehouses took people away from the mosque and into a social arena that encouraged vice and rebellious thinking.[24] Khair Bey, Mecca's governor in 1511, decided he'd had enough when he found that customers in Mecca's coffeehouses were ridiculing him. As it happened, the Mumluk sultanate of Egypt, who controlled Islam's holy places, was a coffee drinker, and he ordered the ban reversed.[25] Still, the brief Meccan prohibition presaged a debate about coffee that would emerge for the next 100 years in every Muslim capital, including Cairo, where coffee spread with Yemeni students who arrived to study at the city's historic Al-Azhar University.[26] Egypt became so crazy about the beverage that marriage contracts included a provision that a woman could divorce her husband if (among other faults) he didn't provide her with an adequate amount of coffee.[27]

After the Ottoman Empire conquered Egypt in 1517 and extended its control over the Arabian Peninsula, coffee became a staple of Turkish society and one of Turkey's most valuable commodities. By 1570, just 15 years after the first coffeehouse came to Constantinople, Turkey's capital had more than 600 of them.[28] The Ottomans named the drink *kaveh*, after the Arabic word *kahwah*, and called their coffeehouses *kaveh kanes*. Turkey imported much of its coffee from the Yemenese city of Mocha, whose name became associated with beans from the region. By the end of the 16th century, Yemen was producing a bulk of the Muslim world's coffee,[29] and Turkey was that world's unassailable coffee capital—a place where nearly everyone wanted to drink *kaveh*. "Coffeehouses [are] thronged day and night," wrote one observer of Constantinople's scene, "the poorer classes actually begging money in the streets for the sole object of purchasing coffee."[30]

It was to the Ottoman Empire of the 16th century that America owed its first taste of coffee, though the connection has as many twists and turns as an *Arabian Nights* adventure. Before helping found the American colony of Jamestown, Virginia, in 1607, Englishman John Smith was an adventurer and mercenary who fought against the Ottomans in Hungary. At one point in Smith's Ottoman adventures, his regiment was overwhelmed by Ottoman soldiers, who decapitated and slaughtered much of the infantry. Somehow, the pillagers at the scene found a wounded Smith amid the piles of bodies and sold him into slavery, to a Turkish "Bashaw" (a noble of the Ottoman Empire), who sent the Englishman to Constantinople.[31] As the story goes, the Bashaw's mistress, Charatza Tragabigzanda, became attracted to Smith. Worried that he could be resold into further slavery and sent permanently away, she arranged for him to go to a brother who lived across the Black Sea in the Ottoman-controlled Crimea. Tragabigzanda hoped that Smith would learn Turkish and return to Constantinople to become her husband, but against his sister's wishes, the brother shaved Smith's head, shackled him, and made him a "slave of slaves," forcing him to do menial labor. During his captivity, Smith noticed the eating and drinking habits of his new Muslim captors, which included both horse entrails and a drink called "coffa." Smith managed to escape from the Crimea after using a "threshing bat" to "beat out [the] braines" of Charatza Tragabigzanda's brother,[32] and he returned to England, where he published a memoir in 1603 called *Travels and Adventure*.[33]

Of the Turks, he wrote: "Their best drink is coffa of a graine they call *coava*."[34]

No wonder that Smith brought to America a drink that would help sustain him in the new English colony.[35] (He also brought with him fond memories of Charatza Tragabigzanda—when he sailed later to northern Massachusetts, he named a peninsula there after her, which is now called Cape Ann.[36]) In the American colonies, coffee became a valuable commodity and, by the 1630s, was sold at inns and taverns in New England.[37] Boston issued its first coffee license in 1670.[38] In New York, the first coffeehouse opened in 1696.[39] By the turn of the century, coffee had begun to displace beer as the drink of choice for breakfast.[40] A century later, America was a full-fledged nation of coffee drinkers,[41] and now the liquid is an iconic part of the culture. Half of all Americans 18 or older drink coffee every day, collectively consuming 400 million cups every 24 hours, making the United States the world's leading consumer of the beverage.[42]

At the 1904 World's Fair in St. Louis, food and culture were inseparable. In his Arab robes, Abe Doumar sold holy water from the River Jordan, then *zalabia* for ice cream. The fair's Arab Bedouin wore Bedouin dress and ate Bedouin food in tents that the paying public could inspect.[43] One Bedouin girl, a 3-year-old named Jetta, was such a hit at the fair—admired for her "beauty and energetic personality"—that ticket holders wanted to adopt her. An American fairgoer offered to pay Jetta's father $10,000 if he would let his daughter stay in the United States.[44] The father refused, even though moving to America was the dream of countless foreigners in the early 1900s.

Abe Doumar had immigrated to the United States a few years before the Louisiana Purchase Exposition,[45] then made enough money from ice cream that he was able to pay for his family and relatives to follow him from Damascus. Generations later, the Doumars haven't forgotten their Arab origins, even if they speak with

Southern U.S. accents. (Ray Doumar, who has lived in Florida since 1953, sounds like former U.S. President Jimmy Carter.) Albert Doumar, who is 86, speaks workable Arabic. Thaddeus, who is 43, knows a little Arabic, including the word *haflis*, which translates into "feast." "In the Norfolk area," he said, "there's a pretty tight Lebanese community. We regard everyone as cousins. They still have *haflis*, where we have Lebanese dancing and food a couple times a year." Lebanese and Syrian Americans who pass through Norfolk and drive by Doumar's Cones & Barbecue will stop in and chat, knowing that the family's last name is from the Levant.

Thaddeus hadn't planned to work there as long as he has, nor did Albert, who is often the Doumar who rolls the cone waffles by hand for customers. Both men stayed in the ice-cream business because of loyalty to their families—a trait that is a leftover from the Middle East. "It's the Lebanese culture," says Thaddeus. "My dad came back after being discharged from World War II—my dad is an engineer—and he told his dad that he was going to go down to Florida and open up a building materials place. And his dad told him, 'No you're not—you're going to run the [restaurant] business with me.' You just did what your dad said. My dad is one of the happiest guys I know, so I know that things turned out like they were supposed to."

As happy as he might be at Doumar's Cones & Barbecue, Albert encouraged Thaddeus to follow his work bliss elsewhere, but when Albert's brother, Victor, a partner in the business, died, he asked Thaddeus to work temporarily at the restaurant. That was more than a decade ago. "I came in to help dad out and I'm still helping him out," Thaddeus Doumar says. "Your family is very important to you."

All of the Doumar family's history lives in Thaddeus. He has strong memories of his grandfather George, who was Abe Doumar's brother and came to America around the turn of the 20th century, just like Abe. Just like Abe, George Doumar would roll up food items into conical shapes—partly as a practical way to eat food, partly as a way to remind himself of the Middle East. "I saw my granddaddy do it often," says Thaddeus. "He would often roll something up into a cone form, like a piece of lettuce, and put food in it and eat it that way. Or a piece of bread, like a piece of pita bread. It was an easy way to eat something and be on the move."

That same principle led to Abe Doumar's brainstorm in 1904. The allure of the ice-cream cone has not changed in the century since it evolved from the *zalabia*. In a black-and-white photo from the 1904 fair, three children are happily holding ice-cream cones as a woman (also with a cone) stands behind them. On the outside of Doumar's Cones & Barbecue, images of cones heaped with ice cream are prominently displayed. "Business is always good," Thaddeus Doumar says. "The ice-cream cone is like our Ronald McDonald—as long as we promote ice cream, it attracts kids, and kids bring the adults."

7

The Height of Orientalism: When U. S. Presidents Donned Fezzes and Said "*Salaam Aleikum*"

The Ancient Arabic Order of the Nobles of the Mystic Shrine is otherwise known as the Shriners. With their bright red fezzes that mimic an old Moroccan and Turkish style, their elaborate buildings that mirror Islamic mosques, and their Arabic sayings that are exact phrases from the everyday Islamic world, the Shriners fall into a category that could be called "absurdist orientalism." From their formation in the early 1870s, Shriners wanted to dress like medieval Muslim men and pretend they were part of a secret society that could trace its origins to Mecca, Saudi Arabia, and to a caliph called "Alee."[1] The Shriners printed documents in Arabic,[2] paraded down streets with camels and mechanical elephants,[3] and consumed lots of alcohol.[4] It wasn't until 1888 that the Shriners began to incorporate charity as one of their principal aims.[5] Today, the Shriners are best known for their fezzes and their hospitals that give free health care to anyone in need. At the start, though, their group was an orientalist playground for a few select Masons, none of whom were Arab or Muslim.

The connection between Shriners and Masons can be confusing for those outside the walls of both organizations. The Shriners came out of the Mason tradition, which claims to stretch back to the Middle Ages, to at least the year 1057, when a guild of men in Scotland were granted a royal charter.[6] Originally, the masons were stoneworkers—men who cut, moved, and engineered hard rock into buildings. Freemasons were those who worked with softer stone, called "freestone," which was made into the artistic façades of cathedrals. Most of the early masons' work was on Christian cathedrals in England, France, and Germany.[7] By the 1700s, when the Church had faced years of division among Protestants and Roman Catholics, the Masons had formed as a society that admitted members who had no connection to stonecutting but were interested in a fraternal organization of "intellectual gentlemen who favored religious toleration and friendship between men of different religions."[8] The only requirement was that members believe in God and in the Masonic tradition of solid citizenship and strong moral foundations.

In the 1700s, Masonry spread to America, where a who's who of founding fathers became members, including George Washington, Benjamin Franklin, Paul Revere, and John Hancock.[9] (Benedict Arnold was also a Mason.) The Masons were a social organization for serious-minded people, and like many such organizations, they adopted rituals and symbols that united their membership. For the Masons, three important symbols became the drafting compass, the carpenters' square,[10] and a builders' apron, all of which connected the Masons to the philosophical ideals of craftsmanship.[11] In 1793, Washington wore a Masonic apron at the laying of the first stone of America's new capital in the District of Columbia.[12] Before and during his two-term presidency, Washington could be seen wearing the Masonic apron.[13] By Washington's time, the Masons had also incorporated a kind of induction ceremony that reenacted the story of Hiram Abiff, a biblical architect who, Masons believed, knew the secret of Solomon's Temple.[14]

The Shriners took the Mason tradition and turned it on its head. They kept the Masons' emphasis on deism and select membership (all Shriners have to be Masons), but they took the ideas of rituals, symbols, and a connection to history and reformulated them through the prism of Arab and Muslim society—or at least of a caricature of that society. While the Masons' buildings were called

Grand Lodges, Shriners called their gathering spots "mosques" and gave the building names like Mecca, Medina, Al Koran, and Al Malaikah, which tied the buildings to Arab and Muslim culture.[15] The fez became the hat of choice for active members, while the Shriners' top officers (called potentates) wore robes and headdresses (including turbans) from medieval Islam,[16] as if they had walked out of the pages of the *Arabian Nights*.

Where did the original Shriners get the idea for acting like Arabs and Muslims? The Shriners' official explanation is that founding member William J. Florence, who was a prominent actor at the time, conceived the idea "for a Near East–themed organization after attending a party thrown by an Arabian diplomat."[17] Walter M. Fleming, a prominent doctor at the time, created the Shriners' name, rules, and rituals and—along with Florence—conceived of the fez headgear and the salutation that Shriners said whenever they met each other: *salaam aleikum*, which is Arabic for "peace be upon you." In his 1959 book, *Parade to Glory: The Story of the Shriners and Their Hospitals for Crippled Children*, author Fred Van Deventer says Florence and Fleming were helped by William Sleigh Paterson (one of the Shriners' original 13 members), who was fluent in Arabic.[18]

From the beginning, the Shriners wanted to be fun Masons. Drinking was a mainstay of early Shriner events,[19] and "relaxation, mirth and merriment" were encouraged.[20] In those early years, the Shriners' official explanation was deliberately campy, as in this passage which—if written seriously—would place the Shriners in the same league as al-Qaeda: "The Order of the Nobles of the Mystic Shrine was instituted by the Mohammedan Kalif Alee (whose name be praised!), the cousin-german and son-in-law of the Prophet Mohammed (God favor and preserve him!), in the year of the Hegira 25 (A.D. 644) at Mecca in Arabia, as an inquisition, or Vigilance Committee, to dispense justice and execute punishment upon criminals who escaped their just deserts through the tardiness of the courts."[21]

Drinking. Merriment. A campy history. All under the de facto imprimatur of the George Washington–approved Masons? Who wouldn't want to join such a group? When word eventually got out about the Shriners, its membership ranks swelled beyond belief. By 1888, 10,000 people had joined, and by 1900, more than 50,000 Americans were a part of the order.[22] Though he didn't become a member of the Shriners, President William McKinley was an ardent supporter because of his background as a Mason. When the Shriners poured into Washington, DC, in May of 1900 for their Imperial Session, they paraded in front of the White House, where McKinley viewed the procession from the South Portico. What happened during their parade of May 23rd made history, of a sort: For the first time in America, the president of the United States stood at attention and heard a fellow citizen address him in Arabic. That man was the Imperial Potentate of the Shriners, John H. Atwood of Leavenworth, Kansas, who greeted McKinley with "*salaam aleikum*."[23] Atwood was the last in a line of some 3,000 Shriners who had passed by.

"It was impressive," wrote the *Washington Post*, "to see the President of the United States stand to receive and to respond to the salutation of his brothers in the Mason's craft."[24]

The people of Washington turned out in large numbers to see the Shriners, with their marching bands and Arabian horses, parade down Pennsylvania Avenue. Downtown merchants—responding to a Shriner contest for best-decorated façade—draped themselves in the Shriner colors of red, green, and yellow. Some merchants "even erected miniature mosques across the fronts of buildings and in store windows."[25] Perhaps the most unbelievable gesture of support came from a section of the Marine Corps band that dressed itself in Arab costume to welcome the Shriners to the nation's capital.[26] Needless to say, Atwood and his fellow Shriners were overjoyed at their reception. "From every clime and from every corner of the continent," Atwood said at the opening of the Imperial Session, "we, the representatives of all these many (Shriner) tribes, have come as Moslems to their Mecca, and as citizens and guests to the city that capitals the mightiest empire seen by the sun, or washed by the waves of any sea."[27]

If Washington, DC, was the Shriners' equivalent of Mecca, then the White House was the Shriners' Kaaba, which they reached the night of May 23, when McKinley held a reception for them, all dressed in their formal wear and fezzes. Five thousands guests milled about in what Van Deventer describes as "McKinley's most lavish reception during his tenure in the White House."[28]

The White House would be the site of another remarkable Shriner reception—this one on May 9, 1921, when they paraded in front of the first American president to be a Shriner, Warren G. Harding. On that May day, according to the *New York Times*, Harding spoke in Arabic to the Shriners, telling them, "*wa aleikum salaam*" ("And peace be upon you")—the Shriners' ritual saying given in response to "*salaam aleikum.*" "Harding Gives Salaam at Shriners' Parade," the *Times* headlined its story, which said that the president preceded his Arabic greeting by politely turning down the Shriners' request to join the parade right then and there.[29] "Smilingly the President declined the invitation shouted enthusiastically at him to 'come and join us,'" the story said, "but he demonstrated his familiarity with the rites of the order by giving the grand salaam in answer to that extended to him."

Two years later at the White House, on June 5, 1923, Harding adorned his head with a bright red fez as he watched 25,000 Shriners parade in front once again. His fez boasted the name of the particular Shriners' lodge that he belonged to: Aladdin, of Columbus, Ohio.[30] Also in the reviewing stand that day was General John Pershing, the legendary military leader who was also an avid Shriner. (Pershing wore his military uniform and a general's hat—not a fez—as he sat next to Harding.)[31] Orchestrating the Shriners' music that day was another prominent member of the order: John Philip Sousa, the composer and band leader whose best-known work, "Stars and Stripes Forever," took a back seat that day to his new march, "Nobles of the Mystic Shrine."[32] At least 50,000 people lined the streets of Washington to witness the Shriners' parade, which featured more than 100 bands.[33] That afternoon in Washington, Harding addressed the Shriners convention with a speech that contrasted their laudatory aims around the United States, including in the South (a year earlier, the first Shriners hospital opened in Shreveport, Louisiana), with those of the Ku Klux Klan. "I think I know the very soul of Masonry, out of which the Shrine has come to lighten our burdens and add cheer to our daily lives," Harding told the assemblage. "There is both quantity and quality in the nobility of the Shrine. It is more than a mere Masonic playground. Conceived in cheer, the order hungered for more than play, though we need more of play in our daily lives. It craved to be helpful, and it is algow in noble achievement."[34]

Speaking indirectly of the Klan, which had a few days earlier organized a large demonstration in Maryland, Harding said, "Fraternities must be just, if they are to survive. . . . I will have said enough if I suggest that men lose their right of fraternal hearing when they transgress the law of the land. . . . I like the highly purposed fraternity, because it is our assurance against menacing organization. In the very naturalness of association [in a group like the KKK] men band together for mischief, to exert misguided zeal, to vent unreasoning malice, in undermining our institutions. This isn't fraternity, this is conspiracy. This isn't associated uplift, it is organized destruction. This is not brotherhood, it is the discord of disloyalty and a danger to the republic."

The Shriners gave Harding a standing ovation,[35] then gathered that night with the president for a banquet reception.[36] The Shriners' Imperial Council Session in Washington, which lasted from June 5 to 7, 1923, was the apogee of their popularity and prestige in America. They boasted a membership of 500,000 that included the president of the United States and the country's most accomplished military officer.[37] They could boast that the Shriners' earlier years of drinking and partying had been replaced with the serious aim of helping children who needed medical attention. And they could boast—even if it hadn't occurred to them—that their campy attire and Arabic sayings had at least helped introduce the idea of Arab and Muslim culture to Americans. "Although the Shrine did not accurately portray Islam," writes author William D. Moore in *Masonic Temples: Freemasonry, Ritual Architecture, and Masculine Archetypes*, "it served as a conduit through which Americans learned about the faith."[38]

Still, it's clear that the Shriners largely saw the Arab and Muslim world through an "orientalist" lens. As explained by Columbia University professor Edward Said in his groundbreaking 1978 book *Orientalism*, this lens misrepresents far-off lands and reduces them to a series of sensationalistic images. In the worst cases of orientalism, Westerners filter lands through a strictly Western prism, never bothering to give voice to actual people from the lands they claim to represent. Orientalism is insidious, Said wrote, because it blatantly misrepresents, commodifies, and domineers people in Arab and Muslim lands. Marx, Napoleon, Dante, Mark Twain, Henry Kissinger, and (in *Orientalism*'s 2003 anniversary edition) American neocons all come under blistering attack, as when Said describes Kissinger's propensity to divide the world into polar opposites—an "us" vs. "them" mentality that links Kissinger to "the traditional Orientalist." Both, says Said, "conceive of the difference between cultures, first, as creating a battlefront that separates them, and second, as inviting the West to control, contain, and otherwise govern (though superior knowledge and accommodating power) the Other."[39]

"The Other" is how the Shriners saw the Arab and Muslim world—until the organization started getting members who were Arabs and Muslims. One of the first Muslim Shriners was Simon Michale, who was a member of the Shriners' El Paso, Texas, chapter in 1910. That year, Michale attended the Shriners' annual meeting in the same white robe that he wore during his *hajj* to Mecca, according to *Parade to Glory*, which said that Michale told his fellow Shriners, "I stood against the sacred stone—that is the Kaaba—

and the sun was so hot it scorched my forehead and my lips when I pressed them against the stone."[40]

Adam Olweean has never done the *hajj*, but the 77-year-old retired electrician is a practicing Muslim—one of about 30 Arab and Muslim Americans in the Detroit area who belong to the Shriners. Olweean, whose father cofounded one of the first Muslim mosques in Michigan, is a member of the Islamic Center of America, a Dearborn mosque that is the United States' largest. (Dearborn has the highest concentration of Arabs in the United States.) What does Olweean think of the Shriners' continuing emphasis on fez hats and Arabic greetings? "I love it," he tells me. "It doesn't bother me a bit." Olweean says that he had adulated the Shriners since he was a small child in downtown Detroit and watched their annual parade. Olweean was dazzled by the procession of men wearing fezzes (though he prefers the Arabic word for the hat: *tarboosh*). In 1960, a year after being married, Olweean joined the Masons (he had cousins who were members), then became a Shriner in 1961 because "I wanted to do something different. Masonry is very dry. The Shriners are like a playground. They get loose."

And loose is what Olweean prefers. An avid motorcyclist, Olweean rode his Honda chopper in countless Shrine parades. He is a member of the Shriners' Southfield (Michigan) chapter which is called the Moslem Shriners. When Olweean has worn in public his "Moslem Shriners" emblem—whether on a fez or on a sweater or jacket—strangers have approached him, particularly during periods of war in the Middle East. "They say, 'Are you Muslim?' And I say, 'I just happen to be one,'" says Olweean. "Then they say, 'Do you have to be Muslim to be a Shriner?' I say, 'No,' then I tell them the [Shriner] story. And two weeks later, they're asking me for a petition to get into the Shriners."

Still, around 1988, when the Iran-Iraq war was going strong and the news out of the Middle East was mostly negative, members of Shriner chapters, including the Southfield "Moslem Shriners," debated whether to change their chapters' names, Olweean says. In the end, particularly after consulting with Shriner higher-ups, they stuck with their chapters' Arab- and Muslim-sounding names, he says. "They [Shriner leaders] said, 'No, you're not going to change your name because of some dumb stuff happening out there,'" remembers Olweean, whose father immigrated to the United States from greater Syria. "They said, 'If someone says something to you about the Arab motif, especially the ['Moslem'] name, explain it the best you can.'"

Over the years, though, the Shriners have eliminated some of their founders' emphasis on Arab and Muslim culture. No longer are Shriner buildings called "mosques." Now, they are called "temples" or "centers." No longer do the Shriners claim their origins go back to seventh-century Mecca. And no longer do they dress up completely in Arab and Muslim robes during during important sessions, as they did a century ago. The fez, however, will always be part of the Shriner motif. And the "*salaam*" ritual that Harding and McKinley took part in at the White House has continued to be an integral part of Shriner functions. "The *salaam* is still used at regular meetings and ceremonials, and when we initiate new members," Jack H. Jones, a member of the Shriners' governing council (his official title: Imperial Recorder), tells me. Asked whether the Arab-influenced rituals are really just another way for the Shriners to have fun, Jones says, "It's light-hearted but it's serious in a way, too—to teach them a lesson of being honest and an upright person, and to treat your fellow man with respect. So, it has a serious part and a fun part, too."

Back in the 1870s, though, the emphasis was strictly on fun. When Florence, Fleming, and the other original Shriners dreamt up the organization, they chose an Arab and Muslim motif partly because they imagined the Arab and Muslim world as a place where men did little if any work.[41] To be light-hearted Masons—to reject the Masons' stringency but still hold on to Masonic ideals—the Shriners imitated their idea of sheikhs in the desert, though they put those sheikhs in imposing mosques that rivaled the fanciest ones in Cairo, Mecca, and Constantinople.

The Shriners' buildings looked so much like real mosques that people became confused. In 1960, a Pittsburgh (Pennsylvania) couple who were hosting a visiting Muslim student from Pakistan took him to what they assumed was an Islamic mosque—but it turned out to be the headquarters of the Shriners' Pittsburgh chapter. The couple's mistake was understandable: The building had a three-story vertical sign, jutting out over the main entrance, that said, "Syria Mosque." Six-foot-high Arabic calligraphy rimming the top of the building said *la ghalib il-Allah* ("There is no victor but Allah"). Horseshoe arches patterned after La Mezquita in Arab-ruled Cordoba greeted visitors as they walked up the main stairs. When the student, Gulzar Haider, realized that the Syria Mosque was a place for Shriners, not devout Muslims, he was flabbergasted. Haider would go on to become a prominent architect and designer of real mosques in America. Recalling the moment he stood in the Shriners' Syria Mosque, Haider said it fueled his desire to create houses of worship that weren't orientalist fantasies. "Two Americans and one Pakistani in search of a mosque had comically ended up in front of an architectural joke, a tasteless impersonation," Haider wrote in a 1996 essay.[42] "Though charity, service, and volunteerism legitimized the Shriners, they could not erase their insensitive and callous misuse of another religion's artistic vocabulary and symbolic grammar."

The Shriners' history of charity and volunteerism legitimized their organization in the eyes of many Americans, including John F. Kennedy, who spoke at the Shriners' Syria Mosque the same year that Haider visited, which happened to be a campaign year for the U.S. presidency. In his Syria Mosque speech of October 10, 1960, Kennedy lambasted Richard Nixon, his Republican opponent, as a naïve "risktaker" who would jeopardize American foreign policy.[43] Harry Truman, who was a devout Shriner, also visited the Syria Mosque, also to warn people about the Republican Party, telling his Shriner audience in a 1952 address, "I do not want to see the American people deceived or tricked into giving up the liberal policies and programs of the New Deal and the Fair Deal. I do not want to see this country bamboozled into switching to reactionary policies that brought us to disaster once, and will bring us to disaster again."[44]

Truman's speech, made while he was president, was broadcast around the United States on radio and televison, giving national exposure to Syria Mosque. The Shriners' building with the greatest history of media coverage, however, is Al Malaikah in Los Angeles, which hosted the Academy Awards 10 times, the first time in 1947, when Jack Benny sauntered onto the Shriners' auditorium stage and wowed the audience with his jokes and banter. Those in the audience (which included Ronald and Nancy Reagan) sat in an auditorium that was as draped in Arab and Islamic motifs as the building's exterior.[45] Inside, pointed and lobed archways were the norm. Towering above the stage was a panorama of a desert kingdom that depicted Muslim men on camels, next to palm trees, next to mosques with minarets and bulbous domes. Outside were actual mosque-like domes that stood atop the Shriners' edifice and could be seen for miles away. Al Malaikah means "the angel" in Arabic. The building's fantastical appearance, its expansive auditorium (with 6,300 seats, the largest theater in North America), and its central location (close to downtown L. A.) have made it the home of countless shows and events, including the Oscars, the Emmys, and the Grammys, but Al Malaikah is known to prompt visitors into orientalist thinking. Here is how a *Time* magazine music critic described the scene in 1945, when the Italian conductor Arturo Toscanini peformed at the Shrine Auditorium: "The first half of the concert was brilliant: Rossini's Overture to Semiramide and Beethoven's Seventh. . . . The 7,000 worshipers that jam-packed the huge Moorish Shrine Auditorium spent half the intermission praising the Allah of music and swearing that Toscanini was his only prophet."[46]

The name *Allah* is a conspicuous part of the Shriners' best-known sports facility—the Medinah Country Club, outside of Chicago,

Illinois, where the main gate has a sign that tells visitors as they leave, "Allah Be With You." The Medinah Country Club was built from 1924 to 1928, at virtually the same time that Al Malaikah was constructed in Los Angeles. Like its West Coast cousin, Medinah is an orientalist fantasy come to life that has been in the media spotlight for more than 50 years. How orientalist? Besides the "Allah Be With You" sign, there is the lake named after the prophet Muhammad's first wife, Khadijah; the clubhouse, with its Islamic domes, columns, arches, and turbaned statues; and the name of the club itself, which is taken from Islam's second holiest city. On televison, millions of people have seen the Medinah Golf Course, which has hosted some of golf's most prestigious events, including the PGA Championship, which Tiger Woods has won twice at Medinah. Inevitably, golf fans who first see the clubhouse are perplexed by its Middle East flavor and cultural connection to the Arabian peninsula. At Medinah's 1999 PGA Championship, a *Chicago Tribune* sports scribe wrote that the country club "was named after the home of the Mohammedan religion,"[47] a naïve and obsolete reference that is reminiscent of the orientalism that so chagrined Edward Said.[48]

Without a doubt, the Shriners' history is full of orientalism gone amok. The debate is whether this "absurdist orientalism" has done serious harm to anyone. The Shriners say no. Little things in their history prove this, they say. For example, in the 1890s, in the years before they admitted their first Muslim members, the Shriners advertised in an Arabic-language newspaper, the *Kawkab America*—the first Arabic paper in the United States.[49] Those ads listed the officers of the Shriners' Imperial Council, which was later headed by Hubert M. Poteat, who said the organization tried to promote "brotherly love" and "toleration of religious opinion."[50] But the Shriners had at least one member who opposed those goals: FBI director J. Edgar Hoover. In 1956, when Hoover asked the U.S. Attorney General to approve a wiretap against the Nation of Islam's director, Elijah Muhammad, Hoover called the Islamic faith "the Muslim Cult of Islam."[51]

Like any organization more than 100 years old, the Shriners have a complicated history. Many of their early buildings (like the Syria Mosque in Pittsburgh) no longer exist, having either been sold off or torn down. Today, with a membership of about 400,000,[52] the Shriners have fewer adherents than they did in the 1920s. Still, the Shriner buildings that remain, and the Shriners' celebrity members—who include Arnold Palmer, Kris Kristofferson, race-car driver Sam Hornish Jr., and country singer Brad Paisley—are testament to the group's resilience.[53] And the group is a testament to some of Arab and Muslim culture's highest ideals. The Shriners' emphasis on charity and free hospital care, for example, parallels the Islamic idea of *zakat*, an almsgiving mandate that is one of the religion's five pillars. When the Shriners *salaam* each other and wear their fezzes in public, they are reaffirming this positive connection to Arab and Muslim culture.

8

The Lasting Appeal of *The Arabian Nights* and the Bearded Mullah from Turkey

America's best-selling poet is not Billy Collins, whose humorous odes won him two terms as U.S. poet laureate. It is not Robert Frost, the four-time Pulitzer Prize winner whose reading at John F. Kennedy's 1961 inauguration ("The land was ours before we were the land's . . .") is still studied by students around the country. And it is not Edgar Allan Poe, whose "The Raven" has been called "probably the best-known poem in America."[1] If you want to meet the most popular poet in the United States currently, you must board an airplane and fly across the Atlantic to Konya, Turkey, where you will find the mausoleum of Jalal al-Din Muhammad Balkhi, who is better known by his Westernized name, Rumi. Born in the early 13th century in what is today Afghanistan, Rumi was a Muslim religious leader whose name in Arabic means "greatness of faith."

Thanks to the faith of Rumi's U.S. fans, his books have sold more than 500,000 copies since 1990, making Rumi a runaway choice for America's top-selling poet. How did a bearded mullah from north of Kabul become so beloved here? To answer that, we must start with a bearded professor from south of the Mason-Dixon line. Coleman Barks taught literature and creative writing at the University of Georgia for 30 years. Barks began studying Rumi's poems in 1976, when the poet Robert Bly gave Barks a book of Rumi's poems that had been translated in 1949 by the British academic

Arthur John Arberry. "These poems need to be released from their cages,"[2] Bly told Barks, by which he meant that Arberry's versions of Rumi were too klunky, too literal, and too uninspired.

Barks did what Bly requested, and Rumi's words were transformed from formal, rhyming English into informal, unrhyming English. Stripped (as it were) of his dusty scholarly robes and redressed in jeans and a turtleneck, Rumi could now be in English what he was in the original Persian: A soulful sage who spoke to people's hearts instead of their heads.

Under Arberry, here is Rumi addressing the subject of jealousy:

Why envious are ye
Of this all generous sea,
These joyous waters why
To each would ye deny?
Shall fishes treasure up
The waters in a cup,
To whom the ocean wide
Will never be denied?[3]

Here is Barks's rewording:

Are you jealous of the ocean's generosity?
Why would you refuse to give
this joy to anyone?
Fish don't hold the sacred liquid in cups!
They swim the huge fluid freedom.[4]

Under Arberry, here is Rumi talking about love:

My heart, thou shalt not find the road
By argument and subtle lore,
Nor enter in to Love's abode
Save at annihilation's door

About this broad and circling sky
Where soar God's birds on pinion free
If thou hast never learned to fly,
No pinion shall be given thee.[5]

Here is Barks's rewording:

The way of love is not
a subtle argument.
The door there
is devastation.
Birds make great sky-circles
of their freedom.
How do they learn it?
They fall, and falling,
they're given wings.[6]

With touches like these, Barks's Rumi found an audience in the United States, first with his book *Open Secret* in 1984,[7] then 11 years later with *The Essential Rumi*—a collection that became a publishing phenomenon after Barks went on PBS and spoke to Bill Moyers about the joy and feeling inherent in Rumi's poems. More than 20 million people watched Moyers's "Language of Life" series, which featured Barks and such other American poets as Gary Snyder, Robert Bly, and Robert Haas. In his Southern accent, Barks recited poems he had reworked from their original translations (besides Arberry, Barks has molded Rumi poems that were originally translated in the 1920s by British academic Reynold Nicholson). He told a national TV audience that Rumi was one of the world's most important muses. Within weeks, bookstores couldn't keep *The Essential Rumi* on their shelves.[8] America had fallen for Jalal al-Din Muhammad Balkhi.

The Essential Rumi tells stories about human desires and the ways that people quench those desires through intimate connections with loved ones and strangers. In Barks's reworkings of Rumi (as in other versions), God and religion are a subtext of these stories, but *The Essential Rumi* goes out of its way to universalize Rumi. "I took the Islam out of it," Barks told me in a phone interview from his home in Athens, Georgia.[9] "Yeah, the fundamentalists or people who think there is one particular revelation scold me for this." For example, Barks told me that he rewrote a Rumi line that originally read, in English, "out beyond what is holy in Islam and what is not permitted in Islam," as "out beyond ideas of wrongdoing and right-doing."

Still, references to the Quran, the prophet Muhammad, and the Arabic language are sprinkled throughout *The Essential Rumi*, as are stories about Moses, Jesus, and Solomon; copulating couples; kings and their servants; and people of all classes who want more than they have. Many of the poems feature a narrator (Rumi) or a character who urges calm, patience, or some other reassuring advice, as in the bird that tells its captor, "Do not grieve over what is past. It's over. Never regret what has happened."[10] Barks opens *The Essential Rumi* with Rumi's metaphorical tales of wine and taverns and sex, and ends the book with Rumi's metaphorical descriptions of death in which a life's passing—and the subsequent union with God—is a time of celebration, not mourning.

The Essential Rumi presents a Rumi that any American adult can understand and relate to. Three years after Barks's appearance on PBS, Rumi's words and practices (including his whirling in circles, which spawned the whirling dervishes of Konya, Turkey) entered American pop culture. Madonna featured dervishes in one of her music videos,[11] Demi Moore publicly read Rumi's verses,[12] and designer Donna Karan used Rumi's words during her fashion shows.[13] Meanwhile, the Hallmark company asked Barks if it could incorporate his Rumi poems in Valentine's Day cards, while director Oliver Stone was telling people he wanted to make a movie about Rumi's life.[14]

In the decade since then, America's embrace of Rumi has only intensified, as has a debate among Rumi experts: Did Barks water down Rumi's Islamic identity too much? During his life in Konya, Rumi was a scholar of Islamic law (*shariah*), the Quran, and the traditions of the prophet Muhammad,[15] and he taught religion at a madrassa, like his father.[16] "I am the servant of the Quran," Rumi once said, "as long as I live. And I am the soil where the foot of Muhammad stepped."[17] All of Rumi's poems about love are meant to enshrine his belief that love is a manifestation of God's will that brings lovers closer to the Divine, according to Sefik Can, author of *Fundamentals of Rumi's Thought: A Mevlevi Sufi Perspective.* In Rumi's most celebrated work of poetry, the six-volume *Mathnawi* (which Iranians often refer to as the "Persian Quran"), the poet writes that "Love, be it real or metaphorical,/Ultimately takes humans to God."[18] Elsewhere, he wrote, "Our prophet's way is the way of love."[19]

"Rumi has acknowledged that all his inspiration comes from the Quran and the prophet of Islam, Muhammad," Postneshin Jelaluddin, who heads the Mevlevi Order of America—the U.S. body of the Sufi order that Rumi inspired—told me in a phone interview from his home in Hawaii. Later, when I interviewed Jelaluddin in person, he told me that even Rumi's stories of sexual relations were another device to bring readers to the conclusion that people shouldn't stray from an honest belief in God (*Allah*).[20] For example, the *Mathnawi* features a story about an ascetic husband who cheats on his wife with their beautiful maid, only to be discovered in the act of coitus. In Barks's reworking, the story's narrator uses words like "jism" and "juices," then concludes by bemoaning the husband's so-called asceticism, saying that "People who renounce desires often turn, suddenly, into hyprocrites!"[21] Jelaluddin, who was born and raised in Konya, tells me that "Sometimes, Rumi brings sex into [the story] as a clever way to make the point with the story he began; to bring a better understanding."

In *The Essential Rumi*, the words "sex" and "intercourse" appear for hundreds of pages before the first reference to "Muslim" or

"Islam."[22] Fatemeh Keshavarz, an Iranian-born professor of Persian language and comparative literature at Washington University in St. Louis, is one of many scholars who believe that *The Essential Rumi* dilutes Rumi's religious (and cultural) foundations too much.

"In one of the translations, Coleman Barks says Rumi's creativity is some kind of fountaining from behind time," Keshavarz told me.

> I know that he sees something very universal in Rumi, that goes beyond all of these things. He's been trying to translate Rumi into valid American poetry, and he's been successful in drawing the attention of American poetry lovers to Rumi, and as long as we know what's been the process, then that's fine. But I do see a problem in taking out the religious references. And I don't think it's a question of fundamentalism; Rumi was so deeply rooted in this [Islamic] tradition that, in order to understand what he's talking about, you need to have those allusions and the context. I know a lot of nonfundamentalists who are upset about [Barks's books]—they wonder what happened to all of Rumi's Quranic echoes and the references to prophetic tradition.[23]

Still, Barks's popularization of Rumi (he has published more than 10 Rumi titles) created an awarness of a mystical Islamic poet that most Americans would likely have never heard of otherwise. Barks has many fans who are Muslim or Persian or who live in the Muslim world, including an Iranian ayatollah named Abbasali Amid Zanjani, who is chancellor of the University of Tehran. In 2006, Zanjani bestowed Barks with an honorary doctorate in Tehran, where he commended Barks for the way he "introduced Rumi to English speakers around the world. You did a great job—magnificent. We appreciate that very much."[24]

Iran, Turkey, and Afghanistan all claim Rumi as their own—Iran because Rumi wrote in Persian; Turkey because Rumi spent most of his adult life there and is bured in Konya; and Afghanistan because Rumi was born and raised there. Hasan Ali Yurtsever, a Turkish-born research scholar at Georgetown University's mathematics department and president of the Rumi Forum, a Washington, DC, organization that promotes interfaith dialogue, told me that the Turkish people became more interested in Rumi because of Barks's books, which have prompted a stream of Americans to visit the poet's tomb in Konya. When Kemal Ataturk became Turkey's leader in 1923, he banned all religious groups, including Rumi's Mevlevi Order. "After his [Rumi's] popularity in the United States," Yurtsever told me, "in Turkey, people became more aware of him. They say, 'Oh, Rumi is a very famous person—people in the United States come all the way from the United States to visit him here.' "

Rumi might never have gone to Konya were it not for the Mongol invasions that swept past the steppes of Asia into what is today Afghanistan. Because of the threat of warfare, Rumi's father took the family out of Balkh, though bloodshed and violence continued to be an everyday part of the region in which Rumi lived—not only from the Mongols, but from Muslim armies, Crusaders, and mercenaries. Mass murders were a routine part of Rumi's 13th-century world. So, where is the bloodshed in Rumi's writing? Where are all the parables about gore and conflict and Mongol atrocities? Nowhere, really, say Rumi scholars, pinpointing a central incongruity of the poet's life: Rumi, a man so advanced in Islamic training that he could issue wartime edicts, divorced himself from talk of revenge, retribution, and eye-for-an-eye killings. Like Jesus, Gandhi, and Martin Luther King Jr., Rumi insisted that violence was an unsatisfying way of resolving issues. In fact, he believed that people could find salvation in their enemies' hatred. "Every enemy is your medicine . . . your beneficial alchemy and heart healing," he says in the *Mathnawi*, as translated by Majid Naini, an Iranian American scholar. "Carry the burden smilingly and cheerfully, because patience is the key to victory."[25]

It is this peace-advocating side of Rumi that is universal—that comes through in Barks's, Naini's, Arberry's, or any other version of Rumi—and helps explain why Rumi would (even after 9/11; *especially* after 9/11) retain his status as a poet sought out by Americans of all races and backgrounds. In Rumi, they discovered a kind man and a great poet—someone whose storytelling skills transcend time and place.

Rumi is only the most recent writer from the Arab/Muslim world who has gained a popular foothold in the United States centuries after his original heyday. Many of these writers are poets (Saadi, Hafiz, Omar Khayyam, etc.) whose writings were resurrected by new English translations, but the most successful book from the Arab/Muslim world is one by anonymous writers whose stories are more prosaic than poetic. The *Arabian Nights* has circulated in the United States for almost as long as the country has existed. Its fantastical stories about magic lamps, secret caves, unimaginable riches, and requited love—along with its story-within-a-story structure that keeps readers in suspense—have appealed to tens of millions of Americans.

New editions of *The Arabian Nights* (which is also called *The Thousand and One Nights*) are constantly being published in the United States, where its popularity has been fueled by movie versions that have taken the book's most popular stories—such as "Aladdin and the Magic Lamp," "Sinbad the Sailor," and "Ali Baba and the Forty Thieves"—and turned them into cinematic juggernauts. These Hollywood movies are toned-down versions of the original stories, which feature a smorgasbord of characters who are motivated by adventure, justice, power, greed, revenge, jealousy, lust, love, kindness, empathy, material gain, and a simple desire to stay alive.

Besides being a sprawling entertainment, *The Arabian Nights* is a window into Islam and Arab and Muslim culture, even if it is a completely sensationalized window, and even though the scenes in that window show a culture that is medieval or older. "A book as important as the Quran for its influence on Western attitudes toward Islam," is how University of North Carolina professor Timothy Marr describes *The Arabian Nights.*[26]

Readers of *The Arabian Nights* learn about mosques, the ways Muslims pray, the Muslim word for God (*Allah*), the practice of veiling, the importance of Mecca, and scores of other concepts. In one of the book's most popular stories, "Aladdin and the Magic Lamp," the central character prays in mosques,[27] meets a princess dressed in a full *hijab*, encounters a magic man known in Arabic as a *djinn* (the source of the English word "genie"), lives in a country to which Islam has spread (China), and is known—at least in the most faithfully translated versions—by a name, Ala al-Din, that in Arabic means "excellence of faith." These Islamic elements are lost in Disney's movie version of *Aladdin*, which situates the story in the Arab world, puts the princess in a midriff-revealing belly-dance outfit, anglicizes Ala al-Din's name, and gives him voice like someone from Kansas City, Missouri. But in book format, ever since it was first published in the United States in the 1790s, *The Arabian Nights* (and its more noticeable Islamic symbols) has commanded the attention of generations of kids and adults, with an impact that goes far beyond literature. Edgar Allan Poe and Herman Melville—not to mention Hans Christian Andersen, Lord Byron, Chaucer, Charles Dickens, the brothers Grimm, James Joyce, Marcel Proust, and Robert Louis Stevenson—have incorporated motifs from *The Arabian Nights* into their work, according to Robert Irwin, a retired professor of medieval history at the University of St. Andrews.[28]

For the centuries that the stories of *The Arabian Nights* have circulated in the Arab world and beyond, adventure has been the book's trademark. Who thought up the work and its story-within-a-story format? No single person gets credit. Nor is there proof that the tales that begat the *Nights* originated in the Arab world. Scholars are still investigating whether the book began in Persia, India, or elsewhere, but as Irwin notes in *The Arabian Nights: A Companion*,

Arabs kept the stories alive for more than 1,000 years, recounting and circulating them anywhere there was interest—a process that added scores of Arab stories to the collection, and solidified the stories' Arab and Muslim template.[29] King Shahrayar and his consort Shahrazad are Persian and Muslim.[30] Ala al-Din is Arab and Muslim and living in China. Ali Baba is Muslim and resides in Arabia. The oldest surviving copy of the book is from Syria—a late-14th-century manuscript from which the first European version of the *Nights* was translated.[31] Antoine Galland called his French translation *Les Mille et Une Nuits*, based on the title of the Syrian manuscript: *Alf Layla wa-Layla*.[32] In English, the title of the Syrian manuscript means "One Thousand Nights and a Night," but when English versions of Galland's translation were published, they used the title *The Arabian Nights Entertainments*—a name that stuck with many of the book's English versions.[33]

For Arabs and Mulims, the book is a source of pride and consternation—consternation because many see it as a series of vulgar, exploitative stories that were popularized in the medieval Muslim world by less-than-high-class citizens.[34] In this view, *The Arabian Nights* has always been a collection of street stories that—emblematic of the entire book—start off with vivid scenes of adultery and mass killings. Still, versions of the book that edit out these graphic details have long circulated around the world, and *The Arabian Nights* was a core part of many Arab childhoods, including that of Husain Haddawy, an Iraqi native who grew up in Baghdad. Haddawy left his homeland for the United States, where he became an English professor at the University of Nevada and a translator of *The Arabian Nights*. Haddawy's translations are based on the 14th-century Arabic manuscript that Galland worked from. This "mother manuscript" has layers of details that Galland ignored and were thus absent from the many English and European version of the stories. Galland, for example, neglected most of the poetry that was in the Syrian manuscript,[35] and left out words and passages he didn't understand. Sir Richard Burton, whose 1885 version of *The Arabian Nights* remains a staple of American libraries, translated his book from another Arabic manuscript,[36] but Burton's translation uses such archaic language (and has so many footnotes that display his overt racism) that it is looked down on by many *Nights* scholars. Haddawy's versions are well-written and gripping without resorting to literary smoke and mirrors—the result of someone who memorized many of the stories as a boy in Baghdad, when his grandmothers' friends would regale him with them in the hours before he went to sleep. "I used to like romances and fairy tales best," Haddawy writes in his 1990 translation, "because they took me to a land of magic and because they were so long."[37]

What boy wouldn't like the story of Ala al-Din, who overcomes his poor circumstances and an evil magician to marry the king's daughter and live in a grand palace? And what boy wouldn't like the story of Ali Baba, a humble man who accidentally discovers a cave of robbers' treasures, then—with the crucial help of a maid—overcomes the evildoings of those same robbers? *The Arabian Nights* portrays a kind of Muslim Wild West come to life—a venue where smart characters thrive in the end, even if they get dirty in the process. The great American architect Frank Lloyd Wright cherished *The Arabian Nights* as a child, even putting a scene from the story "The Fisherman and the Genii" on his playhouse. As an adult in the 1950s, Wright took on an architectural project in Baghdad (a city that figures in many of the tales), motivated by his lifelong love of the book.[38] The Iraqi government commissioned him to design an opera house in the middle of Baghdad. In his letter agreeing to participate in the project, Wright mentions *The Arabian Nights* by name and, unfortunately, conflates Iraq with Iran—an error that did not hurt his gaining the commission. "I am pleased," Wright wrote, "to join Iraq in a Twentieth Century enterprise. . . . To me this opportunity to assist Persia is like a story to a boy fascinated by the *Arabian Nights Entertainment* as I was."[39] In fact, Wright's design for the Opera House called for bronze sculptures that depicted characters from the stories,[40] including Ala al-din, who Wright envisioned holding a magic lamp. Wright called the lamp a "symbol of human imagination."[41]

Wright's imagination and excitement for the project led him to design not just an opera house in Baghdad but a civic auditorium, museums, a post and telegraph building, a bazaar, a public park, a garden, an outdoor amphitheater, and even a casino. In short, Wright's dream was to give Baghdad a new cultural center—one with a thoroughfare called King Faisal Esplanade that would go in the direction of Mecca,[42] and one featuring spires and mosquelike domes that were straight from *The Arabian Nights*. In May of 1957, Wright flew to Baghdad to solidify his contract, but in the summer of 1958, Iraq's King Faisal was assassinated in a military coup, and the country's new leaders dismissed Wright's vision of their capital city. (Wright transferred the Arab-Islamic characteristics of his Baghdad plan into his next project: the Marin County Civic Center, a building in San Rafael, California, that has a blue mosquelike dome and towering antenna that resembles an ancient minaret.)

At least one American project inspired by *The Arabian Nights* did get built: In the mid-1920s, developer Glen Curtiss bought land north of Miami and constructed an entire city with an *Arabian Nights* theme. Under Curtiss's plan, nearly every building in Opa-locka, Florida, has a dome and minaret. The city, which became known as "Baghdad of the South" and "the Baghdad of Florida," boasts of having the largest collection of "Moorish" architecture in the Western Hemisphere. Twenty of its buildings are on the National Register of Historic Places. Streets in Opa-locka include Ali Baba Avenue and Sharazad Boulevard.

"I Dream of Jeannie," one of America's most popular TV shows in the late 1960s (and in reruns), was inspired as a result of *The Arabian Nights*. The sitcom was based on a 1964 movie, *The Brass Bottle*, which was based on a comic novel of the same name that was written by a British author (Thomas Anstey Guthrie) smitten with *The Arabian Nights*.[43] The genie in *I Dream of Jeannie* is the antithesis of the type of genie (a strong, serious male) found in *The Arabian Nights*, but—like Disney's *Aladdin*—*I Dream of Jeannie* corrupted the original to make an entertainment that would sit better with American audiences. Like Frank Lloyd Wright, Guthrie grew up in the mid-19th century, at a time when *The Arabian Nights* were practically required reading for literate families.

The *Nights* contain poetic language, as when a king laments to his adviser, "My heart is contracted, and my patience is overcome, and my strength is impaired, because I have neither a wife nor a child; this is not the usual way of Kings who rule over lords and poor men; for they rejoice in leaving children, and multiplying by them the number of their posterity."[44] According to British scholars Sir Thomas Arnold and Alfred Guillaume, Arabic was the first Western language to "insist on perfect rhyme as an essential element of its poetry."[45] With the spread of Islam to Persia in the seventh century, this rhyming pattern became an integral part of Persian culture,[46] so that by Rumi's lifetime in the 13th century, rhyming in verse was vaunted as high art. Rumi's *Mathnawi* is characterized by seamless lines of rhyming, which is why Arthur John Arberry translated them into English stanzas that also rhymed. The task would have been a Herculean one for any person, even for one as highly trained as Arberry, an Arabic and Persian linguist who also translated the Quran into English, lived in Cairo (where he taught at Cairo University), and headed the Persian studies department at London's prestigious School of Oriental and African Studies. Arberry's Rumi poems may have been "locked in cages," but they were locked in with an obvious Persian and Muslim bent, as in this first stanza from a poem called "Faith":

So long as I shall live
To God's Koran my faith I give
God's chosen one
Mohammed, is my lord alone.[47]

Coleman Barks unlocked Rumi's poems into an American dialect that is touching, but also unrecognizable as Persian Muslim poetry. As Barks writes in the last pages of *The Essential Rumi*, he and his original collaborator, John Moyne, "have not tried to reproduce any of the dense musicality of the Persian originals. It has seemed appropriate to place Rumi in the strong tradition of American free verse, which has the inner searching, the delicacy, and the simple groundedness that also characterizes Rumi's poetry. These are free translations, but I hope they remain true to the essence."[48]

Actually, Barks's "translations" aren't translations at all—they're reworkings of poems that were translated into English by people like Arberry. They are hints of the essence of Rumi—hints that are, themselves, touching and poignant and inspiring, and have led countless Americans to seek more of this 13th-century Persian Sufi mystic.

9

The Trippy Sounds of the '60s: How Dick Dale, The Doors, and Even Dylan Swayed to Arab Music

When it comes to pop music, the '60s will always be remembered for Hendrix, Dylan, Joplin, and groups like Crosby, Stills, and Nash, but the early part of the decade produced a sound that was equally revolutionary in the history of rock 'n' roll. Surf music was the music of choice from 1960 to early 1964, producing hit after hit. Emanating from the beach cities of Southern California, this music featured doo-wop-like harmonies and reverberating guitar riffs that made listeners want to move and dance. The Beach Boys were the most successful group in parlaying surf music's softer side to a mass audience, but Dick Dale was the one who begat the genre with his signature songs, including one that remains a hit to this day: "Miserlou." The tune reached new levels of popularity with its inclusion in Quentin Tarantino's *Pulp Fiction*, which overlayed Dale's aural freneticism with a stylish storyline that produced one of cinema's most acclaimed movies.

In fact, "Miserlou" inspired Tarantino to make *Pulp Fiction*, so taken was the director by the tune's epic sound and the way it could musically anchor a two-hour blockbuster.[1] What was Dale's inspiration for "Miserlou"? His Arab roots. Dale's real name is Richard Monsour—his paternal grandparents were born and raised in Lebanon—and as a young man growing up in Boston, Dale spoke Arabic and listened to Arabic music. Dale's uncle, who was a musician, taught him how to play the Lebanese goblet drum, called the *derbeki.*[2] As importantly, Dale watched his uncle perform a mesmerising song on the *oud*—a composition with Arabic and Turkish origins. That song was "Miserlou," which means "The Egyptian" in Turkish.[3] (*Misr* is the Arabic word for Egypt.) When Dale was 11, his family moved to Southern California, where (besides really learning how to surf) Dale became a professional musician. The way that Dale explains it, he was performing at the Rendezvous Ballroom, a club near Newport Beach, when a young fan around 10 years old asked if he could play a song using just one guitar string. Dale told the fan to attend the next night's concert and he would get his wish—except that Dale had no idea how he'd keep his promise. Later that night, Dale remembered his uncle playing "Miserlou" on one string. Dale also harkened back to the goblet drum, whose fast rhythms he adopted for his rendition of "Miserlou."[4] The result: A surf song with origins in the Arab world. This was in the late 1950s. When Dale released "Miserlou" on a record in 1962, the song quickly became his most demanded number.

"So many people call it a Greek folk song, but it's actually an Arabic song because 'Miserlou' means 'The Egyptian,'" Dale tells me, before repeating some of the song's lyrics—in Arabic. "The words [are], '*Wenak habibi winta habibi.*' That means, 'Where are you, my sweetheart?'"

The impression that "Miserlou" is Greek stems from the fact that the first person who recorded it and credited himself for the song was a Greek artist, Nicholas Roubanis. This was during the early 1940s. Historically, "Miserlou" was performed in Greece, but in the country's east, which has large numbers of Muslims and belongs to the region called Thrace, which overlapped with Turkey. Jewish musicians also adopted "Miserlou" from that region. "It's much older than from the 1940s, and it's obviously something from the 19th century. And the rightful composers, we'll never really know," scholar and author Yale Strom told National Public Radio.[5] "The Greeks will claim it for themselves, and the Turks often say it's theirs. It's definitely from the region where the Greeks and the Turks were."

Because the Ottoman Empire in the 19th and 20th centuries included the Levant, "Miserlou" made its way to Lebanon when Dale's paternal grandparents lived there. Dale's father spent years in Lebanon, too. On his mother's side, Dale is Polish. He looks more Polish than Lebanese, but in so many ways, Dale relates more to his Arab side. For example, his real first name is Richard, but he tells me he was often called "Rashid" growing up, because Rashid is the Arabic version of Richard. In fact, with his close Arab friends, Dale will end correspondence with "Rashid." "A lot of people I talk to on e-mail, I sign 'Rashid.' I have many, many Arab friends that perform and play musical instruments, and from all over the world—they write to me," Dale tells me. "So, I always sign [with] 'Rashid.'"

Back in 1954, when Dale was a teenager trying to break into the music business, he was prodded to change his stage name by a country and western disc jockey named "Texas Tiny," who told Dale that "Richard Monsour" was too complicated for fans, and that "Dick Dale sounded like a good country name," Dale tells me. This was when Dale was emerging as a country artist—not yet a surf guitarist—and performing on a weekly TV show filmed at the Town Hall Party theater in Compton, California. "Texas Tiny wanted me to do a country song called 'White Silver Sands,' and he was going to record me because I was playing with (country musicians) like Johnny Cash and Freddie Hart and Lefty Frizzell and Laurie and Larry Colins—I played with all those people at Town Hall Party," Dale says. "I always wanted to be a cowboy singer."

Cowboy singing was quickly forgotten, though, when Dale made a name for himself with "Miserlou," "Let's Go Trippin,'" and other now-landmark surf tunes. Not long after his stint at the Rendezvous Ballroom, Dale released his version of "Miserlou" (called "Misirlou Twist") on the album *Surfers' Choice*, which catapulted him into national prominence. In 1963, Dale became the first rock musician invited onto the *Ed Sullivan Show*,[6] the first to be given cover treatment by *Life* magazine, and one of the first to be spotlighted performing in toto in a Hollywood feature film. *A Swingin' Affair*, which starred William Wellman Jr. (and Teri Garr in her first feature role), has Dale peforming "Miserlou" in a style that accentuates the song's bending notes and Arabic origins. To see and hear this version is almost to bear witness to belly-dance music—which is what Dale would listen to in his childhood.[7] In *A Swingin' Affair*, Dale plays "Miserlou" for a rabid audience that includes a Jayne Mansfield/Marilyn Monroe lookalike, who twists and shimmies practically in Dale's lap.

When the movie was released, Dale had been crowned "The King of Surf Music." There was nobody like Dick Dale, and everyone knew it—including the Beach Boys, who imitated Dale's sound and recorded their own version of "Miserlou"; and a young Jimi Hendrix, who sought out Dale for musical advice[8] (like Hendrix, Dale was a frenetic left-handed guitarist) and recorded an homage to the Surf King on his seminal 1967 album *Are You Experienced?* Tucked on side two, between "Fire" and "Foxey Lady," is "Third Stone from the Sun," in which Hendrix imagines himself as an omnipotent being over Earth who marvels at the planet's natural beauty, but "Your people I do not understand, so to you I shall put an end, and you'll never hear surf music again." A lengthy, trippy tune bordering on psychedelia, "Third Stone from the Sun" was an aural bridge between the heyday of surf music and the hard-edged rock that, by 1967, had taken over American culture. Arab music, though, remained an anchor of this more psychedelic music, albeit a mostly unknown anchor.

Listen to the Rolling Stones' "Paint It, Black," which bolted to the top of the U.S. charts in 1966, and you hear echoes of Arab music's quarter tones and minor keys. Listen to the 1967 Jefferson Airplane hit "White Rabbit"—especially its intro, which climbs a scale of dissonant notes, and its lyrics, which mention a hookah—and you hear Arabic music fused with psychedelic sensibilities. And listen to The Doors' "The End" or "Light My Fire," both from the group's self-titled 1967 debut album, and you hear the influence of

Arabic music. Ray Manzarek, The Doors' keyboardist, tells me that his group's connection to Arabic music is no accident. The Doors' guitarist, Robby Krieger, was a flamenco guitarist before joining the band, and flamenco is based on centuries of Arab music, which infused Spain's culture during Muslim rule over the country. Also, says Manzarek, all four members of The Doors—he, Krieger, Jim Morrison, and drummer John Densmore—were interested in Latin music, which (like flamenco) has been touched by Arabic music.

"It comes out of the whole Latin influence," Manzarek tells me. "The Doors are a Southern California band, but we're always listening to the roots of things. That combination of jazz and blues and classical music and Robbie's flamenco guitar, and jug band (music)—all of that is sitting on top of that Southern California Latin influence, which is sitting on top of Arabic influence. . . . It's that minor harmony—the Arabic, minor harmonic sense is such an endemic part of The Doors' music." Speaking of flamenco, Manzarek says, "Flamenco guitar incorporates all kinds of Arabic influence. It was just inherent in Robbie's guitar playing because it comes out of his flamenco guitar studies."

At least one reference to the Muslim world is embedded in The Doors collection of songs: On the group's 1967 magnum opus "When the Music's Over," Morrison—after saying, "We want the world and we want it . . . now"—shouts out "Persian night, babe! See the light, babe!" Right after these words, Morrison yells, "Save us! Jesus! Save us!" Says Manzarek: "We blend Islam and Christianity in there."

After Morrison's drug-related death in 1971, the surviving Doors' members made two albums, one of which, 1972's *Full Circle*, featured a song, "The Mosquito," that Manzarek says is their most obvious Arab-inflected song. The Arab influence is noticeable in the tune's keyboard interlude, played by Manzarek, which features a sliding scale of quarter tones. The song opens with a slow Latin flavor and the lyrics, "*No me moleste* mosquito . . . Why don't you go home?," before segueing into the Arab interlude, and then a raucous mix of guitars and keyboards that is The Doors' trademark sound. "It goes from a Latino/Norteño song to an Arabic song," Manzarek tells me. "The beat was from something that (drummer) John Densmore came up with, but we were all into Arabic-style playing because it's so much fun to play with Arabic rhythms and Arabic harmonies. From a keyboard perspective, and certainly from a guitar perspective, we were using Arabic modal lines. That's a great deal of fun to play that stuff. Robbie came up with the [song's] melodic line, John came up with the beat, and I came up with whatever else is left. It's basically Densmore having an affection for the *doumbek* and Arabic music."

Since 2002, Manzarek and Krieger have performed The Doors' music as a group that was first called The Doors of the 21st Century, then Riders on the Storm. "Interestingly enough," Manzarek says of "The Mosquito," "it's one of our most popular songs in Europe. It's a very popular song in [Europe's] Northern countries. The Scandinavians and Germans are very fond of 'The Mosquito.' When Robby and I are out playing as Riders on the Storm, it's one of the songs that's always asked for, and when I do interviews [there], the northern Europeans ask, 'Will you play "The Mosquito"?' They just love it. It brings passion. It's got the passion of Mexico, and it's got the passion of the Arabian Peninsula."

This passion is also inherent in a new version of "Strange Days" that Manzarek penned for his reworked Doors group. Manzarek and Krieger have performed this version of "Strange Days" in Europe and the United States. "The introduction I've added is completely Arabic," Manzarek tells me. "We did it in this last European tour. Everybody loved it. We got rousing applause. I'm looking forward to getting the re-recording on a disc one of these days." This "Strange Days," Manzarek tells me, is emblematic of "music that [acts] as a perfect bridge. Rock 'n' roll, our Western beat music, and Arabic music, the harmonies and loveliness of it. Music will bring us together. We have to get together with Islam." Referring to Arab music, Manzarek says one of his regrets is that "I wish we had gotten in more of it [into The Doors' music]. You can't do everything. You just don't have time to do everything you want to do, dammit."

Manzarek lets out a laugh as he finishes his thought. Later on in our conversation, he tells me I was the only observer in his 40 years of playing to ask him about The Doors' connection to Arab music. "People don't even get as far as the flamenco connection," he says, "let alone to the origination of the connection."

The connection to Arabic music remained alive in the American pop-, rock-, and folk-music scene long after the '60s were over. In 1975, the Grateful Dead released *Blues for Allah*, an album whose title track is a spare medley of Islamic praise music. Against a backdrop of bending guitar notes, the song begins with the Dead as a chorus singing the words, "Arabian wind,/The needle's eye is thin . . . /What good is spilling blood?/It will not grow a thing;/Taste eternity the swords sing:/Blues for Allah Inshallah." The Dead modulate their voices according to centuries-old principles of Arab musical scales, which employ deep quarter tones that are nonexistent in traditional Western music. *Blues for Allah* is an atmospheric eulogy for Saudi Arabia's King Faisal, a Grateful Dead fan who was assassinated in early 1975. Dead lyricist Robert Hunter, who wrote *Blues for Allah*, once described Faisal as "a progressive and democratically inclined ruler," a reference to Faisal's championing of women's rights, his prohibition of slavery, and his other [for Saudi Arabia] liberal measures.[9] Three years after releasing *Blues for Allah*, the Grateful Dead performed in the Muslim world's historic cultural capital, Cairo, where they jammed with a Nubian *oud*ist, Hamza el-Din, whose songs are an amalgamation of African and Arabic music. El-din, who arranged for the Dead's performance at the base of Egypt's great pyramids, was a strong influence on American music of the 1960s and 1970s. Like Ravi Shankar, el-Din performed at U.S. folk festivals (most notably the 1964 Newport Folk Festival), and though Shankar had a much higher profile because of his association with the Beatles, el-Din—who was born and raised in Egypt—was a musician's musician. Among his fans was Joan Baez, who helped secure el-Din a contract with Vanguard Records,[10] which released albums in 1964 (*Hamza El Din: Music of Nubia*) and 1965 (*Al Oud: Instrumental and Vocal Music of Nubia*).

Guitarist G.E. Smith, the former *Saturday Night Live* music director who has performed with Bob Dylan, tells me that "His [el-Din's] records were around, and people listened to that stuff. Guitar players would listen to it. It might not be heavy rotation, but we'd listen, and we'd go, 'Oh, listen to that. Listen to how he negotiates those notes.' It [his music] is similar to [American rock music] but it's different. You'd throw in little things. The sitar thing was much easier to go, 'OK, here's a little phrase; here's seven notes that I can just lift and play, and if I do the vibrato right, use really slinky strings, I can kind of make it do that.' The oud was much subtler. I think the Arabic influence is certainly around, but not as overt as the Indian was."

Some bands blended both Indian and Arabic music into a rock mélange that listeners gravitated to. Led Zeppelin, whose songs have long been mainstays on American and British music charts, was the most successful group to break through using this banquet-table approach to rock 'n' roll. "Kashmir," Led Zeppelin's 1975 hit from the album *Physical Graffiti*, is a supercharged paean to Arab music. Robert Plant wrote the song's lyrics (". . . All I see turns to brown,/as the sun burns the ground,/And my eyes fill with sand . . .") while traveling in Morocco's Sahara Desert. The song's bending notes, and Plant's interpretation of those notes, conjure up images of an Arabian Nights orchestra playing not in India's Kashmir but North Africa's sand dunes. "They probably overtly used Arabic music more than anybody," Smith, who is half-Lebanese, says of Led Zeppelin. "Me and my buddies would talk about the difference between, 'Oh, that's the Indian thing, and that's the Arabic thing.'" Plant freely talks about his blending of different music styles, telling rock critic Robert Palmer that he learned to love Indian film music at age 17 ("it was all very sensual and alluring") and that his multiple visits to Morocco "moved me into a totally different culture. The place, the smells, the colors were all very intoxicating, as was the music. On the radio you could hear a lot of Egyptian pop like Oum Kalsoum, and depending on where you were, Berber music. I never tried to write anything down or to play it. I was just developing a love affair. But I know it did something to me, to my vocal style. You can hear it in the longer sustained notes, the drops, the quarter tones. You hear that in 'Friends' [from Led Zepplin's 1970 album *Led Zeppelin III*] or in 'In the Light' [from 1975's *Physical Graffiti*] for instance, lots of other places too."[11]

Plant's reference to Oum Kalsoum is another important connection between American and Arab music. Kalsoum, whose last name is often spelled Kalthoum or Khulthum, was Egypt's greatest singer—the equivalent of Barbra Streisand, Billie Holiday, and Maria Callas rolled into one inimitable voice. The daughter of a Muslim cleric, Kalsoum was taught to recite the Quran before she found fame as a secular singer of love songs—songs that were as musically intense as Quranic recitations but eschewed religious proselytizing for lamentations about heartbreak, longing, and planning for a better day. Dylan found inspiration in Kalsoum's music, telling *Playboy* magazine for a 1978 interview that "She does mostly love and prayer-type songs, with violin-and-drum accompaniment. Her father chanted those prayers and I guess she was so good when she tried singing behind his back that he allowed her to sing professionally, and she's dead now but not forgotten. She's great. She really is. Really great."[12] G.E. Smith, who got to know Dylan well, even going to Istanbul with him for a 1989 concert, told me, "He is the most erudite musicologist I've ever been around. The guy has spent his life listening. I was with him for four years. We sat on the bus and talked. He'd go [imitating Dylan's voice], 'Well, there's this song by . . . ,' and he'd tell you about it. He absolutely told me about African stuff, and we talked about Arabic stuff, because he knew I was Lebanese. He named specific Arabic musicians that I had never heard of."

Many Americans had never heard of the Egyptian pop singer Hakim (he goes by just one name) before his collaboration with the Godfather of Soul, James Brown, in 2003. In their video of "Lela," Brown shouts out three times the Arabic greeting, *salaam aleikum*, which means "peace be upon you." The video, which was filmed in Brown's native Georgia, features Brown and Hakim clasping hands and embracing. Another prominent match of East and West came in 1995, for the movie *Dead Man Walking*, whose soundtrack spotlights Pearl Jam singer Eddie Vedder and Pakistani singer Nusrat Fateh Ali Khan. The Muslim world's greatest exponent of the devotional Sufi music known as *qawwali*, Khan performs in Urdu on the tracks "The Long Road" and "The Face of Love," both of which feature Vedder in a kind of call-and-response format with Khan and his fellow *qawwali* masters. The soundtrack helped introduce *qawwali* and Khan's haunting voice to audiences beyond those in the world-music realm who were already fans of the Pakistani icon.[13]

The *Pulp Fiction* soundtrack resurrected "Miserlou" for a generation of young Americans who had never known of surf music. When the movie starts, a couple (Tim Roth and Amanda Plummer) sit in a restaurant booth discussing their future and the most efficient way to make money—including the differences between robbing a bank, a liquor store, and a restaurant. The couple decides to rob the eatery right then and there—at which point Dale's "Miserlou" is unveiled, along with the opening credits. Violence, humorous dialogue, and "Miserlou" anchor the movie. After watching Dale perform in an Amsterdam venue, Tarantino personally asked him for permission to use the song, though it took the director two tries to get through to Dale.

"It's funny," Dale tells me. "He gave a note to my bass player and said, 'I'm Quentin Tarantino; I want to talk to Dick Dale.' And my bass player didn't know who he was, so he threw the note away.

Then he got me in my dressing room and said, 'I've been listening to your music for so many years, and 'Miserlou' is a masterpiece.' He said, 'Can I use that song? I want to play it over and over and over again, so I can get the energy from it. I want to get the energy from it, to create a masterpiece of a movie, to complement the masterpiece of your song.' Most people make a movie first and then they put music later. Well, Tarantino does it the other way: He gets a song and plays it over and over again and creates a movie from the song."

The machete killings, gun splatterings, and sexual violence in *Pulp Fiction* are the antithesis of the innocence of "Miserlou," whose lyrics describe a longing for a dark-eyed Egyptian woman. When Tarantino finished the movie and sent a limousine to Dale's house to take him to a screening at Universal Studios, Dale was apprehensive. He had given Tarantino permission because he liked the director's humility and his rebellious nature, which Dale identified with. Violence was another matter and one that Dale accepts in the real world—to a degree. "I was born and raised in Boston, and when I was a child, we were watching a parade, and a Chinese man fell at my feet with a hatchet in his back. My father grabbed me and we ran—that was the beginning of the 'Tong Wars.' I've witnessed violence," Dale tells me.

After *Pulp Fiction*, "Miserlou" was used in every possible commercial way—in TV commercials and children's cartoons; in pop albums and rap records; in documentaries and Hollywood blockbusters. In its first incarnation under Dale, "Miserlou" was also sampled multiple times. It even helped inspire the James Bond theme, which borrows Dale's surf twang to evoke the daring life of Agent 007.[14] On stage, Dale—now a septuagenarian—is like a James Bond figure, with endless amounts of energy and resolve. When I saw him perform at a San Francisco club, he bounced around for more than two hours, saving "Miserlou" for the end of the concert, after which the audience—comprising mainly people in their 20s, 30s, and 40s—went wild with applause and hollering.

Dale relates to a younger audience. He often peforms with his son Jimmy, a professional guitarist who was 15 at the time I saw Dale in concert. Dale has made sure Jimmy knows some Arabic. "I got a whole bunch of Arabic tapes, because I don't hang around with the people who speak Arabic, and it's such a beautiful, disgustingly terrible language to learn," Dale says, starting to laugh. "I miss listening. But when I go throughout the world, I know enough words to get me in trouble. And so when I meet people in different stores all over the world, I'll speak to them and say, *kayf halak* ["how are you"] and *mapsut* ["pleased"]. And I knew all the swear words, because I used to listen to my father swear. But I wanted my son to learn, so I went and got these Pimsleur Egyptian speaking [tapes], and it's amazing—my son was actually speaking in full paragraphs. I wanted him to learn, because if he travels, there isn't a place that you don't run into someone who speaks Arabic. It's a beautiful language. I love listening to it. In fact, when I would drive down the highway, I'd listen to nothing but Arabic speaking lessons on the CD. It soothes me."

10

East Meets West in Memphis: Elvis and the Poet from Lebanon

Brunettes were his type. So were redheads and the occasional blonde, as long as they were shapely, and as long as they would flatter him with their bodies and their devotion to his Kingliness. They all flocked to Elvis Presley—to his concerts, to the stores he frequented, to his home in Memphis, anywhere they could approach him in the flesh, which is what they wanted. In the summer of 1956, when he was still only 21 years old, Presley could have almost any woman he desired. In subsequent years, Presley's list would include Ann-Margret, Ursula Andress, Natalie Wood, Connie Stevens, Cybill Shepherd, Rita Moreno, and Priscilla Presley (nee Beaulieu),[1] but that summer of '56, Presley was in love with a new high school grad named June Juanico. Presley first spotted her in Biloxi, Mississippi, at one of his nightclub performances. He had seen Juanico walking out of the lady's bathroom, and as she strolled past the stage, Presley grabbed her arm and said, "Where're you going? You're not leaving, are you?"[2]

She wasn't. Not anymore, anyway. After the show that night, they went to a lounge for drinks, drove to the beach, walked on the pier, and stayed up until 6 A.M. For the next year, Presley and Juanico—a dark-haired teen who was only 17 when they met—became so close that they met each others' parents and talked about marriage. Elvis confided his most intimate feelings to Juanico, including the fact that he felt insecure about acting (he would make his first film, *Love Me Tender,* in August of 1956) and insecure about her. He wanted Juanico to stand by him all the time, including his public appearances, while she preferred to give him room. "I keep thinking you don't care," he told her. "You're never next to me when I need you. . . . Whenever a crowd is around, you back off and stand on the outside. I'm always looking around to see where you are."[3]

Though three years younger than Presley, Juanico seemed to have more maturity than he did, telling the pop star that while she loved him dearly, "I'm not going to hang on your every word, or hang all over you, either. That's not who I am." Thinking that Presley needed something to "calm him down," Juanico retrieved her copy of *The Prophet* by Lebanese-American poet Kahlil Gibran, which offers mystical advice about love, work, and 24 other subjects. Juanico had read the book often since getting it as a graduation present. "Here," she said to Presley as she handed him the book, "read a little of this. It might make you see things a little differently. Who knows, it might even make you a little wiser."[4]

Originally published in 1923, *The Prophet* features a prophet named Almustafa (which in Arabic means "the chosen" or "the beloved") who has lived in the city of Orphalese for 12 years. Just before embarking on a return to his homeland across the ocean, Almustafa dispenses wisdom to the Orphalese people, topic by topic, beginning with love. "When love beckons to you, follow him,/ Though his ways are hard and steep,"[5] Gibran's Almustafa tells them from the town's great square. "And when his wings enfold you yield to him,/Though the sword hidden among his pinions may wound you."

The Prophet's words of assurance comforted Presley, who days later pulled up to Juanico's house in a new lavender Lincoln, opened thc car's glove box, and showed her the book. "I love it," he told her. "Can I keep it?"[6]

Presley would keep *The Prophet* for the rest of his life. He told Juanico that he read the book whenever he felt "uptight," and that it helped him "relax and forget everything."[7] So enamored was Presley with *The Prophet* that he regularly quoted from it (especially the sections on love), bought multiple copies, gave them to his closest friends, and—just before his death in 1977—planned to make a movie version.[8] *The Prophet* was on Presley's bedroom nightstand when he died. One of his copies is still on display at Graceland, the Memphis home that remains a much-visited shrine to the pop star's life. "He knew that book inside and out," Larry Geller, Presley's longtime advisor and hairdresser, told me. Geller, who (like Juanico) recommended *The Prophet* to Presley, said, "This was a book that really touched him deeply."

The depth of *The Prophet* has touched millions of Americans over the past 80 years. During the 1991 Persian Gulf War, General Norman Schwarzkopf had a copy with him (along with the Bible) in his Saudi Arabian military headquarters.[9] In his childhood, Jimmy Carter listened to his mother read from *The Prophet*.[10] In the 1960s, hippies bought *The Prophet* by the thousands.[11] Its passages have been read at countless weddings, including the 1981 Beverly Hills nuptials of Ronald Reagan's eldest daughter, Maureen.[12] Johnny Cash was a lifelong devotee of Gibran, and in 1996, he narrated an audiobook of new English translations of Gibran's Arabic writing called *The Eye of the Prophet*.[13] Comedian Flip Wilson memorized *The Prophet*, and would recite parts to friends and at churches. Eight years before his death, Wilson told an interviewer, "I spend 50 hours a week studying Gibran, listening to tapes of his sermons and meditating on them."[14] President George H.W. Bush once said of Gibran, "Perhaps his greatest bequest was the key by which we opened our own imaginations."[15]

From the start of writing to the book's publication, Gibran's creation of *The Prophet* took 11 years.[16] With its biblical-sounding verses and Gibran's background as a Maronite Christian, *The Prophet* can be mistaken for a book of empathetic Christian doctrine, but from the very first words, the book reveals itself for what it really is: wisdom that combines notions of Christianity with the mystical tenets of Islamic Sufism and general elements of Arab and Islamic culture. Take, as one example, the name of the book's prophet. "Almustafa" (the very first word of the text) is one of the alternative names that Muslims have for the prophet Muhammad. In the book's second paragraph, when Gibran refers to *Ielool*, he is using an Arabic word describing the rising of the moon.[17] When, on the third page, Almustafa looks toward the sea and says he shall soon "come to you, a boundless drop to a boundless ocean,"[18] he employs a Sufi metaphor that compares God to the never-ending expanse of the ocean.[19] When, in the book's section on prayer, Almustafa tells the Orphalese people that "God listens not to your words save when He Himself utters them through your lips,"[20] he is reworking a *hadith* (saying) of the Muslim prophet Muhammad, who said (channelling the words of God), "A servant draws near to me in prayer when I become the eyes with which he sees and the ears with which he hears."[21] *The Prophet*'s section on crime and punishment features a saying, "Like a procession you walk together toward your god-self,"[22] that echoes a Quranic idea that people's journeys begin and end with God.[23] *The Prophet* is not a facsimile of the Quran or a Sufi text like Rumi's *Mathnawi*, but it reflects both books, which—along with the Bible and other works—influenced Gibran during the many years he spent in Lebanon before immigrating to America.

"While the language and the sentiment of *The Prophet* puts one constantly in mind of the Bible and the English Romantics, the spirit and message is Sufi to its very core," write Gibran biographers Suheil Bushrui and Joe Jenkins in *Kahlil Gibran: Man and Poet*. "The book is the sum of Gibran's Sufi thought and his social creed."[24]

The Prophet was Gibran's way of melding what he believed were the best tenets of Islam and the best tenets of Christianity. As a college student in Beirut, Gibran once drew plans for an opera house with two domes—one representing Christianity, one representing Islam.[25] As a resident of New York, Gibran co-founded an Arab literary circle, Arrabitah, whose emblem featured a *hadith* ("How wonderful the treasures beneath God's throne which only poets' tongues can unlock") that Gibran personally chose.[26] Two years before *The Prophet* was published, Gibran wrote a play in Arabic, *Iram Dhat al-'Imad* ("Iram, City of Lofty Pillars"), that featured a prophetess bemoaning sectarianism and telling a Christian, "There is no God but Allah . . . there is nothing but Allah. You may speak these words and still remain a Christian, for a God Who is good knows of no segregations amongst words or names."[27] *The Prophet* was another manifestation of Gibran's attempt to unify two religions that, in the Lebanon of Gibran's youth, were often at war with each other. The prophet Almustafa is, "above all," write Bushrui and Jenkins, "Christ and Muhammad merged into one."[28]

This merging is noticeable to those familiar with Sufi and Muslim traditions and with Gibran's background in Lebanon. Before his death in 1977, Presley would often ask Larry Geller about the poet from Lebanon. "He was curious about Gibran," says Geller, who began working for Presley in 1964. "He had several other Gibran books [besides *The Prophet*], but I don't think at the time there was a real definite biography of Gibran." Actually, a good biography, *Kahlil Gibran: His Life and World*, came out in 1974, three years before the King's passing, and if Presley had read it, he would have discovered many things about the Arab poet he could identify with. Like Presley, Gibran was born into a poor, small-town family struggling to make ends meet. Like Presley, Gibran had a father who was in trouble with the law.[29] (Gibran's dad, an uneducated tax collector, was charged with embezzlement; Presley's dad served time in Mississippi's infamous Parchman state prison for forgery.) Like Presley, Gibran was determined to advance beyond his family strata, and like Presley, Gibran accomplished this through his artistry rather than the working-class life that his parents were embedded in. (Presley's parents were happy for their son to be a truck driver and an electrician;[30] in America, Gibran's mother worked as a peddler and then operated a small-goods store, which Gibran ran when his mom became ill.)[31] Like Presley, Gibran had striking good looks that helped get him notice and advance his career, and like Presley, Gibran believed he could use his work to unite people who had a history of enmity. (In the case of Presley, he envisioned his music bringing blacks and whites together, along with rebellious youth and an older generation of Americans.)[32] And, like Presley, Gibran succeeded in his art and professional life, only to self-destruct and pass away in his 40s. Gibran drank himself to death, and in the end—his body bloated and battered—he was a shell of the handsome, dark-haired man who attracted so many people at the height of his career.[33] Just like Elvis.

The circumstances of Gibran's demise have not diminished the sublimity of *The Prophet*, which has sold 9 million copies in the United States,[34] making it by far the most popular book of poetry ever published by an American author. The majority of those sales have come after Gibran's 1931 passing. Like Presley, Gibran is as popular today as he was during his lifetime—more so, really. Besides being a continuing bestseller, *The Prophet* is taught at universities around the United States (including the University of Memphis—the most prominent institution in Presley's hometown). Several public U.S. schools are named after Gibran, including one in Yonkers, New York, and one in Brooklyn, while countless parents have named their sons Kahlil after Gibran.[35] In 2004, Boston's mayor declared "Kahlil Gibran Day" in the city that Gibran's family first settled in on their move to America.[36] In 2003, Massachusetts senator Edward Kennedy—speaking at the annual Kahlil Gibran Spirit of Humanity Awards given by the Arab American Institute (recipients of these awards have included Muhammad Ali and Sting)—said that "Gibran has . . . come to symbolize the very best of this country as a nation of immigrants." And in 1991, a who's who of political Washington, led by President George H.W. Bush, celebrated the opening of the Kahlil Gibran Memorial Garden, located in a posh part of the nation's capital, on Massachusetts Avenue close to Dupont Circle. The garden, which took eight years to plan and fund, is the embodiment of everything Gibran wanted

The Prophet to be: A space for people to go and contemplate issues big and small. Gibran's words are chiseled in marble and stone throughout the garden. (The first words that a visitor sees are, to the right of the water fountain: "I love you my brother, whoever you are, whether you worship in your church, kneel in your temple or play in your mosque. You and I are children of one faith.") Cedar trees from Lebanon are part of the landscape, along with rows of plants, shrubs, and other trees; so are benches to sit on, an intricate water fountain, and walkways that have patterns of Islamic stars. When I visited the garden one early summer evening, with the sun still buoyant overhead, a lone deer was standing at the edge of the garden, enjoying an hors d'oeuvre of grass. In the trees, cicadas were making joyous noise. A sculpture of Gibran, who craved being in nature, occupied the center of the garden. As I stood there taking in the scene, a jogger along Massachusetts Avenue stopped and walked toward the fountain. She read the stanzas of poetry there (including "we live only to discover beauty; all else is a form of waiting"), then strolled around the grounds, where I asked if she was a frequent visitor there. "I live not far from here, and have passed by it many times, but this is my first time to look at the quotes," said Andrea Fereshteh. "I was curious to see them. They're very inspiring and insightful."

Raised Catholic in West Virginia, Fereshteh had recently purchased a copy of *The Prophet* ("It's been on my nightstand for a couple of months") after her mother encouraged her to buy it. "My mom said that, in her day, everybody was reading it at my age," said Fereshteh, who is in her late 20s and married to a Persian American man. Fereshteh and her husband had two wedding ceremonies—one a traditional Catholic ceremony, the other a traditional Persian ceremony that featured the poetry of Hafez, whose work (like Gibran's) is draped in Sufism. The Persian ceremony was held in Fereshteh's hometown of Asheville, North Carolina, which posed a slight logistical problem when they were planning the food.

"We were Googling 'Persian restaurants in western North Carolina,'" Fereshteh says, "and we found a guy named Reza with a place called 'Reza's,' but it's more Mediterranean fusion, and we weren't sure if he could do Joojey kabob [a kabob of game hen] or lamb or basmati [rice], so my husband's mother went to a Persian restaurant up here, and she brought the sweet rice desserts, and basmati ice cream, on dry ice. We had a Persian rehearsal dinner in the mountains of North Carolina. [The non-Persians] loved the Persian ceremony. They loved the traditions, which include a table that has symbolic items, like apples for fertility. It wasn't your normal church wedding."

With her blonde hair, blue eyes, and Catholic upbringing, Fereshteh is what many people think of when they imagine America. But she says America and its new pluralism is reflected by Gibran's words from another century—words like those at the memorial garden that say that people are all "children of one faith." "I feel his words are universal," says Fereshteh, who works at Georgetown University. "We're all part of the same world, we're all part of the same God, no matter what faith we practice."

Presley felt exactly the same way, saying, "We're all part of God."[37] Besides his love of *The Prophet*, Presley wore the Hebrew word for "life" (*chai*) around his neck[38] and sported a wristwatch that flashed a Star of David[39]—symbols of his Jewish ancestry, which he strongly identified with.[40] (Presley's maternal great-great-grandmother, Nancy Burdine Tackett, was Jewish—a fact that Presley's mother told him when he was a boy.) Under Geller's influence, Presley also studied Hindu and Buddhist philosophy through the book *Autobiography of a Yogi*,[41] New Age theories through Geller's subscription to the *New Age Voice*, and mystical Christianity through Manly Palmer Hall's *The Mystical Christ: Religion as a Personal Spiritual Experience*.[42] Presley also knew historic Christianity through the King James version of the Old and New Testaments,[43] but while Presley was a practicing Christian, he was—in the last decade of his life—committed to seeking nontraditional paths of spirituality, and no other book besides *The Prophet* inspired him to want to make a film.

In the movie version of Gibran's work, Presley did not aspire to star as the prophet Almustafa. Instead, Presley was going to be the film's producer, in what would have been his first major behind-the-scenes role. Presley wanted his cinematic adaptation of *The Prophet* to be a breakthrough for him as well as for audiences. He discussed the project with Geller in a Pittsburgh, Pennsylvania, hotel suite, after performing a New Year's Eve concert for thousands of fans. This was the early morning of January 1, 1977—seven months before Presley would die of drug-related causes at age 42. Presley, whose dependency and weight problem were frequently discussed by his fans and in the media,[44] told Geller he wanted to change his dietary and drug habits before it was too late, and that *The Prophet* was part of his plan for rehabilitation. He would do no more pedestrian films like 1969's *The Trouble with Girls* (in which Presley portrays a show manager opposite Vincent Price) and no more Vegas performances like the one in December of 1976 that prompted him to say onstage, "The other night I had the flu real bad. Someone started the report that I was strung out. If I ever find out who started that, I'll knock their goddamn head off."[45]

"Elvis wanted to quit touring," Geller tells me. "He knew he was at a point of crisis in his life. And he had to change or go down. He knew it—he knew his life was on the line. He was going to quit touring, which he had been doing incessantly for 7–8 years. We had the house picked out in Hawaii. He was going to quit for a year, rejuvenate himself, get off the pills, get on the diet that I was on. He wanted to come back to Hollywood to become an actor again—a real actor without singing in films, and he wanted to produce movies. And we started talking about *The Prophet*, and what a great movie that would make."

As Geller and Presley were talking, one of Presley's longtime concert producers, Tom Hulett, came into the suite. Hulett also knew and loved *The Prophet*, according to Geller. "Tom Hulett came over, and so Tom, Elvis, and I are in Elvis's suite talking about *The Prophet*, and Tom says, 'I own the rights to this for a stage play.' Elvis and I look at each other and say, 'What? This is one of Elvis's favorite books.' And we got into the subject of *The Prophet*, and what an extraordinary movie it would make, and that some kind of creative screenplay could be done. And Tom said, 'Don't worry. I'll get the rights. We'll make this movie.' Elvis said, 'Well, I'm not going to be in it, but this is a film that I'd love to get behind and produce.' "

Presley never realized his ambition. In fact, he never got off tour, continuing to perform around the United States until he was hospitalized in late June of 1977.[46] Weighing close to 250 pounds,[47] he was addicted to prescription pills[48] and felt he was going to die soon. Eerily enough, in earlier years, Presley had quoted from *The Prophet*'s passages on death "a lot," says Geller. In *The Prophet*, Gibran's Almustafa takes a quintessential Sufi approach to death by saying that it is a time to celebrate, not worry—a time even more important than life for a person to connect to God and His spirit. Only in death, argues Almustafa, can a person's soul "sing" and "truly dance."[49] In his final years, Presley echoed these words in his own way, saying many times, "I'm not afraid of death. Only the ignorant, the unenlightened person is afraid of death. And that's because they're afraid of living. People, man, they go to funerals and everyone wears black, and everyone's crying. They should be rejoicing. The soul's free. The soul is going back to God, going home again."[50]

In a similar way, *The Prophet*'s words on love helped Presley understand (and get over) relationships with women. The book's section on love was his favorite, says Geller. Presley tried to interest his wife Priscilla in *The Prophet* when they were were first together at Graceland, but Priscilla—then 20 years old—was not interested, Geller told me. Presley even tried to persuade his retinue of friends/assistants/bodyguards known as the Memphis Mafia that *The Prophet* was must reading.

"I can remember one time, we were in Vegas, and he had an entourage of guys, and he handed one of them [Lamar Fike] the book, and he [Presley] said, 'Just open the book anywhere and start reading,'" Geller says. "So, the guy started reading, and after 6–7 lines, he put the book down and said, 'Elvis, I don't know what the hell I'm even talking about here.' And [without looking at the book] Elvis picked up the last word, verbatim, and he said it till the end of the page. He would do that with the whole book. He loved it."

The Memphis Mafia didn't love Geller. Nor did Presley's manager, Colonel Tom Parker. They all distrusted Geller for the way they thought he "put ideas" into Presley's head about spiritual matters. Parker and the Memphis Mafia could care less about *The Prophet*, and they believed Presley's focus on Gibran and other spiritual authors made the King too serious-minded and less focused on his singing and acting. "I just couldn't stomach it," one of Presley's Memphis Mafia, Marty Lacker, said of Presley's "religious thing."[51] Though Geller rejoined Presley's inner circle in 1973 (at Presley's insistence), Parker had forced Geller out in 1967, after which Priscilla had made her husband burn all the spiritual books that Geller had given him.[52] The pyre and Geller's exile were supposed to wean Presley off of his "religious kick,"[53] but Presley remained on his spiritual quest[54]—a fact that Parker and many of the Memphis Mafia eventually accepted, and that is acknowledged in Graceland, where *The Prophet* is on display in a room that recreates Presley's personal library. Other spiritual books of Presley's on display there are Herman Hesse's novel about the life of the Buddha, *Siddhartha*; Ernest Holmes's *The Science of Mind: A Philosophy, a Faith, a Way of Life*, which explores such subjects as "mental healing" and "the nature of man"; Thomas Troward's *The Creative Process in the Individual*, which gets into the concept of "self-contemplation of spirit"; and a Holy Bible. "He read all the time—always of a spiritual nature," Lisa Marie Presley, the singer's only child, says on the audio tour that describes Presley's personal library. "[He was] always searching for something."

The Prophet was not the only spiritual book Presley read that had undercurrents of Arab and Muslim culture. In 1962, Presley was a fan of *Leaves of Gold*,[55] a compilation of wisdom from the ages that featured the Persian Sufi poet Saadi (in a parable about a Muslim father telling his son to ignore the way their neighbors prayed),[56] a saying from the 19th-century Algerian Sufi writer Abd al-Qadir ("It is with a word as with an arrow—once let it loose and it does not return"),[57] and an old Arab proverb ("All sunshine makes the desert").[58] Presley was comfortable with Arabian motifs, as is evident from the pool room at Graceland, which he modeled with wall and ceiling fabrics that created "an Arabian Nights décor."[59] At Graceland's "Elvis After Dark" exhibit, a blown-up photo shows Presley wearing an Arab headdress. With his *kaffiyeh* and *agal* (an Arabic word for the black cord that wraps around the headdress), Presley has a confident look on his face. It is unclear when the image was taken, but there is a good chance that this Arab Elvis was captured around the time he made *Harum Scarum*, his 1965 spoof set in a mythical Muslim kingdom. Presley wore an Arab headdress throughout *Harum Scarum*, a movie that has the King of Rock 'n' Roll singing such songs as "Go East, Young Man," in which Presley croons, "Out on the burning sands, in some caravan, I'll find adventure, while I can." When I arrived at Graceland's ticket lobby, where fans have to queue before setting foot in Presley's old home, the TV monitors were all playing clips from *Harum Scarum* as part of a continuous loop of movie snippets from Presley's career. *Harum Scarum* is a campy *Arabian Nights*–like adventure film in which Presley's character goes to a country called Babalstan, becomes embroiled in a plot to kill a Persian monarch named King Toranshah, and (of course) meets a beautiful woman called Princess Shalimar (played by former Miss America Mary Ann Mobley). *Harum Scarum*, which has Arab characters talking of Ramadan and Allah, is *Arabian Nights* meets Hollywood orientalism meets Elvis, Inc. Universally derided by critics, the movie was designed to take advantage of Presley's popularity—which it did. It grossed millions for MGM and was thought of highly enough by Presley's heirs that they have the movie's memorabilia on display on prominent walls at Graceland. One poster uses Arabic-like calligraphy to spell the names of Presley and the movie. Presley was genuinely interested in the Middle East and the Arab world, according to Geller. One reason Presley was curious about Gibran and Lebanon was that "The whole Bible takes place in that area," Geller told me.

For the general public, Presley's spiritual side was a little-known fact, yet the singer told Geller that his meditating, reading of spiritual books, and quest for a higher purpose were as important as anything in his life.[60] Presley was a mediocre student, never went to college, and was insecure about his lack of education and occasional stammering.[61] Throughout his life, he related to the underdog and to people who were marginalized. As a teenager at Memphis's Humes High School, Presley once came to the aid of an Arab American student whose parents he had worked for. The student was being bullied by other students, one of whom called him a "dirty Arab." According to a recounting of the story, Presley saw what was happening, walked over, and told the toughs, "Hey, you leave him alone. I know him and his family and they are very nice people. These 'Arabs' treat me well and you better treat him well also." The bullies backed down.[62]

For Presley's millions of fans, their idol's history with Arabs and Arab culture[63] may not change their opinion of the King one iota. In their mind, Presley will always be—first and foremost—the man who infused rock 'n' roll with a freedom and a sexiness that revolutionized the music and pop culture in general. When Presley fans go on a pilgrimage to Graceland, they see their hero frozen in his time of splendor. The video screens in the lobby screen clips of Presley in his physical prime. Trim and athletic, Presley prances around stages and movie sets like he owns them. On screen, women in the audience go wild. They still do. As I stood in front of Graceland with other first-time visitors, a woman in her 50s looked at the mansion and asked the nearby tour guide, "Which one was Elvis's bedroom?"

Presley hated it when women saw him just as a sex object.[64] He wanted to be taken seriously. He wanted to discuss issues, feelings, and concerns. At one point, he planned to leave the glitz and glamour of show business for a monk's life in a monastery.[65] Books like *The Prophet* filled the inner void that Presley grappled with. He embraced their pages in a bid to clarify the contradictions in his life. Seen as a man who had it all, Presley carried around anger that occasionally resulted in him hitting people.[66] Women he fell in love with did not love him the way he wanted them to. Presley's last girlfriend, 20-year-old Ginger Alden, exasperated Presley for the way she disliked accompanying him on tour and the way she often preferred her family's company to his. One day in June of 1977, when Geller walked into Presley's room at Graceland, the singer told him that Alden—by then his fiancée—was "always letting me down. I don't know whose team she's on. . . . One minute she's here, and as soon as everything is together she runs home to mama and her sisters. That's why it says in *The Prophet*, 'For even as love crowns you, so shall he crucify you.' "[67]

The copy of *The Prophet* on display at Graceland is an oversize one that, on its cover, features an image of Almustafa drawn by Gibran. The prophet looks like an Arab man—in fact, he looks like Gibran. Dark mustache, dark eyebrows, and dark skin connect the fictional Almustafa to the real Gibran. Gibran put much of himself into his best-known work. The book's link to Elvis Presley was a merging of the minds (and souls) that helped the pop icon sustain himself during the full arc of his incredible and unpredictable life.

11

Islam and the World Trade Center: Minoru Yamasaki Plants a Dream for Peace in New York

The year 1959 was a banner year for American architect Minoru Yamasaki. At age 46, he was finally getting the recognition he had always wanted—not just in the United States, where his conference center at a Michigan university won a national award,[1] but in India, where his U.S. Pavilion at the World Agricultural Fair was a hit with Prime Minister Nehru and the Indian public.[2] Another country was also lavishing praise on Yamasaki in 1959—a country that would become one of the architect's favorites, and one that would influence his work from that point onward: Saudi Arabia.

The country was in transition when Yamasaki received a commission to create an airport terminal in Dhahran, a desert city on the edge of the Persian Gulf. Saudi Arabia had been a united kingdom for just 27 years, and its architecture—influenced by decades of outside rule by Turks and Egyptians—was a mishmash of styles. Oddly enough, a European aesthetic prevailed over many Saudi buildings. Yamasaki returned to traditional Muslim architecture for his project, but he also fused it with a modern flourish. The result: Five-story-tall archways that crested in a point, like those of the Taj Mahal, and—within each grand archway—a lineup of tall, slender arches whose intersecting lines produced a honeycomb effect, almost like a *murqana*, the Islamic decorative pattern that is prominent in Persian mosques. Seen today, the Dhahran terminal is still impressive for its perfect proportions. In 1959, the design was hailed by King ibn Saud, the patriarch of Saudi Arabia's modern monarchy.

"The King and the principal leaders of Arabia were delighted with the fact that we had designed an Arabian-looking building," Yamasaki said in a 1959 interview, in which he also said, "There was a deliberate attempt to set a Moorish character or Arabian character in the building because we felt that an Arabian building should look Arabic. Curiously enough, 99 percent of the buildings in Arabia are patterned after European modern buildings—and very bad patterns. So the rather Arabian-looking building that we are constructing will be all by itself in Arabia."[3]

Not for long. The Saudis were so impressed by Yamasaki's vision that they quickly adopted his arch plan into a cross-section of other buildings, then put a likeness of the Dhahran terminal on their five-riyal banknote. Yamasaki was ecstatic, but the Dhahran terminal segued into another project that would bring "Yama" (as he was known to friends and associates) even more fame and fortune.

The World Trade Center in lower Manhattan was his dream job. Selected over other high-ranking American architects, such as Philip Johnson, I. M. Pei, and Louis Khan (who were the equivalent of architecture's Three Tenors),[4] Yamasaki put into practice everything he held dear, with Islamic architecture most visible at the base of the Twin Towers. There, pointed arches resembling those at Dhahran ringed each building. Yamasaki's inner circle knew that the World Trade Center had an Islamic sheen that spilled over from his work in Saudi Arabia, and from his intense admiration of Muslim architecture. Yamasaki was in love with the Taj Mahal (which he first visited in 1954) and with other buildings evoking Persia's once-vaunted empire. In 1961, exactly a year before he was awarded the World Trade Center commission, Yamasaki told the *New York Times* that his favorite building of all time was Iran's Shah Mosque, whose intricate *muqarnas*, towering pointed arch, soaring minarets, Persian blue motif, and swaths of Persian script have awed visitors for almost 400 years. "Its delicacy and beautiful proportions are very thrilling," Yamasaki told the paper. "It is my belief that buildings should not be overpowering in their grandeur; here there is no sense of feeling overpowered or overwhelmed. One feels in touch with it and uplifted by it."[5]

At the end of his career, Yamasaki would help design a mosque—this one for King Fahd International Airport in Damman, Saudi Arabia. Yamasaki's firm designed the whole airport, which was completed after the architect's death in 1986. Yamasaki was not alive when Mohammed Atta and his fellow hijackers crashed kamikaze-style into the top floors of the World Trade Center. Before his own death from cancer, Yamasaki believed that the World Trade Center would bear the impact of a 707 jetliner.[6] He also believed that the buildings had accomplished the goal he had set for them: to be a welcoming place for people of all nationalities to conduct world trade. Yamasaki wanted the Muslim world to be at this Manhattan nexus where trade and—by extension—peace could be achieved. "We were sold on the idea that having a place of commerce like this for all the products that are produced throughout the world would lead to a better society for everyone," Kip Serota, an architect in Yamasaki's practice who worked with him on the World Trade Center, tells me. "All the motivation and enthusiasm on the architects' part was that it was something that would contribute to a better world."

To that end, Yamasaki wanted the plaza fronting the towers to be a meeting place where people would congregate—day and night—around cafés, restaurants, a garden, and a cascading water fountain. Employing language harkening back to his time in the Middle East, Yamasaki envisioned the plaza as "an oasis"[7] and "a mecca."[8] His plan for a fully functioning plaza was never realized ("it wasn't financially viable at the time," says Serota), but Yamasaki made sure the Twin Towers were festooned with representations of Muslim architecture. The pointed arches were the most obvious manifestation. More subtle was the way the two towers were sheathed in rows of thin, exterior columns that were as much decorative as they were functional. From a distance—from, say, the waters off Manhattan—the World Trade Center towers looked just like any other steel skyscraper, but as you approached the buildings on foot, these columns (and the pointed archways they extended from) were more clearly in focus. Like the Taj Mahal, the Twin Towers became more arresting on closer inspection. Like the Taj Mahal and the Shah's mosque in Esfahan, the Twin Towers were sheathed in straight and curved lines of interlocking proportions—Yamasaki's way of "following the Islamic tradition of wrapping a powerful geometric form in a dense filigree," according to one American architect.[9]

Les Robertson, the World Trade Center's structural engineer and Yamasaki's longtime colleague, tells me that Yamasaki "really liked the intricate detailing (of Islamic architecture) and all the decoration that went with that. It was clear in looking at his work. Maybe the World Trade Center is not the one that would hit you in the face, but a lot of his earlier buildings—they definitely realize that. Sometimes it was very subtle. The synagogue in Chicago is an example. Looking inside, it was a synagogue, but it could very well have passed for a mosque in terms of the detailing inside."

Robertson is referring to the North Shore Congregation Israel synagogue in the Chicago suburb of Glencoe. The first thing that's noticeable about the temple's main sanctuary is the majestic pointed archway that is about the same height (five stories) and shape as the main archways in Yamasaki's Dhahran terminal. The same pointed arch is repeated—in window form—along both walls of the synagogue sanctuary, while atop the building's front entrance is another pointed arch, almost two stories tall, that mirrors the domes atop the Taj Mahal. At least one Jewish author has criticized the synagogue for its resemblance to the Taj Mahal,[10] but many Jewish leaders in Chicago continue to herald the temple for its aesthetic beauty. The house of worship was commissioned in 1959, around the same time that Yamasaki completed his Dhahran design. When *Time* magazine put Yamasaki on its cover in January of 1963, it noted that the architect was "putting up a gracefully vaulted synagogue in Glencoe, Ill."[11] Still, it was the World Trade Center, not the synagogue, that prompted *Time* to spotlight him that January. Four months earlier, Yamasaki had been officially named the architect of the World Trade Center project, and many Americans said, "Who?"

Yamasaki was known among fellow architects, but his name was a blank beyond the world of structural design. *Time* helped rectify that by detailing Yamasaki's life, which began in a Seattle slum where his parents had settled after emigrating from Japan in 1908. Their home, according to *Time*, was "a shabby wooden tenement whose foundation was so eroded that the house had a tilt."[12] It had no indoor bathroom,[13] and no plumbing at all.[14] In the world beyond their rickety wooden walls, Yamasaki's family struggled to make a living and survive the discrimination that was then rampant against Japanese Americans. Yamasaki's father, John Tsunejiro Yamasaki, worked as a stockroom manager of a shoe store,[15] until he was fired the day after the Japanese attacked Pearl Harbor.[16] Yamasaki's mother, Hana, was a piano teacher who, one day, came home crying because of a bus incident: She had sat next to a white woman, who immediately moved away.[17] To pay for his college, Yamasaki spent summers in Alaska's fish-canning factories, where—for $2 a day,[18] working from sunup to sundown—he shoveled fish from unloading bins into processing machines.[19] After getting an architecture degree from the University of Washington, Yamasaki left Seattle because of the anti-Japanese bias that he believed would stunt his career there.[20] In New York, Yamasaki eventually found good work as an architectural designer, so that by 1942, before the U.S. government rounded up Japanese Americans on the West Coast and put them in internment camps, he sent for his parents to live with him. Yamasaki's mom and dad were among the lucky ones, even though—like all the Japanese Americans who fled—they were forced to part with prized possessions. "Our people had to sell everything for 10¢ to 15¢ on the dollar," Yamasaki told *Time* for the article. "The people who bought their businesses and houses knew they had them over a barrel."

Professionally, Yamasaki got a big break in 1945, when the Detroit office of Smith, Hinchman, and Grylls brought him on as their chief designer. In 1949, he and two colleagues started an architecture firm that built a new terminal at Lambert–St. Louis International Airport[21]—a commission that brought Yamasaki high acclaim and a bleeding ulcer that forced doctors to take out more than half of his stomach.[22] In a bid to regain his health and take it easy, Yamasaki traveled in 1954 to Europe and Asia, a four-month excursion that brought him face-to-face with the Taj Mahal for the first time. The architect's encounters with monumental buildings in India, Italy, and Japan inspired Yamasaki toward a new architecture—one that emphasized decorative, almost fanciful exteriors. In mid-1950s America, the steel-and-glass minimalism of the Bauhaus was a prevailing architecture, as embodied in New York by Le Corbusier's United Nations Secretariat building. Yamasaki turned against these steel-and-glass "boxes," what he called "the dogma of rectangles,"[23] and helped instigate a kind of architectural revolution that—like all revolutions—divided people into polarized camps.

People either loved Yamasaki's decorative works or hated them. Not surprisingly, Philip Johnson and other Bauhaus advocates hated them.[24] The first building that Yamasaki created in his new style was Wayne State University's McGregor Memorial Community Conference Center,[25] which showcased rows of decorative triangles that jutted out from walls inside and outside, a skylight entrance with lozenge pattern that extended over the whole building, and rows of exterior pointed arches whose top thirds were draped in an intricate mesh pattern. "He was an architect, but now he's nothing but a decorator," one rival architect told *Time*,[26] referring to the McGregor Center, which opened in 1958. "Artistic caprice" is how I. M. Pei referred to another Yamasaki creation, the 1962 Seattle World's Fair Science Pavilion, whose tall, overlapping arches were a facsimile of those at Yamasaki's Dhahran terminal.[27]

In fact, the arches had become a staple of Yamasaki's architecture, and he would employ a variation of them to ring the base of the World Trade Center towers. Looking at *Time*'s 1963 cover, which shows Yamasaki and his Seattle Pavilion, is to see a snapshot of what would later rise in lower Manhattan. The future was here, and Yamasaki was its messenger.

In designing the World Trade Center, Yamasaki was guided by his likes and idiosyncrasies. As the buildings developed, his fear of heights prompted him to demand narrow windows for each floor. At their interior width, the windows were just 18 inches—tight enough that his shoulder span could not push past the opening. Still, Yamasaki was forced to compromise on his vision for the World Trade Center—so much so that the final product was really a constellation of his ideas and those of the Port Authority of New York, which ordered him to create the world's tallest buildings. Bigger was not better in Yamasaki's view. He wanted (as noted in his application for the commission) to design office space that was "a beautiful solution of form and silhouette."[28] The Port Authority cared more about the bottom line. For its $280 million, it required buildings that would maximize the amount of rentable floors. "This is not a trophy we are building. It is a speculative office building," Malcolm P. Levy, the Authority's chief planning engineer, reminded Yamasaki's architectural team in the initial stages of planning.[29]

A year or so later, the clash of ideals between Yamasaki and the Port Authority reached a climax when Yamasaki flew back to Detroit and threatened to quit the project.[30] He soon retracted his threat, though, and ultimately stripped away much of the detailed ornamentation from his original plan. The arches at the base of the buildings, for example, were supposed to be much closer in style to the elaborate interweaving arches at Dhahran and Seattle, but he vastly simplified the World Trade Center arches for the final design.[31]

As it turned out, Yamasaki was still able to create buildings with a more obvious Islamic bent—just not in the United States. In 1973, as he was still putting the finishing touches on the World Trade Center, Yamasaki was offered a commission to design the headquarters of Saudi Arabia's central Monetary Agency. Yamasaki flew to Riyadh (Saudi Arabia's capital) to confer with the governor of the Saudi Arabian Monetary Agency, Anwar Ali, who asked the architect to draft a central bank building that would "reflect Islamic tradition and yet have monumental qualities appropriate to its intended use."[32] Yamasaki happily accepted, delivering a white, six-story building with a central gilded entranceway that swooped practically to the roof. A high, pointed arch anchored the entranceway, giving visitors the feeling they were entering a sacred and stately space. To the left and right of the entrance were a series of Yamasaki's trademark pointed arches—but unlike the simplified World Trade Center versions, these were filled with swirling lines of geometry that made them into *mashrabiya*, the decorative Islamic window coverings that are found on historic homes throughout the Muslim world. Some Arab designers saw the World Trade Center façade as Yamasaki's idea of a giant *mashrabiya*,[33] but here in the heart of Riyadh, overlooking King Fahd Road, was the real thing. The Saudi government was so impressed with Yamasaki's Monetary Agency building that, in 2007, they put its image on the back of the country's new one-riyal note. (The front of the bill features a beaming King Saud.)[34]

Yamasaki would undertake one final project in Saudi Arabia: King Fahd International Airport in the country's eastern province of Damman. The assignment took Yamasaki full circle from his first major U.S. work (Lambert–St. Louis International Airport) and his first major Saudi work (Dhahran, which is in Damman), but this one dwarfed those two projects in size and expense. At 300 square miles, King Fahd International Airport is one of the world's largest airports. In 1985, when Yamasaki was overseeing the first phase of construction, the Saudis had earmarked $1.5 billion for its completion[35]—a budget that ballooned by the time the airport was completely finished in 1999. Like the World Trade Center, King Fahd International Airport was practically a city unto itself. Yamasaki's task in Damman was to outline a destination that would be suitable for king and subject alike. All modern Saudi airports have to have a Royal Pavilion where the country's king can conduct business and host heads of state. These reception halls are the equivalents of royal palaces. Interviewed in 1985, Yamasaki promised that the Damman pavilion "will be the best part" of the airport[36]—a vow that led to a building of stunning detail and dimensions. Seven fantastical archways, each five stories tall and hooded like a bandshell, connect around a central corridor. The effect is reversed inside, where the hooded archways create a wide circle of curving columns that soar upward. Light pours in through the archways' grilled windows, so that during the day, the pavilion is lit like a spectacular chamber. At night, elaborate chandeliers maintain the grace that Yamasaki had intended for the heptagonal edifice.[37]

Only one other building at King Fahd International Airport commands more attention than the Royal Pavilion, and that is the mosque. With room for upward of 2,000 people,[38] the sanctuary resembles the Al-Aksa Mosque in Jerusalem, which is one of Islam's holiest sites. Similar to Al-Aksa, the perimeter of the King Fahd Airport mosque features arch after arch after arch—a repeated pattern that implies that all entrances lead to God and Islam. Yamasaki was planning for the mosque when he passed away in February of 1986. Yamasaki's firm finished the airport without their founder, who cherished his time in Saudi Arabia for three very practical reasons: The commissions kept his office busy—especially in the mid-to-late 1970s, when the U.S. economy soured and architects struggled to find well-paid work;[39] the projects let him continue working on buildings whose funders favored the archways and decorative patterns that he did; and he was treated like royalty by Saudi royalty. In the eyes of the Saudis, Yamasaki was like kin. "He was very well-received in Saudi Arabia," Robertson told me. "In Saudi

Arabia, he dealt with people of very high rank, and they treated him very well."

Aesthetically, Yamasaki's Saudi buildings are closely connected to the World Trade Center towers destroyed on 9/11 and to Yamasaki's surviving buildings that incorporate Muslim architecture: Seattle's Pacific Science Center (the former World's Fair Science Pavilion); the McGregor Memorial Center and Education Building at Detroit's Wayne State University; the Conservatory of Music at Oberlin College in Ohio; and the North Shore Congregation Israel temple in Glencoe, Illinois. All of these buildings play with forms, arches, and decorative patterns in ways "in which you cannot quite distinguish ornament from construction," Oleg Grabar, an emeritus professor of Islamic art and architecture and a former Harvard professor, told me. "The idea of construction and ornamentation balancing each other in a way so that you never quite know what is part of the construction principle and what is decoration—that certainly is true of Islamic art. Yamasaki was interested in that."

The link between Yamasaki's buildings and Islamic art and architecture was (and is) mostly unknown to the general public. The Islamic roots of many other prominent U. S. buildings have also gone largely unnoticed. At the turn of the 20th century, New York's biggest entertainment venue was the old Madison Square Garden, a colossal edifice that architect Stanford White modeled partly after Spain's Moorish past. Archways at White's Garden featured the familiar red-and-white bands of La Mezquita, the one-time mosque in Cordoba. More astounding, the Garden's thirty-two-story tower imitated the Giralda, the Seville bell tower that was formerly a mosque minaret.[40] White's Madison Square Garden was demolished in 1925, and in its final months, the *New York Times* noted its architectural brilliance (it "stands out as one of the most famous buildings in the city from the architectural point of view").[41] The newspaper's biggest concern, though, was for the curvy, female statue that topped the minaret-looking tower. Would this image of the goddess Diana, done by the great American sculptor Augustus St. Gaudens, be rescued from the wrecking ball? The *Times* devoted four articles to Diana's plight before announcing that New York University had agreed to adopt the statue—and that, under the terms of the deal, the Garden's Moorish tower would also be preserved in reconstructed form at the Manhattan campus.[42] In the end, only the Diana statue was saved, and the Moorish tower is today remembered—if it is remembered at all—through old photographs and postcards. But another famous tower modeled after the Giralda, built around the same time as White's Madison Square Garden, survives to this day. This is the tower of the Ferry Building,[43] which watches over San Francisco Bay and is one of three famous, historic sights along the city's waterfront. (The other two are the Golden Gate and Bay Bridges.)

The most unusual American buildings to incorporate Islamic architecture may be those at the Citadel, the military college in Charleston, South Carolina, that trained many of the soldiers who have fought in Iraq and Afghanistan. Soon after the college was established in 1842, it adopted the citadel architecture of Spain's Moorish rulers, undoubtedly inspired by the wave of interest in Moorish architecture brought on by Washington Irving's books on the Alhambra. Like the Moorish citadels that still stand in southern Spain, the Citadel's buildings feature crenellated rooftops and turrets. On its web site, the military college boasts of its Moorish-looking buildings, saying that they follow a "Spanish-Moorish style."[44]

For visitors to the Citadel, the Moorish influence may be blurred or unrecognizable, just as Yamasaki's arches are sometimes confused for Gothic pointed arches. The confusion is exacerbated by the fact that Gothic architecture borrowed the pointed arch from Islamic architecture around the 12th century. This adaptation likely occurred via Italy, according to Jean Bony, a French-born art historian who taught at the University of California at Berkeley. In *French Gothic Architecture of the 12th and 13th Centuries*, Bony speculates that two Italian sites—the port city of Amalfi, which like

Venice had important trade relations with Muslim countries, and Monte Cassino, a historic Christian abbey about 100 miles south of Rome—were conduits. "The pointed arch . . . had been adopted first in Islamic architecture of the Near East in the course of the eighth century and had propagated itself through Egypt and Tunisia to Sicily, then under Arab domination," writes Bony. "The exact course of its transmission to western Christendom is uncertain. It is commonly thought that the pointed arch must have first been adopted at Amalfi, then the main centre of trade with the Islamic countries, and that from there it passed to Monte Cassino at the time of Abbot Desiderius, who rebuilt the main church of the monastery between 1066 and 1071."[45]

Yamasaki's colleagues knew about the history of architectural borrowing among cultures, so when the architect approached them about adapting arches into the World Trade Center that were influenced by the Taj Mahal and Moorish and Islamic architecture, they supported him, even if they were reticent at first. "I sort of grew into it," Robertson tells me. In fact, Robertson was more open to it because of his interest in Islam. After his stint in the Navy for World War II, he attended mosque services in Berkeley, in addition to synagogue services in the city. "When I got out of the Navy, I guess I had lost my faith in God," Robertson says. "And I spent time with all the great religions. I was probably more familiar with Islam than [was] Yama. I'm now talking about the religion, not the architecture. I came out of the Second World War and lost good friends, and was searching. I did a lot of reading, and I went to services."

During his life, Yamasaki left many hints that he had infused his most spectacular buildings with the architecture of Islam. At the World Trade Center, he deliberately mimicked the Taj Mahal's entrance plan. Like the great Moghul building in Agra, India, the World Trade Center had a relatively far-off entranceway (at Church Street) designed to give visitors a taste of what they would soon see. "There's an arch as you go into the Taj Mahal, and at the World

Trade Center [Yamasaki put] a directional thing in the plaza at the Church Street entrance," Serota tells me. "You can see the influence of the Taj Mahal in the Trade Center because he was deeply moved by it. He paid for me to go to see the Taj Mahal to have a better understanding of what he felt as far as its form, silhouette, proportions—everything about it."

Back in 1963, Yamasaki told *Time* just how much the Taj Mahal—including its layout—had touched him, saying, "You go through this narrow deep gate, opening in total shadow. You emerge beyond the wall into the sharp contrast of a peaceful and silent setting, and there is the gleaming Taj Mahal in front of you. Then you walk along the fabled pools, then up a dark stairway, so narrow you have to walk sideways. Finally you emerge again into the sunlight, and the Taj is so blinding you can barely see it. But you notice as you get closer the fine details and the wonderful inlays of marble."[46] In *A Life in Architecture*, Yamasaki uses virtually the same themes to describe his approach to the World Trade Center, writing, "The Trade Center towers are set well back from the Church Street entrance—the entrance from the city—to the project. Their changing quality as one approaches across the plaza is, to me, especially interesting. So many tall building say nothing at all when one is next to them; their great beams and columns may be gloomy and fearsome from directly below, as they sit so solidly and so close to the sidewalk and street."[47]

Critics of the World Trade Center did not care about Yamasaki's explanation, influences, or circuitous backstory. They knew one thing: They hated the North and South Towers. Soulless behemoths, they said. Maybe the archways were interesting, but these looked like Gothic ripoffs, they said. *New York Times* architecture critic Ada Louise Huxtable led the procession of naysayers. "These are big buildings but they are not great architecture," she wrote in 1973. "The grill-like metal façade stripes are curiously without scale. They taper into the more widely spaced columns of 'Gothic trees' at ten lower stories, a detail that does not express structure so much as tart it up. The Port Authority has built the ultimate Disneyland fairytale blockbuster. It is General Motors Gothic."[48]

For almost 30 years, Yamasaki's spires loomed over lower Manhattan. Not long after the complex was officially opened in a ribbon-cutting ceremony in 1973, Yamasaki was photographed standing in the main plaza. In the background, the arches inspired by Muslim architecture are standing straight up. Yamasaki is smiling, and why not? The World Trade Center did succeed where Yamasaki had most wanted it to, by connecting people in the business of world trade. Men and women from practically every country on earth made their way to the North and South Towers. In 1989, a group of apparel and textile manufacturers from Egypt ventured to the World Trade Center to promote their products to an American audience. At that point, Egypt exported few garments to the United States, focusing instead on Europe, the Middle East, and their own country. "We think we can do good business in the American market," Mohammed Aboul Enein, chairman of the Egyptian Textile and Garments Association, said from the exhibition that his association had set up at the World Trade Center.[49] Aboul Enein was right: By 2006, Egypt was exporting fully 60 percent of its garments to the United States, providing the Arab country with an important economic foothold in the American marketplace.[50] That year, the United States' biggest export to Egypt was corn.[51] Yamasaki would have welcomed the developments. "The Trade Center," he wrote in *A Life in Architecture*,[52] "with its location facing the entry to New York harbor, could symbolize the importance of world trade to this country and its major metropolis and become a physical expression of the universal effort to seek and achieve world peace."

12

Fashion, Tattoos, and Arabic Calligraphy: The Nexus of Style, Design, and Angelina Jolie

Murrysville, Pennsylvania, is the sort of place that people imagine when they think of "small town America." Located 20 miles east of Pittsburgh, Murrysville has just 20,000 residents, is overwhelmingly white, has a bountiful number of churches (almost 20, including Lutheran, Presbyterian, Baptist, Methodist, and Episcopal),[1] and, in the summer, radiates with families that gather for barbecues. "A beautiful suburban community," is how mayor Joyce Somers describes Murrysville.[2]

Cory Pontinen says he is proud to be from there, proud it has given him, at age 23, a social network of friends and employers who support his aspirations. Some day, Pontinen tells me, he wants to work for the FBI. Ideally, he would be an FBI linguist who specializes in Arabic. Pontinen knows the language and has put a tattoo of Arabic calligraphy—the words for what he says is "morning view" (*mathda sahbah*)—on his forearm. "I'm a white kid in America who has a love for Arabic culture," Pontinen says.

The story of that love connects Pontinen to other love stories, all of them involving Arabic design patterns, calligraphy, and fashion, and all of them involving non-Arab Westerners who found in these Arabic shapes and schemes a beauty and sublimeness that motivated them to want more. If there is a poster child for this cross-cultural exchange, it's actress Angelina Jolie, who—like Pontinen—has a tattoo of Arabic calligraphy on her forearm. Jolie's tattoo says al-Azima, which means "strength of will."[3] (It covers a spot that once featured a tattoo of Billy Bob Thornton, her former lover and husband.)[4] While Jolie apparently had her calligraphy done during a visit to the Middle East,[5] Pontinen didn't have to go any farther than a tattoo parlor in Pittsburgh. And he didn't have to go any farther than Murrysville to encounter genuine Arab culture. Several Iraqi Americans have settled in the Pennsylvania hamlet, including Haider Rasheed, whose father was a prominent dissident during the reign of Saddam Hussein. Rasheed opened a Murrysville pizzeria called Amili's. When Pontinen applied to work there, he got to know Rasheed, who quickly invited Pontinen into his social circle. "I hang out with all his Arabic friends," Pontinen tells me. "I've pretty much surrounded myself with Arab Muslims for the past 2–3 years. I can speak Arabic fluently—at least a little bit. I'm still learning."

For his Arabic tattoo, Pontinen did the calligraphy himself, after consulting with Rasheed, who made sure the writing was perfect. Pontinen says he loves the Arabic writing and calligraphy because "when you look at it, it's just fascinating. You can tell it's an ancient language. The Middle East is where all life started. Just the language in itself, just looking at it, is amazing." Soon after the tattoo was inked in his flesh, Pontinen posted a photo of it on a tattoo web site, which led to scores of non-Arab Americans contacting him for a favor: Could Pontinen translate Arabic writing for their tattoos? "I get e-mails every week from people online to translate their tattoos for them," Pontinen says. "Ever since I posted it, I've been getting e-mails left and right to translate for people." Several people now have Pontinen's calligraphy on their bodies. Pontinen says he enjoys it when strangers notice that his tattoo comprises Arabic calligraphy. "Sometimes I'll run into people who know what it is, like college students that are learning Arabic, and they'll be like, 'I know what that says.' And I'm like, 'Dude—what does it say?' And they say it. And I say, 'That's good.' "

Not everyone, though, is ecstatic to see the Arabic calligraphy.

Pontinen says that the first week he went out with *mathda sahbah* on his forearm, "I almost got into a fight at a bar with a guy. He came up to me, was being friendly, bought me a drink, and we were bullshitting. He was a little drunk. He saw that I had it. And as soon as he saw it, he copped an attitude with me. He said, 'I ought to put you through this glass window. My brother's over there fighting the war.' And I'm like, 'Your brother is fighting the wrong war.' I was working at the bar at the time. And I said, 'Get the hell out.'" Several other times, people have confronted Pontinen about his Arabic tattoo, but in those cases, he says, "I just explained to them, and it kind of opened their perspective on it, as really not being something bad."

Jolie's Arabic tattoos have also garnered suspicion. Conservative columnist and talk-show host Debbie Schlussel cited Jolie's tattoo as one of many reasons the actress should be shunned on Capitol Hill,[6] where Jolie is a frequent political guest. Another blogger derisively dismissed Jolie as "Arabina Jolie" because of her tattoo, as well as the facts that Jolie named a daughter Zahara (after the Arabic word for "luminous") and the fact the actress visited Iraqi refugee camps in Syria.[7]

The most notable U.S. display of Arabic calligraphy also generated derision and condemnation. Ten days before 9/11—in a coincidence that fueled conservative critics—the United States Postal Service issued the first American stamp with a Muslim religious theme. In English, the 34-cent stamp said "Eid Greetings." In classical Arabic calligraphy, the stamp said *Eid Mubarak*, which means "Blessed Festival" or "May your religious holiday be blessed."[8] *Eid* refers to two major Islamic celebrations: *Eid al-Fitr*, which is the end of the Muslim holy month of Ramadan, when Muslims fast from sunup to sundown to commemorate the transmission of the Quran to the prophet Muhammad; and *Eid al-Adha*, which comes at the end of Muslims' annual pilgrimage to Mecca, when they celebrate with a feast of sacrifice. In issuing the Eid stamp, the Post Office was following its new policy of holiday stamps with religious or ethnic themes. Previous stamps showcased the Jewish tradition of Hanukkah, the African American celebration of Kwanzaa, and the Mexican American ritual of Cinco de Mayo.[9] "This is a proud moment for the Postal Service, the Muslim community, and Americans in general as we issue the first postage stamp to honor and commemorate two important Islamic celebrations," said Azeezaly S. Jaffer, Vice President, Public Affairs and Communications for the Postal Service, before the Eid stamp's official unveiling. "The Postal Service has a strong commitment to diversity in the workplace. The Eid stamp will help us highlight the business, educational and social contributions of the millions of Muslims in this country whose cultural heritage has become an integral part of the fabric of this great nation."[10]

The stamp's release was a high point for American Muslims—and a low point for the Free Congress Foundation, a conservative think tank that, in November of 2001, lobbied Washington to rescind the stamp. Foundation president Paul Weyrich sent a letter to House Speaker Dennis Hastert and Majority Whip Tom DeLay that read, "I am writing to suggest that the current stamps be withdrawn, to be overprinted with the image of the Twin Towers and then reissued. I have no doubt a majority of Americans would find the altered stamps a more appropriate commemoration of Islam than the current celebratory version."[11] Weyrich's pleas—and those of other critics like *Mekeel's and Stamps Magazine* publisher John Dunn, who wrote a column that said, "I am not a Muslim, my country was attacked by fanatics who happened to be Muslims, so I don't see any particular reason for using the Eid stamp"[12]—were too little, too late. Americans purchased millions of Eid stamps not just in 2001 but in subsequent years, prompting the Post Office to make the stamp a regular part of its holiday releases. "It's an exquisite stamp," Judith Hatcher, a 52-year-old Episcopalian from Virginia Beach, told the *Virginian-Pilot* newspaper in December of 2001. "I've never seen anything so beautiful."[13]

The postage's calligrapher, Mohammed Zakariya, says the stamp's beauty stems from its inviting, angular script, which is called *thuluth* in Arabic, and from its decorative allure: The *thuluth* has a gold luster, which is set against a background of azure that's almost the color of a heaven-sent sky. Like the best art at the Metropolitan Museum and the Louvre (Monet, Michelangelo, Picasso, Rothko, etc.), the stamp appeals to people's eyes because it is balanced and proportioned in ways that mimic nature. Since the inception of Islam, Arabic calligraphy—what Zakariya prefers to call "Islamic calligraphy" ("historically, it was never called 'Arabic' calligraphy, and a lot of calligraphers are not Arabs")—has been a highly valued art form. Because Islam frowns upon pictorial representations in religious settings, calligraphy took on an exalted role—whether it was in the pages of Qurans, the exteriors of mosques and mausoleums (like the Taj Mahal), or some other public function. In mosques, elaborate lines of calligraphy became the equivalent of stained glass in churches. Out of this centuries-old tradition came scripts that—even to non-Arabs and non-Muslims—are, upon first sight, beautiful. That's what Judith Hatcher recognized in Zakariya's Eid stamp.

"If you see a flight of butterflies or a flight of geese, there's a natural order about it that attracts you," Zakariya tells me. "We look at things in the natural world—cats' whiskers, leaves on water, ripples—all these natural phenomenon, and we see them as beauty, because they have an order behind them. They have a harmony with the mathematical, and physical. In calligraphy, we try to consciously catch some of that natural beauty. And it's very hard to do it naturally. If you try to draw ripples in a pond, or leaves falling, you get an unnatural look. If you try to use the yellows and greens of nature as they are, they look funny. It can be done. But it takes a lot of work and observation. When you see a pretty good bit of calligraphy, and it has that reflection of natural characteristics, people are drawn to it."

Zakariya studied calligraphy for years in Istanbul, where he is the only American to have two diplomas from the prestigious Research

Center for Islamic History, Art and Culture—the Muslim world's equivalent of Harvard, the Sorbonne, and the Art Institute of Chicago, all rolled into one. When the U.S. government was looking for someone to capture the spirit of Eid on a stamp, they chose Zakariya because of his outstanding reputation. Zakariya's calligraphy has been exhibited in galleries and museums around the United States. Many people who buy his art are non-Arabs and non-Muslims who see in his work an attractiveness that is absent in typical Western art.

"The graphic aspect of the writing itself is extremely seductive, because it comes in different kinds of shapes," Zakariya says. "There's a script I use a lot, which is very sinuous and powerful. All the big motion is horizontal. It's like a living spring or a snake. It's got this very rich and attractive power to it. It's loaded with power. The other scripts have a strong vertical aspect of it. That vertical aspect of it expresses itself in terms of delicateness and motion. There's both forward motion and backward motion."

"The other thing," Zakariya tells me, "is that [Muslim] scripts have a huge variation in letter height, above the line, under the line. As a matter of fact, the work doesn't sit on a line. It sits on an invisible, slanted line that you don't draw. And a lot of it is, the line goes through the letters, rather than sitting on it. So the positioning is very complex. That gives it a position and space that's different from, say, a line in Russian or something like that."

Zakariya's love of Islamic art and calligraphy was set up during his teenage years in Southern California, when—besides studying architecture and visiting old movie theaters ("they're architectural wonders")—he was a tattooist. This was the late 1950s, a decade before Zakariya converted to Islam. In the '50s, he wanted to earn money from a creative endeavor, and tattooing was it. "I've always been drawn to an art that had a nonpainted background, and in tattooing, you have the human skin," says Zakariya, who attended Santa Monica High School. "The ink and the patterns go over the skin, but the panel, the skin itself, plays a huge part in the look of the thing." Zakariya says he would travel around L.A. with a tattoo kit. His customers were people on the margins of society. "Most of the people you dealt with in those days were Hells Angels and black gangs—I used to do a lot of tattooing in downtown L.A. hoods," he tells me. "They were all underage at that point. You had to be 18 to get a tattoo. I was running a kind of illegal outfit. I met a lot of really interesting characters. It was a phase of my life, and then I moved on. But in a sense, it was my introduction into professional art."

Zakariya has tattoos on his own body that testify to his teenage years: "Mine are kinds of hodgepodges—mostly bunches of flowers and stuff like that. I have a small dragon somewhere, and a snake, but most of them are just flowers." Islam generally forbids tattooing, so why didn't Zakariya remove his flowers and dragon after becoming a devout Muslim? "You couldn't do it well; it meant enormous scarring," he says. "On the other hand, I never cried about spilt milk (laughs). There's no point in trying to erase them." As a man in his 60s, Zakariya cautions young people—especially Muslims—about getting tattoos that incorporate Arabic calligraphy. "Let me work in an Islamic fashion here and say there are pros and cons to this," he says. "Being a tattooist and having quite a number of them myself, Arabic is a very unsuitable vehicle for getting a tattoo. Because Arabic relies on the precision of its angles and its thickness and thinness, and as you get older, they spread, your body changes, and all the proportions get wrecked. So I never advise people to get an Arabic tattoo because of that. It's just going to look really funny. The other part of it, of course, is that for Muslims, there are religious objections."

Islam prohibits the degradation of the body, whether from tattoos or some other form of deliberate marking. Also, Arabic is a sacred language—the language in which the Quran was transmitted—so to put it on human skin in a decorative way (however well-intentioned) is, in the eyes of some devout Muslims, committing a kind of blasphemy. Abu Musab al-Zarqawi, the Jordanian-born al-Qaeda operative who was killed in 2006, had green tattoos all over his forearms, including Bedouin tribal tattoos and one of an anchor.[14] When Osama bin Laden saw the tattoos, he reportedly viewed them as un-Islamic.[15] Still, after moving to the United States, Haider Rasheed went ahead and got a tattoo: An image of his father, whom Saddam Hussein had murdered. "I inspired him to get the tattoo," Pontinen says. "It's to honor his dad."

Rasheed's dad, Aziz Al-Sayed Jassim Ali Rasheed, was one of Iraq's most notable writers and opposition figures. The author of 40 books,[16] he criticized Hussein's 1990 decision to invade Kuwait,[17] which led Hussein to murder him. "My dad published a book against Saddam about how he was dictatorial," Rasheed told the Pittsburgh *Tribune Review*. "They arrested him from the street, and we never saw him again. They killed him in prison."[18]

The face of Aziz Al-Sayed Jassim Ali Rasheed is now permanently on his son's arm, according to Pontinen. Arabic writing accompanies the image. "He's pretty much Westernized now," Pontinen says of Rasheed. "He still has his faith. His house is covered with artifacts from Iraq. He has [prayer] beads that they [religious Muslims] all tinker with. He still has his culture. He definitely will never lose his culture." Asked whether Rasheed considers Pontinen's Arabic tattoo to be inappropriate, Pontinen says, "I think he knows my meaning behind it is right, therefore he [approves]. If it were obviously something bad or negative, that would be a different question. A lot of other Arabic people I run into who see [my tattoo] stare at it and give me a smile. They're like, 'Wow, a white American that has my language written on him.' They kind of look at me as a friend from America, as opposed to people who criticize them for 9/11. . . . For the most part, people like it. Most of my American friends think it looks really cool."

The adoption of Arabic calligraphy for tattoos is just the latest manifestation of a longstanding cultural commingling, but these days, the commingling is much easier to do, thanks to web sites such as www.tattoonow.com, www.rankmytattoos.com, and http://community.livejournal.com/translateplease, which have forums that let users ask about tattoos, request translations of Arabic (or other languages), and compare notes. Here is one sign of the times: Near Haight and Ashbury—an intersection that defines San Francisco and its counterculture, where famous musicians pranced around in the 1960s' Summer of Love—a tattoo parlor called Soul Patch specializes in Arabic tattoos. "Write anything in Arabic script. Professional Arabic calligrapher," advertises a sign in its window on Haight Street. Customers request whatever words they want in Arabic on their skin. Soul Patch then contacts a calligrapher in Jordan, who—from his home in the Middle East—e-mails the calligraphy to the store. Most of the people requesting Soul Patch's Arabic tattoos are non-Arabs in their 20s and 30s who don't understand Arabic but still love its form in calligraphy.

The American (and European) fashion industry has long looked to the Muslim world for inspiration, but in the past decade, the cultural borrowing has magnified. In the 2006 fall season, for example, New York designer Marc Jacobs and Paris designer Karl Lagerfeld created clothing that enveloped women's legs with lengthy fabrics akin to those in Islamic countries. Skin was out; wrapping was in. "Thoughtful designers are putting the change of mood into a different context, as they talk about the 'Muslim-ization' of fashion," wrote Suzy Menkes in her fashion report for the *International Herald Tribune*. "They are referring both to drawing, deliberately or unconsciously, on a culture of female sobriety."[19] Jacobs bundled his New York runway models with what Menkes described as "hefty knits, leg warmers and thick layers of clothes shrouding the body." Jacobs said he used cultural references of women from the Arab world, while Lagerfeld said he modeled his ankle-length skirts on women's garments from the Muslim world. "It was very strange," Lagerfeld told Menkes. "It goes in your mind and out of your fingers. You don't do it on purpose. It is about sensitivity and one cannot escape this kind of influence. It also has something mysterious, a mood of danger, something exciting."[20]

A year later, the fashion designer John Galliano adopted a Moroccan "*souk* look" into his new line of clothing, which he debuted in New York to the sounds of Crosby, Stills, and Nash's "Marrakesh Express."[21] One of Galliano's runway models sported an ornate gold-and-magenta headscarf that looked like it came straight from a Moroccan *amira*—except that Galliano's model also wore pumps and a short pink dress that, let's just say, would prompt a few stares in Marrakesh's famed marketplace.[22]

There's a thin line between orientalist fashion and fashion that respects other cultures—a line that Saks Fifth Avenue crossed repeatedly in its 2005 spring fashion catalog, which was shot on location in Morocco.[23] On the one hand, the catalog spotlighted a canvas sandal by designer Jimmy Choo that incorporated the Magrebi eight-pointed star into the shoe's floral motif.[24] This type of star is synonymous with Moroccan and Arab culture—in Washington, DC, the star can be seen throughout the Kahlil Gibran Memorial Garden, and on the walls of the nearby Islamic Center of Washington. (This is the center that President George W. Bush visited in the days after 9/11 to meet with Muslim leaders and to tell a national audience that Islam was a religion of peace.) Choo's sandal is a tasteful homage to Arab culture, but then in later pages, we see a model in tank top and head wrap lounging seductively next to two camels, with two older Moroccan men dressed in traditional desert garb;[25] two models—one of whom wears a paisley tunic that barely covers her naked thighs—standing in a *souk* alleyway, watched from the distance by four Moroccan males;[26] and a model in skimpy dress and head veil who lies on a tent carpet somewhere in the Moroccan desert.[27] It is all so exotic—at least that was the word Saks Fifth Avenue used[28] to describe its spring catalog, which was titled "Into the Mystic." Saks deserves credit for getting one thing right: The catalog's first sentence says, "The influence of North Africa extends well beyond the vast expanse of the epically romantic Sahara,"[29] which is true.

The whole Muslim world has a cultural influence that extends far beyond its borders, and if one Muslim country tops all others in its influence on design, that country is Iran. Carpets put the country into a category of its own. For half a millennium, Westerners have craved and collected Persian rugs. In the United States, these rugs have been popular from the country's very infancy. George William Fairfax, a friend of George Washington's who lived near him in Virginia, had an elaborate Persian carpet in his mansion.[30] Two hundred years later, Americans buy thousands of Persian carpets every year—so many that the United States accounts for 22 percent of Iran's Persian carpet exports.[31] When the U.S. military wanted to spruce up its Guantanamo Bay prison complex in 2006, it added (among other things) a faux Persian carpet.[32] What is the attraction? For many people, it's a combination of qualities—from the carpets' sterling reputation to the types of knots and materials—but the carpets' intricate design patterns are what elevate them to high art and explain why museums hang them on walls next to galleries of Baroque and Renaissance art.

The most acclaimed Persian carpets in the Western world are the two known as the Ardabil Carpet—16th-century rugs on display at the Los Angeles County Museum of Art and at London's Victoria and Albert Museum. The carpet's vines, flowers, medallions, and ovals are a breathtaking sight—a geometry of exquisite proportions that was originally meant for worshippers in a Persian mosque. The carpet's central pattern is really a celestial look at heaven, according to Persian art scholar Schuyler V.R. Cammann, who says that the carpet's inner four corner designs represent the lesser gates of the universe as imagined by Islamic symbolism.[33] Adding to this religious motif is the fact that the carpet has a small inscription of poetry from Hafiz that talks metaphorically of entering God's kingdom: "But for thy Gate, I have no refuge in the world;/My head has no place of trust except this Door."[34] The carpet's outer, patterned border symbolizes the Quranic idea that a screen (*parda* in Persian, *hijab* in Arabic) serves as a screen, net, or covering between Paradise and mankind. "This concept of a screen or barrier between man and Heaven is essential for an understanding of many Persian rug patterns," notes Cammann.[35] "The border of the Ardabil Rug . . . is more than just a window frame through which to catch a view of the Ultimate Destination beyond the Sky. The border represents the *parda* or *hijab*, formed by interlinked panels or plates of different shapes." Further, according to Cammann, the flower that is central to the carpet design, the peony (whose stems wind throughout the rug) is a deliberate choice for one major reason: The old Persian word for peony was *zakar*, which is related to the Arabic word *zikr*, which describes the circular religious chanting that Sufis employ to reach states of religious ecstasy.[36] "The idea of forming a circle for endless repetitions of the *zikr*," Cammann writes, "is symbolized by the [carpet's] continuous vine, which suggests unending action."[37] Klaus Brisch of Berlin's Museum für islamische Kunst summarizes his view of Persian carpets in this way: "The art of the oriental carpet is religious art."[38]

The Ardabil Carpet, whose design has been copied onto scores of other Persian rugs,[39] is from northwest Iran, where another important Persian carpet was made: the one that supported Pope John Paul II's casket in 2005. At the pontiff's funeral, his coffin was placed on the carpet in front of the Vatican, where Rome's vicar said a prayer, and the church's other cardinals stood at attention in solemn tribute. Like the Ardabil, this pontifical carpet was more than 20 feet in length, featured a border and flower motif, and was awe-inspiring to look at. "Amazing" is how one CNN analyst at the funeral described the carpet.[40] "The Persian carpet was watched by the world," noted an Iranian newspaper.[41] For its main front-page photo of the procession, the *New York Times* published a blown-up overhead shot that showed Pope John Paul's casket resting on the Iranian rug.[42]

The choice of the carpet continued a historic connection between the Catholic Church and Islamic design. In 1519, the Holy Roman emperor of newly reconquered Spain, Charles V, dressed for his coronation ceremony in "robes very much in the Islamic fashion," with the hem of his cape embroidered in Arabic calligraphy.[43] In the 12th century, the Archbishop of Canterbury, Thomas Becket, was said to own an outer garment covered in Islamic imagery and inscription. Becket would have worn the garment, called a "chasuble," during the Eucharist ceremony, at a time when the Crusades were in full throttle.[44] War may diminish the exchanges between cultures on different continents, but it never snuffs them out completely, as is evident from Americans' post-9/11 embrace of Arabic tattoos, Persian carpets, and *kaffiyehs*—the Arabic head scarves that, like Che Guevara T-shirts and Chuck Taylor lowtops, are a staple of college wardrobes from Hawaii to New York. In the United States, fashion, calligraphy, and design from the Arab and Muslim world are now prominent from the street level to high society. What links them all is a beauty that is unmistakable—at least to the owner. Pontinen has had to defend his artwork against the judgment of strangers, and he is happy to do it. In the long run, he says, it clarifies the meaning of his tattoo for others, even if they maintain their distance from it.

13

Arabs and Muslims in the United States: Today and Tomorrow

The United States was founded on the premise that all people and all cultures were equal in the fabric of American society. In reality, of course, the country was dominated by European descendants who saw dark-skinned native Americans and black American slaves as inferior and culturally backward.

In saying that "a multicultural America is impossible because a non-Western America is not American,"[1] Samuel P. Huntington voices a sentiment that stretches back four centuries. Under this mindset, an influx of Arabs and Muslims—and their culture—undermines America's welfare and well-being. A fear is that Arabs and Muslims will try to convert every apostate who does not believe in Allah or Arab values. But go to the most Arab city in the United States—Dearborn, Michigan, where 30 percent of the 100,000 residents have Arab roots—and you will find an America that looks like the America of most other U.S. cities. Restaurants, grocery stores, and fast-food outlets—not houses of worship—dominate the city's Arab-oriented thoroughfares, which are also dotted with beauty parlors, furniture stores, dental clinics, drug stores, and gas stations. The big difference between Dearborn and other U.S. cities is that, in Dearborn, Arabic is as likely to be spoken as English in the aisles of the neighborhood Walgreens—not just by customers, but by the clerks who work there. And in Dearborn, the signage in that Walgreens is likely to be in English and Arabic, just as it is at the Dearborn Walgreens at Schaefer Road and Warren Avenue, where every customer who walks in sees this at the entryway: *Ahlan wa sahalan.*

In Arabic, these words mean "Welcome," though they can also be translated "You Are Entering as Family and Are Trodding on Welcome Land." In the Arab and Muslim world, people who open their doors to guests make this pronouncement as a sign of courtesy and respect. Businesses around Dearborn, including a prominent Italian American car dealership,[2] have the same Arabic greeting in their entryways. Dearborn's Arab residents do not banner their homes with *Ahlan wa sahalan*, which would be redundant anyway, since—like other cultures—Arab culture treats visitors like royalty. So it was when I visited the Dearborn home of Fouad Zaban, the head football coach at Dearborn's Fordson High School.

First came an offer (actually more like a demand) to drink tea, followed by a plate of Arab pastries served by his wife, Zaynab, then a large bowl of freshly cut cantaloupe, then a request to stay and watch Michigan's college football teams play on television. Fouad Zaban's professional life revolves around football. His personal one revolves around his wife, their four children, and Islam. Religion and football sometimes mix at Fordson, where 95 percent of the players (and student body) are Arab American. Though he is a devout Muslim and a member of the largest mosque in the United States, Dearborn's Islamic Center of America, Zaban never pushes his players toward Islam. Instead, it is the players themselves—a smattering of the tackles, linebackers, running backs, and others—who incorporate Islam into their day-to-day school lives, as when they listen to Muslim religious chants to perform better on the field.

The chanting features Arabic pronouncements about the death of Hussein ibn Ali, the revered seventh-century imam who was assassinated in the Battle of Karbala in what is today Iraq. The death of Ali, who was the grandson of the Muslim prophet Muhammad, is remembered by Shi'ite Muslims around the world on the tenth day of the Muslim month of Muharram. That day is called Ashura, which in Arabic is the word for 10.

"You know Karbala and the history of Ashura—you know how they commemorate the martyrdom of Hussein, and they have those rituals and chants—that's pretty much what some of [my players] listen to," says Zaban.

Before their team's matchups, Fordson's players often pray. And during contests, some players invoke religion. "At times during a game, when they feel it's time to do something really important—a big play, for example—they may say, 'God is the greatest,' '*Allahu Akbar,*'" says Zaban, a former Fordson player who grew up in Dearborn. "They do that before the actual play—something to motivate them."

Referring to the chants and the music that his players listen to for inspiration, including rap and hip-hop, Zaban says, "From a coach's point of view, if this is what's going to get them up, let them do it—as long as I don't think it's in bad taste." Referring to the players' incorporation of religious prayers into games, Zaban says, "As a teacher in a public school, I stay away from it. I cannot be the one leading the prayer or anything. I can't deny them that, but I can't encourage them to do that."

However they apply it, the players' use of religion seems to work: As a team, the Fordson Tractors (both names stem from the life of Ford Motor Company founder Henry Ford) are one of the Detroit area's most successful prep gridiron squads. They've won four state championships, more league titles than any other Dearborn team, and went undefeated one year—even though some of their most crucial games are played during Ramadan, the Islamic holy month when Muslims are required to fast from sunup to sundown. At Ramadan, Fordson's fasting players can't even drink water during games. Still, the Tractors continue their winning ways. In the 2007 season, which was Zaban's first as head coach (he was assistant coach before that), Fordson went 8–3 and won its big matchup against rival Dearborn High School, 16–14, in a thrilling come-from-behind effort. The heroes were quarterback Mohammed Bazzy, who engineered two long touchdown drives; running back Hassan Amen, who ran for the first and last scores; kicker Ali Alaboody, whose field goal was the difference; and Zaban, whose "no excuses" mantra helped propel the Tractors to another winning season.

Zaban is himself a Dearborn success story. As a young boy, he came to the United States in 1976 when his father was lured by a job in a Dearborn factory run by Chrysler. In the '70s, Detroit-area car factories regularly recruited workers from the Arab and Muslim world, continuing a practice that stretched back to the 1920s. (The auto industry was the primary lure for the first wave of Arab immigrants to Michigan.) But Fawad Zaban says his dad, Mohamed, was "unlucky" at work: Chrysler laid him off within six months, and for the next decade, Mohamed Zaban worked intermittently, which meant the family was usually in a precarious financial state. Fouad's upbringing was "lower middle class" ("we didn't necessarily have toys in the house"), but he has earned enough money to move his family to an upscale, tree-lined part of Dearborn that has multilevel houses and well-manicured lawns.

The Zabans are Sunni—the dominant faith in Islam—and attend services at the Islamic Center of America, a $15 million mosque just minutes from the Ford Motor Company's headquarters. Fawad has Palestinian heritage—his grandfather on his dad's side was Palestinian—but nearly everyone from his mother's and father's side is from the area around Tebnin, a small village south of Beirut. Mohamed Zaban died in 2001. Fouad's mother, Samiha, is still alive—she lives minutes away from Zaban and his family, and spends most weekends with them. Growing up in Dearborn, Zaban was not overly religious, but that changed once he got married and had kids. Now, he is more observant than his mother, and he makes sure his own children continue this new line of religious piety. His house is a mix of everything Zaban holds dear: On the day I visited, football was on the television, and Zaban's young children were playing on the first floor, where a picture of SpongeBob was prominently displayed.

This merging of cultures—especially the emphasis on religion, football, and family—is common in Dearborn, though it was not when Zaban was raised there. He had no real role models in football. He followed the career of Ali Haji-Sheikh, the Iranian American kicker who played for the New York Giants, Atlanta Falcons, and Washington Redskins from 1983 to 1987, but Zaban was a running back at Fordson who gravitated toward other offensive-minded players who were on the field all the time. "There were football players you tried to imitate—I was a Steeler fan, so I loved Franco Harris, Lynn Swann, Terry Bradshaw," he says. "I was also a Lions fan, but they weren't that great." Pausing to consider his thoughts, Zaban says, "In all honesty, my role models were basically my parents—this is who I looked up to."

The long journey that Mohamed and Samiha Zaban took from Tebnin, Lebanon, to Dearborn, Michigan, mirrored the paths of thousands of other Arabs and Muslims who found their way to Dearborn and beyond. Dearborn's Arab American National Museum, a gleaming, white-domed edifice that opened its doors in 2005, features exhibits that extol the lives of previous immigrant Arabs and Muslims, including Anna Yousef, a Tebnin native who was one of 154 Arabs who traveled to America on the Titanic.[3] Only 29 of the Arab passengers survived the Atlantic Ocean sinking, according to the museum's exhibit, which lists such victims as Khalil Saad, a 25-year-old farm laborer from Syria, and Ali Ahmed, a 24-year-old laborer from Argentina.[4] The vast majority of Arabs on the Titanic were third-class passengers who paid the minimum fare to get to their new homeland. A dozen families from Tebnin died in the Titanic tragedy because, as third-class passengers, they were put in steerage and had no way to escape the ocean liner's quick submergence, according to an account by Yousef, who lived to be 91.[5]

Besides its surprising display on Yousef and the other Titanic passengers, the Arab American National Museum has exhibits on every imaginable aspect of Arab life in the United States. Not surprisingly, the museum emphasizes Arabs' positive contributions to American society, whether they be the songwriting of Paul Anka, who is of Lebanese Christian descent; the acting of M*A*S*H's Jamie Farr (real name: Jameel Joseph Farah), who is also Lebanese; the volunteer work of the Syrian Ladies Aid Society of New York, which raised money for Syrian immigrants from its start in 1907; or the feats of Hadj Ali, the Greek-Syrian convert to Islam who, in the 1850s, was a camel trainer for the U.S. Army in the American Southwest, where his military colleagues called him "Hi Jolly" because they could not pronounce his real name. Fordson High School is also memorialized (with a life-size photograph of a football player), as are, among others, ukulele player Tiny Tim (real name: Herbert Khaury), Edward Said, Queen Noor, and Joseph Arbeely, a Damascus man whose family arrived in New York on August 20, 1878—the first recorded Arab family to come to the United States with the intention of becoming citizens. By 1924, about 200,000 Arabs lived in the United States, according to the museum. (Today, just in the greater Detroit-Dearborn metropolitan area, about 400,000 Arab Americans reside, while about 500,000 live in Michigan—the highest concentration of Arabs outside the Middle East.[6]) Most of the early Arab immigrants were Christian Arabs from the Syrian-Lebanese Levant, such as Jamie Farr's grandfather, who immigrated to America at the turn of the 20th century, and whose actual pocketknife is displayed at the museum.[7]

More than 50,000 people a year visit the museum, which is the first of its kind in the country, and one of the most ornate: Its indoor water fountain, inlaid tile and limestone floor, and mosque-like dome with intricate Arabic calligraphy give it the feeling of a great Arab palace. Costing more than $16 million, and funded by donations from Arab Americans and people (both Arabs and non-Arabs) around the world, its location across from Dearborn's City

Hall is a powerful statement of how far Arab Americans have come in the United States.

When I visited the museum, the most jarring moment was not seeing a Jewish menorah and tallith (prayer shawl) in a display that explained monotheistic religions; nor was it seeing a typewriter and manuscript that showed that the author of *The Exorcist*, William Peter Blatty, was of Lebanese descent; nor was it encountering the uniform of Jamal Baadani, a Yemenese-Egyptian-American Marine who fought in the Iraq War and, right after 9/11, founded the Association of Patriotic Arab Americans in Military (their slogan: "Our History Validates Our Presence"). No, the most jarring moment was going to the library on the museum's ground floor, perusing their collection, and seeing a 1977 book published by the American Enterprise Institute for Public Policy Research, a conservative think tank, that delved into the subject of Arab and American culture—and whether the two cultures could happily intersect. (The think tank is closely associated with architects of the Iraq War. Among its scholars and fellows are Paul Wolfowitz, Richard Perle, and John Yoo—the law professor whose legal opinions bolstered the Bush administration's mistreatement of prisoners.)

Based on a 1976 Washington, DC, conference sponsored by the Institute, "Arab and American Cultures,"[8] the volume features a roundtable discussion, "Can Cultures Communicate?," involving academics on opposite ends of the spectrum, including Edward Said and Samuel P. Huntington. Their conclusions: No and yes. Said and Huntington actually agreed with each other—to a point.

"I am happy to start off by sounding an optimistic note, that it is indeed possible for Arabs and Americans to interact culturally in the fullest possible sense," Said said, beginning the roundtable.

> But, having said that, I should add, realistically, that in the present context there are two principal obstacles to an optimal relationship between the two cultures.

> First, cultural relationships do not exist in the abstract: they take place in the world. The relationship between Arab and American cultures is highly politicized. . . . The second obstacle is that, for reasons of both language and of cultural or religious tradition, Arab culture is not widely known in this country. The problems of translation are many, but that is only part of it. If you were to ask a generally literate American about what is now taking place culturally in the Arab world—in poetry, in fiction, in the arts generally—he would be very hard put to name a single figure of any importance. That is to say, of any importance to Arabs. He might mention Kahlil Gibran, but he is not of this time. So one feels that the possibilities of intercultural relationships at this moment are severely limited.[9]

Then it was Huntington's turn. Two decades before publishing *The Clash of Civilizations and the Remaking of World Order,* Huntington decried what he called Americans' "ignorance" of Arab culture, then asked,

> How do we go about establishing trust between Americans and Arabs? One can have trust only where one has communication; communication is a necessary but not a sufficient qualification for trust. In order to establish trust, one has to have dealings with individuals. Trust is something which exists within, or rather between, individuals. . . . Related to that is the need to eliminate from American thinking many stereotypes of Arabs, which are based on ignorance.[10]

Huntington, Said, and the other panelists were addressing the relationship between Arabs in the Arab world and Americans in the United States, but their answers could easily apply to the relationship between Arab Americans and other Americans. Stereotypes? Lack of communication? Politicization? The possibility of interacting "in the fullest possible sense"? Yes, yes, yes, and yes. In retrospect, what made the conference even more remarkable was its 1976 setting—a time that followed the first modern American backlash against Arabs and Muslims, and preceded an even more violent one against Iranian Americans. Both backlashes involved oil and the pernicious use of scapegoating.

In 1973, Arab oil producers directed an embargo against the United States for its support of Israel in the Yom Kippur War. Gasoline prices skyrocketed—from about $3 a barrel to $12, leading to resentment (and worse) against Arab Americans, and those perceived to be Arab Americans. Afraid of being targeted by neighbors or strangers, many Arab Americans changed their first names: Farid became "Fred"; Mohammed became "Mo."[11] As war raged in the Middle East, and Arabs there and in America were blamed for the ballooning price of gas, Arab Americans felt helpless. "Suddenly we were being held responsible for things we had nothing to do with and no control over and maybe didn't even support in the first place," Don Unis, a Dearborn fire captain, told the *Los Angeles Times*.[12] James Abourezk, the first U.S. Congressman of Arab American descent, told the same paper that "racism against Arabs has been endemic since the Crusades. But it was stimulated [in the United States] by the 1973 oil embargo. Anytime there's a lot of violence or huckletybuck in the Middle East, you find rising animosity toward Arab-Americans here."[13]

For both Arabs and Iranians in the United States, the pattern continued in 1979, after the Ayatollah Khomeini overthrew the Shah of Iran and oil prices spiked again. In November of 1979, just two weeks after Iranian militants stormed the U.S. embassy in Tehran, bricks were thrown through the windows of Iranian-American homes, and Iranian Americans were subjected to bumper stickers, verbal slogans, and graffiti that said, "Iranians Go Home."[14] In Chicago, a liquor store owner posted a sign that said, "No Dogs and No Iranians Allowed."[15] In Washington, DC, a restaurant owner said he would serve Iranian diplomats only if they agreed to be blindfolded.[16] In Silver Spring, Maryland, customers of an Iranian American furniture store boycotted the business, ultimately forcing it into bankruptcy. Out of a fear their business would suffer a similar fate, scores of Iranian restaurant owners changed their establishments' names, eliminating all references (however subtle) to Iran. In Manhattan, for example, the owners of the Shah Abbas Restaurant in the Waldorf-Astoria Hotel shut their doors and reopened under the name of Tapestry.[17]

Many Iranians hid their identity from people who asked, or pretended they were Italian or German. At Boston's Wentworth Institute of Technology, anti-Iranian students pledged to rape Iranian American women.[18] Around the country, toughs threatened to beat up those suspected of being Iranian American.[19] One Iranian American woman in Denver told a reporter, "I don't sleep at home any more because I am scared they will come and hurt me. All night long young kids keep playing with my door, knocking on it and keeping me awake all night."[20]

Ironically, during this period, more Iranians immigrated to the United States than ever before, spurred by their desire to escape the religious fervor gripping their own country. Their preferred destination was Los Angeles, where a growing number of Iranians had already settled. Iranian American communities exist in all 50 states, especially Washington, Texas, New York, and Virginia, according to U.S. Census data culled by the National Iranian American Council, a Washington, DC, group that encourages Iranian Americans to be politically active. Official Census figures put the Iranian American community at 330,000, with almost half of that number (159,000) in California, but most scholars and experts say those numbers are badly under-reported—that Iranian Americans number at least 1 million, with 500,000 living in "Tehrangeles," the name given to the city of Los Angeles by Iranian Americans who live there. Outside of Iran, the highest concentration of Iranians in the world is in Los Angeles.

Walk down Westwood Boulevard as it heads south of UCLA and you'll find storefronts with Persian signs, establishments where

Persian is more widely spoken than English, and people like Ali Akbar Helmi, who is testament to the progress that Iranian Americans have made in their adopted country. Helmi runs Damoka, which bills itself as the largest Persian rug importer in the United States. Sitting in his office on the ground floor of his business, Helmi surrounds himself with photos of the most important people in his life, which include his son but also Antonio Villaraigosa, the mayor of Los Angeles, whom Helmi campaigned for and helped get elected in May of 2005.

In the late 1970s and early 1980s, when Iranian Americans first settled in Los Angeles in large numbers, they preferred to remain anonymous. The backlash from the hostage crisis only reinforced their desire to keep a low profile. Many were not sure if they would stay in the United States—they thought the Iranian revolution would be a short-term blip in their homeland's history, and they would return at a moment's notice. When it turned out that the blip was a blob, and they found themselves making professional inroads in their adopted country, Iranian Americans elected to remain. Some, like Helmi, changed their first names to fit in better (Helmi's business card lists him as "Alex"). Others, like Mohammad Sadegh Namazikhah, who moved from Tehran to Los Angeles in 1978, not only kept their name but established organizations that fostered Persian culture and their Muslim faith.

Namazikhah heads the Iranian American Muslim Association of North America (IMAN), a cultural center in Palms, California, that also has a mosque inside. I met Namazikhah in the summer of 2005, when I began researching the story of Muslims in Los Angeles. His story—an immigrant success story that has put him in contact with Washington bigwigs and such Hollywood celebrities as Sylvester Stallone—begins in Iran, where Namazikhah's ancestors lived for centuries. In Qom, the country's religious capital, Namazikhah's maternal grandfather, Assadollah, was so prominent he had a street named after him. Qom is where Namazikhah grew up before moving to Tehran for his undergraduate degree. He had known mullahs in every city. He could have easily decided that religion was his calling (in Persian, *Namazikhah* means "a person who prays"; his first name originates with Islam's prophet), or that he would enter his father's car-selling business, but Namazikhah had always been attracted to higher education, medicine, and dentistry, so when USC's advanced endodontics program (think root canals) accepted his application for graduate school, Namazikhah did not hesitate to move 7,000 miles away with his wife, Saiedeh, and their two small children, 5-year-old Sepideh and 1-year-old Saman. Namazikhah was the first in his family to leave his longtime homeland.

Twenty years later, Namazikhah had opened two dental practices, begun IMAN, and moved his immediate family to a mansion near the Pacific Coast Highway. Namazikhah's connection to Sylvester Stallone starts, like many stories in L. A., along the streets of Beverly Hills. One of Namazikhah's dental practices is near the famous David Orgell boutique, owned by Rahim Soltani, another prominent Iranian Muslim in Los Angeles. Soltani befriended Stallone after the actor became a regular customer at David Orgell, where the elite buy sapphire shoes for $2,000, diamond watches for $50,000, and pearl earrings for $70,000. In 2001, Stallone was remodeling his house and asked Soltani what to do with all his Persian rugs. A short time later, those carpets were put in the mosque in the IMAN complex, which Soltani also runs as a member of its board of directors.

"We thank him for the carpets," says Namazikhah, speaking to me in an IMAN office whose shelves are lined with Qurans and other religious books. "He [Stallone] gave us other things that we put up for auction."

That auction raised money to pay for IMAN, which first opened in 1996. What used to be an old mechanic's shop and carpet-cleaning business is now Los Angeles's largest Iranian center, a complex whose architecture reflects the Islamic arches and geometric designs that are common on mosques and other religious buildings in

Iran. IMAN may be the most liberal center frequented by Muslims in Los Angeles. Inside its mosque, men and women worship side by side. While other American mosques have partitions that separate the sexes, or force women to pray in an adjoining area (sometimes a basement, where they can watch the mosque's orations on closed-circuit television), IMAN's higher-ups, led by Namazikhah, say that it is crucial for men and women to remain unsegregated. IMAN, in fact, was the first Muslim center in Los Angeles to practice desegregation, Namazikhah says.

As IMAN's president, Namazikhah has other policies that are considered unorthodox—if not heretical—by other Muslims. For example, he regularly invites Jews and Christians into the IMAN center for interfaith talks, and he allows music during religious and cultural ceremonies. On one of the most important days of the year for Shi'ite Muslims, August 19—the birthday of Imam Ali, the prophet's son-in-law whom Shi'ites believe was Muhammad's rightful successor—I attend a celebration at IMAN that features a singer who, besides belting out religious numbers, showers the audience with Persian love tunes. The crooner's trio includes a keyboardist who looks and dresses like Elvis Presley, complete with bouffant hairstyle and an unbuttoned mauve shirt that reveals his chest hair.

"I was the first person who brought music to an Islamic center," says Namazikhah. "In Wahabism," he says, citing the orthodox sect of Islam that is centered in Saudi Arabia, "you can't have music. You can't have a picture. That's mostly cultural. The way women cover their face—that's not religious, that's cultural; it's because of sunburn they get there. If you go to North Africa, you can see the men cover their faces, too. In Iran, the veil and the *chador* are from Zoroastrian [pre-Islamic] culture. These are practices that people brought into religion. It's a mixture of the country's culture with Islamic teaching."

In my company, Namazikhah's wife, Saiedeh, never wears the head scarf that all Muslim women are required to don in Iran. Still, as I sit across from her and her husband at their kitchen table, surrounded by a mix of Iranian and American food (everything from Persian chicken salad to Florida orange juice), I learn that they, too, have orthodoxy mixed into their lives, even in the most profound way: Their marriage was arranged by their parents, who knew each other. At the time, Namazikhah was 16, Saiedeh 14. This was the early 1960s in Iran, when arranged marriages were practiced throughout society. Though Namazikhah and Saiedeh would wait until 1969 to formally wed, and say they were not pressured to complete their families' wishes, it is clear that "love" was not their original motivation. "Later," they say, almost in unison, "it was love."

Saiedeh Namazikhah has returned to Iran many times, as has her husband. Even their two sons, Saman (28 when I met him) and Soroush (14) have traveled to Tehran, to see relatives and to connect linguistically and culturally to a country that still nurtures their lives. Both speak fluent Persian. When Soroush was last in Iran, people thought he was a native Iranian—at least until little clues emerged, such as the fact he cannot read Persian script, or the fact that he uses "like" a lot when he speaks in English. Saman also uses "like" in a way that was once limited to Valley Girls in the San Fernando Valley. Both sons have picked up other habits that would be considered thoroughly American. At all hours of the day, Soroush plays video games such as Grand Theft Auto, and he worships professional sports, especially the NBA. When I met him, he played point guard in a league of grade-school kids and hoped to be in the NBA one day, just like his idol, Shaquille O'Neal, or Kobe Bryant, whose poster he had on his bedroom wall.

Like his brother, Saman hangs out with non-Muslims. Saman has even dated a non-Muslim woman who consumed alcohol—a no-no for many Muslims but (for Saman) a lesson in how he could apply his religiosity in a country whose popular culture seems so at odds with his Muslim faith. During that relationship, Saman never drank liquor or wine. Nor does he consume alcohol when he "chills" with friends.

"At bars," he says, wearing jeans, Nike flip-flops, and an expensive long-sleeved shirt as I speak to him at his parents' house, "you'll see me holding tomato juice. My [non-Muslim] friends are shocked—they're like, 'Shouldn't you not be here?' My thinking is, 'I could still be here and benefit from it.' They see that they don't need to drink to have fun. My ex-girlfriend had this drive to want me to drink with her, but because of my influence, she doesn't drink anymore. I never told her, 'You're going to go to hell [if you drink].' Islam is a progressive faith to me."

Islam's progressiveness has been a subject of rancorous debate in the United States since the events of September 11, 2001. Does Islam encourage violence against non-Muslims? Cherry-picking from the Quran, Islam's harshest critics point to passages they say are a kind of smoking gun—a revelation, as it were, of Islam's true motives.

"What kind of religion is this?" radio host Michael Savage asked in the fall of 2007 on his nationally syndicated program, which reaches an estimated 8 million people. "What kind of world are you living in when you let them in here with that throwback document in their hand, which is a book of hate. Don't tell me I need re-education. They need deportation."[21]

Evidence of Islam's apparent disregard for non-Muslims is found, say the religion's critics, in the blatant words of Osama bin Laden, Ayman al-Zawahiri, and every al-Qaeda zealot who says "death to Americans" and "death to the infidels." The horror of 9/11, the killing of 3,000 innocent people, is the most egregious evidence of Islam's deceitful ways, say Savage and other public figures who have used their platforms to warn America about the tenets and principles of Muslims.

Regretfully, the U.S. backlash against Muslims was predictable. In times of war and violence, retribution is always commonplace. What was not predictable was America's embrace of Islam. In the wake of 9/11, tens of thousands of Americans who discovered more about the religion converted to Islam, and hundreds of thousands of other Americans (especially college students) studied Islam and can claim further understanding of the world's second most popular faith. True Islam, says its adherents, does not propagate willful killing of innocent people.

"In Islam, it says that, 'No one will have complete faith until he loves for his brother what he loves for himself'—this is part of the religion's foundation," says Chernor Sa'ad Jalloh, an assistant imam at the Islamic Center of New York, as we sit on the third floor of the 96th Street mosque, near rows of children (one of whom is wearing a Disney *Cars* sweatshirt) who are learning to memorize the Quran. "Islam forbids killing innocent life. It is not allowed to harm your brother, it is not allowed to harm your neighbor, it is not allowed to harm your community. We are all servants of God."

Jalloh is from Sierra Leone, where Americans of an earlier century once shopped for African slaves. Since 1975, perhaps the most dramatic trend in U.S. immigration has been from Africa. More than 1 million Africans—almost twice as many as were taken forcibly to the United States in the span of the transatlantic slave trade—have arrived in the United States in that time.[22] How many of those are Muslims is difficult to gauge, but the largest immigration bloc—35 percent—has been from West Africa, where Islam is the dominant faith.[23] In New York City alone, African Muslims have established more than 20 mosques since the mid-1990s.[24] Harlem between 116th Street and 140th Street is the epicenter of Muslim African life in New York, where West African languages—including Wolof, French, Bambara, Fulani, and Arabic—are spoken with more regularity than English, and where stores such as the Djiguiya Market on Malcolm X Boulevard sell halal meat that is bought by both Muslims and non-Muslims.

The influx of African Muslims to Harlem helped transform this part of Manhattan from an area of crime and prostitution to one where Senegalese-Muslim restaurants and other family-run businesses are flourishing—and drawing people from across Manhattan for the unique foods and goods.[25] Islam and its abhorrence of vice worked in Harlem's favor, Linda Beck, a professor of African politics at Columbia University, told United Press International. "Senegalese immigrants . . . have played a fundamental role in terms of going into neighborhoods and basically cleaning them up—physically and also in terms of crime," Beck said. "They did this first by setting up as peddlers in the streets, but also buying stores and living in the area. Senegalese communities are Muslim and they have a very strong network and that has permitted them to emphasize Muslim values. Westerners may think that's not a good thing, but actually it's been wonderful because the emphasis is on family, on responsibility and strong condemnation of drugs and alcohol."[26]

As noted by Beck, Senegalese immigrants gravitated toward selling goods in the street, following the traditions of previous immigrant communities, including early Arab Americans. The job does not require an academic degree—just an ability to carry wares to corner streets and convince passersby that you have what they need. African-Muslim street peddlers are common in Manhattan. Tragically, the best-known peddler was Amadou Diallo, who—unarmed and surrounded by four police officers—was shot 41 times in a 1999 killing that made international headlines for weeks and months afterward. A Muslim from the West African country of Guinea, Diallo was trying to make a new life in America. At the time of his death, Diallo worked six days a week in lower Manhattan selling gloves, socks, and videotapes.[27] After his passing, Diallo's parents, Saikou and Kadiatou, discovered their son's Quran and writings where "he had written the names of all the prophets along with the dates of their birth. He had highlighted passages in the Quran that spoke about the dialogues between Christians and Muslims. Amadou was on a spiritual journey."[28]

Diallo, who prayed five times a day, was just 23. His parents established a foundation in his name that gives scholarships to students from Africa or of African descent to study at four New York colleges, and it also plans to organize cultural exchanges between students from America and Guinea. When I visited Manhattan for this book, I went to Harlem and to the World Trade Center grounds, where I met an African-Muslim peddler named Ibrahim Djita. An immigrant from Gambia in West Africa, Djita had set up his T-shirt table near the intersection of West Broadway and Vesey Street, next to the World Trade Center site that is being rebuilt. Djita has been in the United States for more than five years. His stand has T-shirts memorializing the site, including one showing firemen raising the U.S. flag over the 9/11 rubble. I asked Djita what he thought of the 9/11 hijackers. As he looked in the direction of the World Trade Center, Djita shook his head. "That's not Islam," he said. "Good Muslims don't hurt people."

Walking a few yards away, I came across the fenced-off site of the World Trade Center grounds, which have become an all-encompassing shrine to what happened that day in September. As I stood there with others peering through the chain-link holes to the rough ground below, a nearby woman told a young girl what had happened on 9/11. The woman had her arm around the girl, who appeared to be six or seven years old. Were they a mother and daughter? Aunt and niece? Not wanting to disturb their time together, I didn't ask. Instead, I watched as the woman and girl scanned the whole site. First, they looked at the bulldozers, cranes, and other equipment that were preparing the earth for the next tower. Then they looked up to the sky. "There were two buildings here," the woman explained. "They were taller than that building"—she pointed to a nearby high-rise—"and they came crashing down."

There was no mention of the hijackers. No mention of the bloody chaos that ensued when the towers fell to earth. The girl was too young to be told the whole truth, anyway, and besides, this bloody version of 9/11 is absent from the official display that marks the World Trade Center entryway. There, city officials have put a pictorial that explains the new tower—about how its base will be the exact same dimensions as the old World Trade Center towers, about how (once completed) it will be strong and gleaming and magnificent. The exhibit dwelled on the future, not on the past. Optimism over pessimism. The most prominent flashback to 9/11 was a list of names on a vertical sign that overlooked the World Trade Center grounds. The names were alphabetized under a heading that read "The Heroes of September 11, 2001." Were these all the innocent people who died that day on this very site? I recognized the name of Ronald Michael Breitweiser, whose widow I interviewed for a story about the attacks. I recognized names belonging to Jewish Americans and Russian Americans and Indian Americans and other ethnic groups and cultures, including Arabs and Muslims. Shabbir Ahmed. Syed Abdul Fatha. Waleed Joseph Iskandar. Muhammadou Jawara. Taimour Firaz Khan. Abdu Ali Malahi. Khalid M. Shahid. Mohammed Shajahan. Arabs and Muslims listed as 9/11 heroes. Who were they exactly? What were their stories? The sign had no biographical information on any of the people. Nothing but their names.

A few days later, after doing research, I learned that the first Arab and Muslim name on the list, Shabbir Ahmed, immigrated from Bangladesh, lived in Brooklyn, and worked as a waiter at the Windows of the World restaurant, which helped him pay for his three kids' schooling. Ahmed, 49, loved his job, which required him to serve people of all faiths and nationalities. "He was punctual, never missed a day of work," Abdul Mosobbir, Ahmed's brother, told *Newsday*. "He was always early at work. He left at 4 A.M. to be there at 6."[29]

Syed Abdul Fatha, 54, originally from India, was a customer service associate at the Trade Center's Pitney Bowes copy center. Fatha once told a Spanish-speaking colleague, Beatriz Solo, that he would buy her a Quran "because he wanted me to know about his religion," she told the *New York Times*.[30] Another colleague, Joanna Lewis, told the paper that Fatha put her at ease when she made a mistake on a large copying task: "He'd say, 'No problem; we just have to do it over again.' "[31]

Waleed Joseph Iskandar, born in Lebanon, came to the United States in 1984 to attend Stanford University. Besides a bachelor's degree, he earned an MBA from Harvard before joining a management consulting group in Cambridge, Massachusetts, for whom he worked in Istanbul and London. Fluent in English, French, and Arabic, he was engaged to a woman named Nicolette Cavaleros, whom he planned to marry in July of 2002. On the morning of September 11, 2001, Iskandar, 34, boarded American Airlines Flight 11 in Boston to visit his parents in Los Angeles. After the flight crashed into the North Tower, Iskandar's loved ones established a foundation in his name and organized a blood drive in Los Angeles that saw 29 people donate their blood. In a tribute to his son posted at foxnews.com, Iskandar's father, Joseph, said that "Waleed was one of those rare and remarkable individuals who managed to touch the lives of everyone he knew."[32]

Muhammadou Jawara, 30, was from the Gambia in West Africa. He was working as a security guard at Windows on the World when Flight 11 slammed into the tower. Friends and acquaintances mourned a man they considered "a gentle giant."[33] Posting her memories on a web page that honors Jawara, Nerva Ramos remembered the time when Jawara was at a night spot and "he played tag with me outside the club when I [was] tired of dancing in the crowd. He made me laugh and would laugh out loud at my antics."[34] Another woman, Mia Venster, said in a posting that she visited Jawara's native city, Gambia's capital of Banjul, after 9/11. "I was told to look for his family in Banjul but did not have an address," she wrote. "After a few hours of walking through the city streets while showing Mohammed's photo to various town elders, I did locate the Jawara family's compound. His father and mother were still deeply saddened by his loss but were very appreciative of my efforts to bring greetings to them from their son's former home."[35]

Taimour Firaz Khan, 29, a trader at Carr Futures, grew up in the Long Island hamlet of Syosset, captained the Syosset High School football team (where he was a cornerback), played point guard on its basketball team, and then got his undergraduate degree from the

University of Albany before joining Carr and working in its World Trade Center office, where he was on 9/11. At a tribute page to Khan, Jessica Katz writes that Khan was her husband David's best friend, that Khan "was a special person. He always watched out for me at parties like a big brother."[36]

A native of Yemen, Abdu Ali Malahi, 35, was raised in Brooklyn. His life in America was a mix of both countries' cultures. He went to Yemen to find a wife, with whom he had two young sons, and was trying to get visas for them to come to the United States. In the meantime, with dreams of being a recording engineer (he loved the music of Prince), Malahi was an audiovisual engineer at the Marriott Hotel that was sandwiched between the two World Trade Center towers. Malahi was at work when 9/11 happened. He could have left the hotel but stayed behind to help hotel guests evacuate—a decision that put him in the building when it was destroyed by the falling towers. Malahi was loyal and formal with people. His manager, Vipan Khullar, told the *New York Times* that Malahi would always start his letters with "Greetings." "Even," said Khullar, "if it was just a note to accept a meeting, he would say, 'Greetings, yes, I will meet you at that time.' That's something that always impressed me about him."[37]

Khalid M. Shahid, 25, grew up in Union, New Jersey, and never strayed far from his home. For college, he went to nearby Montclair State University. For work he went to nearby Manhattan, where he was a network systems administrator for Cantor Fitzgerald. On 9/11, Shahid was on the 104th floor of the World Trade Center's North Tower. Shahid was a practicing Muslim—the product of a father from Pakistan and a mother from Colombia who were happily married. He would tell them he wanted to be like them, and was engaged to his high school sweetheart, Jamie Castro, at the time of his death. He and Castro had already picked out a house in Mount Olive, a New Jersey city close to his parents. His mom was looking forward to babysitting the child her son and daughter-in-law had planned to bring into the world. "His idea was to create a family just like ours," his mother, Leonor Shadid, told the *New York Times*. "He'd tell us all the time, he was so proud."[38]

Mohammed Shajahan, 41, was a systems administrator from Bangladesh who was at his job on the 95th floor of the North Tower when it was hit by Flight 11. Shajahan, who believed in religion and love, would pray in his office if he could not attend prescribed mosque services. The father of four young children, he lived with them and his wife in Spring Valley, New York. Shajahan abided by the Islamic commandment to give alms to others who are less fortunate. Shajahan's sister-in-law, Ruby Zigrino, told the *New York Times* that he was constantly helping people in his native country who asked for his help—financial and otherwise.[39] He also aided strangers he met in the United States and loved being in a country where people of all faiths lived side by side. At a web site memorial for Shajahan, a loved one said that Shajahan "often said, 'We come from all parts of the world, and we are able to get a fair chance, and one's opportunities are only limited by hard work.' He was proud to be a part of the American dream."[40]

The American dream. All of these men were living it when they died on 9/11. During work and in their personal lives, they all interacted with non-Arabs and non-Muslims. Their lives in the United States were reflections of many things, including their faith in the future. If the past—their past and this country's past—is a prelude to the future, then the United States in the decades ahead will be a further blending of peoples and cultures. At some point, Islam will be the second most followed religion in the United States. At some point, Arabic will be taught at every major American university. And at some point, Arab and Muslim culture—absent its extreme elements—will be recognized by a majority of Americans as a vital, integral part of this country's culture. They will look back on 9/11 and see it as a turning point, both for the worse and for the better. For now, like the World Trade Center itself, American Arabs and Muslims are trying to rebuild their cultural legacy—trying to begin again from their own Ground Zero. Despite bin Laden and al-

Zawahiri, the foundation of that legacy was undisturbed by 9/11. From its beginning, America intersected with Arab and Muslim culture, borrowing from it, admonishing it, fearing it, co-existing with it. The most recent manifestations of this intermingling—from the widespread American use of Islamic architecture, to the pairing of James Brown and Egyptian pop star Hakim—are further evidence of an alchemy that has become more pronounced since 9/11, not less. *Alchemy.* A word from Arabic that means the chemical mixing of metals into gold. The idea of alchemy may be based on wishful thinking, but so is every endeavor of culture and creativity. Discussing the subject of Arab poetry, Syrian poet Nizar Qabbani—one of the Arab world's greatest modern poets, and a former diplomat whose works on love and relationships have been popularized by many Arab singers and also translated into English—said this at the American Enterprise Institute's 1976 conference on "Arab and American Cultures":

> Any culture should be open to all other cultures. It should affect them and be affected by them continuously. . . . Culture should strive to bring the world together and unify its dreams.[41]

This book is dedicated to those dreams. History shows that the world can commingle peacefully, and that even in times of war—even in the aftermath of an apocalyptic tragedy like 9/11—people divided by borders, language, and apparent differences eventually understand they have more in common than they ever, ever realized.

Notes

Preface: The Irony of 9/11

1. Lynn Elber, "Muslims, Arab Communities Around Nation Targeted for Abuse; Political Leaders Call for Calm," Associated Press, September 14, 2001.
2. Ibid.
3. The "I did it to retaliate" comment was reported in a November 15, 2002, article by Alexander Lane, "Family's Fate in the Balance," (Newark, NJ) *Star-Ledger.* The "I did what every American" comment was reported on February 16, 2002, in an unbylined article by the Associated Press, "Felon Charged in Death of N.J. Man in Dallas."
4. The description of WorldNetDaily can be found at www.worldnetdaily.com/resources/about_WND.asp. The letter, which was written by a man identified as Stephen P. Hamburger, was found at http://web.archive.org/web/20010911000000-20010919235959/http://www.worldnetdaily.com/letters.asp.
5. "Bunch of savages" and "Islamic way of life" postings were reported by correspondent John Donvan on ABC News's *Nightline* program of September 12, 2001. Donvan also reported the comments on that day's *World News Tonight* program anchored by Peter Jennings.
6. For Gallup's 2001 poll, see Michael Paulson, "U. S. Attitudes Toward Arabs Souring, According to Poll," *Boston Globe*, September 24, 2001, and Dana DiFilipo and Myung Oak Kim, "For Bigots, Someone New to Hate," *Philadelphia Daily News*, September 24, 2001. For Gallup's 2006 poll, which was conducted with *USA Today*, see Lydia Saad, "Anti-Muslim Sentiments Fairly Commonplace," and Marilyn Elias, "USA's Muslims Under a Cloud," *USA Today*, August 10, 2006.
7. "Newsweek Poll: Americans Are Mixed on U.S. Muslims," U.S. Newswire, July 20, 2007. A description of the poll can be seen at www.pluralism.org/news/article.php?id=16956.

8. This estimate was given at Oxford University during a spring 2006 seminar sponsored by St. Antony's College that I attended as a Reuters Foundation Fellow.
9. See p. 120 of *Report of the Lemmon Slave Case: Containing Points and Arguments of Counsel on Both Sides, and Opinions of All the Judges*, New York: Horace Greeley & Co., 1860. O'Conor was defending Jonathan Lemmon and his wife, Juliet.
10. Ibid.
11. See especially pp. 29, 34, 254–265 of *The Clash of Civilizations and the Remaking of World Order*, New York: Touchstone, 1996 (paperback ed.).
12. Ibid., p. 318.

1 The Seeds of Islam in America

1. The conditions of Columbus's ship and his own health: John Boyd Thacher, *Christopher Columbus: His Life, His Work, His Remains*, New York: G.P. Putnam's Sons, 1903, Chapter LXXXXI, "Narrative of Third Voyage," pp. 374–408. Reference to his gout and lack of sleep: p. 382. References to intense summer heat: pp. 380–382. Reference to "miracle," p. 383. Reference to Salve Regina: p. 383.
2. Cecil Jane, *Select Documents Illustrating the Four Voyages of Columbus*, Hakluyt Society, London, 1933, p. 22. The book features Columbus's journals in both Spanish and English.
3. Kees Versteegh, *The Arabic Language*, New York: Columbia University Press, 1997, p. 228. Some scholars believe that *almirante* derives specifically from the Arabic words *amir al-bahr*, which mean "commander of the seas." See Walter William Skeat, *An Eytmological Dictionary of the English Language*, Oxford: Clarendon Press, 1884, p. 775. For a document featuring Columbus's Almirante signature, see pp. 180–181 of Thacher, *Christopher Columbus*.
4. Columbus's quote: Paul Lunde, "Al-Farghani and the 'Short Degree'," *Saudi Aramco World*, May/June 1992, available at www.saudiaramcoworld.com/issue/199203/pillars.of.hercules.sea.of.darkness.htm. Fernando Columbus's biography: Benjamin Keen, trans. and ed., *The Life of the Admiral Christopher Columbus, by His Son Ferdinand*, New Brunswick, N.J.: Rutgers University Press, 1959, p. 16. Fernando writes that his father had five principle reasons for believing he could "discover the Indies." Fifth was "the opinion of Alfragan and his followers, who assign a much smaller size to the earth than all the other writers and geographers." Columbus studied al-Farghani's calculations in *Imago Mundi* (Image of the World), an authoritative com-

pendium of astronomy that was written and organized by Catholic Cardinal Pierre d'Ailly.

5. See Robert E. Krebs and Carolyn A. Krebs, *Groundbreaking Scientific Experiments, Inventions, and Discoveries of the Ancient World*, Westport, CT: Greenwood Press, 2004, p. 42. See also Salma Khadra Jayyusi and Manuela Martin, *The Legacy of Muslim Spain*, Brill, 1992, p. 293; and Josef W. Meri, *Medieval Islamic Civilization: An Encyclopedia*, Volume 1, A–K, London: Taylor & Francis, 2006, pp. 379–381.
6. Felipe Fernandez-Armesto, *Columbus*, New York: Oxford University Press, 1991, p. 5.
7. Mariners' compass: See p. 7 of Resat Kasaba, "By Compass and Sword!—The Meanings of 1492," *Middle East Report*, No. 178 (September–October 1992), pp. 6–10. *Nina* and *Pinta* were caravels: p. 325, Abbas Hamdani, "Ottoman Response to the Discovery of America and the New Route to India," *Journal of the American Oriental Society*, Vol. 101, No. 3 (July 1981), pp. 323–330. Caravels adopted from *qarib*: Ibid., p. 324. Parry quote: Ibid, p. 325. Kramers quote: J.H. Kramers, "Geography and Commerce," *The Legacy of Islam*, ed. Sir Thomas Arnold and Alfred Guillaume, London, 1931, pp. 93–94, noted in Jayyusi and Marin, *The Legacy of Muslim Spain*, p. 278.
8. Mistreatment by Columbus: Spanish historian Consuelo Varela, a Columbus expert who documented the abuse in *The Fall of Christopher Columbus* (*Caida de Cristobal Colon*), found that Columbus and his brothers prohibited natives from being baptized so they could use them as slaves, who were auctioned in the main square of Santo Domingo. "One woman happened to say that Columbus came from a working-class family and that his father had been a weaver," Verala told the Spanish newspaper *El Pais*. "Columbus' brother Bartolomeo had her tongue cut out, after parading her naked through the streets on a donkey. Christopher congratulated his brother on defending the family honour." See Graham Keeley, "Columbus Exposed as Iron-Fisted Tyrant Who Tortured His Slaves," the (London) *Independent*, July 21, 2006. Columbus's maltreatment of Native Americans was foreshadowed on October 12, 1492, when within hours of landing at San Salvador, Columbus said he would try to convert the natives to Christianity—but would wait until they trusted him. Here's what Columbus said: "I in order that they might develop a very friendly disposition towards us, because I knew that they were a people who could better be freed and converted to our Holy Faith by love than by force, gave to some of them red caps and to others glass beads, which they hung on their necks, and many other things of slight value, in

which they took much pleasure. . . . They ought to be good servants and of good skill, for I see that they repeat very quickly whatever was said to them. I believe they would easily be made Christians." See pp. 64–65 of Samuel Eliot Morison, trans. and ed., *Journals and Other Documents on the Life and Voyages of Christopher Columbus*, New York: The Heritage Press, 1963.

9. William C. Fischer, *Identity, Community, and Pluralism in American Life*, New York: Oxford University Press, 1997, p. 93.
10. Jack D. L. Holmes, *A Guide to Spanish Louisiana 1762–1806*, New Orleans: Laborde, 1970, pp. 1–35.
11. Martin A. S. Hume, *The Spanish People: Their Origin, Growth and Influence*, New York: D. Appleton & Co., 1901, pp. 110, 169–170.
12. Stanley Clisby Arthur, *Old New Orleans: A History of the Vieux Carré, Its Ancient and Historical Buildings*, New Orleans: Harmanson, 1936, pp. 109, 226. Arthur actually refers to 339 Royal Street, but he meant 343—the building that was formerly a branch of the United States Bank. In *Memoirs, Eight Decades, 1926–1998: Memories Are Forever*, (Xlibris, 2005), Juan Silverio Latour writes on p. 54 that, "So it is today the French Quarter of New Orleans has the curious formation of possessing streets with French names (Bienville, Bourbon, Chartres, Burgundy), but the architecture is purely Spanish. Most houses have a central open patio and balconies surrounded by typically wrought-iron work made in Seville, Spain."
13. Dome spirals at Mission Nuestra Señora de la Concepción de Acuña: Thomas Drain, *A Sense of Mission: Historic Churches of the Southwest*, San Francisco: Chronicle Books, 1994, p. 13. Columbus's quote: *Christopher Columbus: His Life, His Work, His Remains*, p. 554.
14. R. Brooks Jeffery, "From Azulejos to Zaguanes: The Islamic Legacy in the Built Environment of Hispano-America," *Journal of the Southwest*, Vol. 45, Nos. 1–2 (Spring–Summer 2003). Jeffery notes in his article that "use of the *alfiz* to define the entrance portal extended as far north as the mission churches of San Antonio de Valero, commonly known as the Alamo (1744), in Texas and San Diego de Alcala (1774) in California." The definition of an *alfiz* can be found in Joseph A. Baird Jr., "Style in 18th Century Mexico," *Journal of Inter-American Studies*, Vol. 1, No. 3 (July 1959), p. 268, in which Baird writes that an *alfiz* is "a *mudejar* feature; it consists usually of a stepped rectilinear molding (occasionally with new world modifications—as at Huejotzingo, where the Franciscan cord is used in place of an architectural molding for the purpose) that outlines a portal and limits the decoration around that portal to a distinct right-angled area of enclosure."

15. James Early, *The Colonial Architecture of Mexico*, Albuquerque: University of New Mexico Press, 1994, pp. 31, 119.
16. Barbara Berkenfield, "At the Heart of Santa Fe," *The New Mexican*, June 14, 2004. The article can be seen online at www.freenewmexican.com/sfguide/701.html.
17. Frank Thompson, *The Alamo: A Cultural History*, New York: Cooper Square Press, 2001, pp. 25–28. Thompson also details the Army's use of the Alamo on pages 80–87.
18. An Alamo docent used the word during my visit there. As we stood in the former sacristy, I asked him why the military whitewashed the frescoes, and he said the Army considered the drawings "frilly."
19. David McLemore, "Team Works to Preserve Colorful Frescoes Uncovered in Alamo Chapel," *Dallas Morning News*, October 7, 2000.
20. Doğan Kuban, *Muslim Religious Architecture*, Leiden, Netherlands: Brill, 1997, pp. 1–4.
21. Brian Edwards, *Courtyard Housing: Past, Present and Future*, New York: Taylor & Francis, 2004, p. 235. Edwards writes that "the courtyard house arrived in Spain with the first wave of Arab Muslim conquest from North Africa. . . . The concept took root and its development began."
22. Jeffery, "From Azulejos to Zaguanes."
23. Malcolm Heard, *French Quarter Manual: An Architectural Guide to New Orleans' Vieux Carré*, Jackson: University Press of Mississippi, 1997, p. 21.
24. Church of the Immaculate Conception in New Orleans, describing why its architecture is Moorish: http://jesuitchurch.net/parish_history.htm.

2 Slavery and Islam

1. C.B. Wadstrom, *An Essay on Colonization, Particularly Applied to the Western Cost of Africa with Some Free Thoughts on Cultivation and Commerce*, London: Darton and Harvey, 1794.
2. George Gordon, Lord Byron, "The Giaour: A Fragment of a Turkish Tale," published in 1813. The version used for this book was published in *The Poetical Works of Lord Byron: Complete in One Volume*, London: John Murray, 1847, p. 697, footnote to reference on page 70.
3. John L. Esposito, *What Everyone Needs to Know About Islam*, New York: Oxford University Press, 2002, p. 169.
4. Ira Marvin Lapidus, *A History of Islamic Societies*, Cambridge, UK: Cambridge University Press, 2002, p. 204.

5. Gerhard Kubik, *Africa and the Blues*, Jackson: University Press of Mississippi, 1999, p. 193.
6. Lorenzo Dow Turner, *Africanisms in the Gullah Dialect*, Columbia: University of South Carolina Press, originally published in 1949, reprinted in 2002, pp. 154 (*sali*), 152 (*sadaka*), 52 (*anebi* and *araba*), 50 (*alansaro*, *alkama*, and *alura*), 49 (*ala*), and 202 (*saut*).
7. *Shout Because You're Free: The African American Ring Shout Tradition in Coastal Georgia*, Athens: University of Georgia Press, 1998, p. 4.
8. Lydia Parrish, "Slave Songs of the Georgia Sea Islands," originally published 1942, reprint edition 1992, Athens: University of Georgia Press, p. 164.
9. The closure was an apparent result of Hurricane Katrina, which damaged the area just north of Congo Square.
10. See Paul Oliver, *Savannah Syncopators: African Retention in the Blues*, London: November Books Limited, 1970, p. 78.
11. This Latrobe quote can be found in *African-American Traditions in Song, Sermon, Tale, and Dance, 1600s–1920*, compiled by Eileen Southern and Josephine Wright, Westport, CT: Greenwood Publishing, 1990, p. 60.
12. W. C. Handy, *Father of the Blues, An Autobiography*, New York: Da Capo Press, 1991, p. 74, reprint of 1941 book, New York: Macmillan.
13. Kubik, *Africa and the Blues*, pp. 18–19.
14. Ibid., p. 93.
15. Ibid., p. 94.
16. Ibid., p. 94.
17. John Storm Roberts, *Black Music of Two Worlds*, New York: Praeger, 1972, p. 13.
18. Ibid., pp. 212–213.
19. See www.afropop.org/multi/interview/ID/57/Al-Andalus-Dwight+Reynolds.
20. See Cornielia Walker Bailey, *God, Dr. Buzzard, and the Bolito Man*, New York: Doubleday, 2000, p. 134.
21. Ibid., p. 160.
22. Ibid., pp. 287, 289.
23. See Allan D. Austin, *African Muslims in Antebellum America*, New York: Routledge, 1997, p. 89. The historian is William S. McFeely.
24. Austin, *African Muslims in Antebellum America*, p. 85.
25. Ibid., pp.85, 88.
26. See page 25 of Richard Brent Turner, *Islam in the African-American Experience*, Bloomington: Indiana University Press, 1997. See also pp. 51–62 of Austin, *African Muslims in Antebellum America*, and Bluett's

biography of Diallo, which can be read at http://negroartist.com.

27. For notes about Omar ibn Said's biography, go to http://docsouth.unc.edu/nc/omarsaid/omarsaid.html. See also pp. 129–156 of Austin, *African Muslims in Antebellum America.*
28. Page 73 of Austin, *African Muslims in Antebellum America: A Sourcebook*, New York: Garland Publishing, 1984, is where I found the quotes about Abd ar-Rahman and his White House meeting.
29. On p. 22 of Austin, *African Muslims in Antebellum America*, Austin estimates that 40,000 African Muslim slaves lived "in the colonial and pre–Civil War territory making up the United States before 1860."
30. Ibid., p. 73.

3 Emerson and Persian Poetry

1. See Caroline Hinsey, "Fantasy 'World'," *New York Daily News*, December 16, 2007.
2. TV ad by Orchard Supply Hardware, aired in the San Francisco Bay Area during the week of March 10, 2008.
3. Ray McGovern, "Don't Look for Much from the 'Bipartisan' Iraq Study Group," November 14, 2006; available at www.buzzflash.com/articles/contributors/558.
4. Emerson, *Essays: First Series*, Boston: Houghton, Mifflin & Co., 1876, p. 84.
5. Ibid., p. 91.
6. Ralph Waldo Emerson, "Self-Reliance," in *Self-Reliance and Other Essays*, New York: Courier Dover, 1993, p. 24. See also www.emersoncentral.com/selfreliance.htm.
7. Ibid., p. 19.
8. Ibid., p. 34.
9. Ibid., p. 37.
10. *Essays: First Series*, p. 157. See also www.emersoncentral.com/friendship.htm.
11. Ralph Waldo Emerson, "Love," in *Essays: First Series*, Flin and Company, 1889, p. 135. See also www.rwe.org/works/Essays-1st_Series_05_Love.htm.
12. George Sampson ed., *The Works of Ralph Waldo Emerson, Vol. IV*, London: George Bell and Sons, 1905, p. 283.
13. Ibid., pp. 283, 285, 290.
14. Francis Gladwin trans., *The Gulistan*, fourth edition, Lucknow (India): Newul Kishore Press, 1883, p. 1.
15. Ibid., p. 17.

16. Ibid., p. iii.
17. Ibid., p. iv.
18. Ibid., pp. 160–161.
19. See Arthur John Arberry, *Shiraz: Persian City of Saints and Poets*, Norman: University of Oklahoma Press, 1960, p. 122.
20. Ibid.
21. The poem "Saadi" appeared in Vol. III, No. II (October 1842), of *The Dial*. A reprint can be seen in Jean F. Terry, *The Dial: A Magazine for Literature, Philosophy and Religion*, pp. 265–269.
22. The number of times that Saadi went to Mecca—like other details of his life—is unclear. Among those who cite the figure 14 is Ella Constance Sykes, *Persia and Its People*, Boston: Adamant Media, 2001, p. 305.
23. Arthur Christy, *The Orient in American Transcendentalism: A Study of Emerson, Thoreau, and Alcott*, New York: Octagon Books, 1972, pp. 304–305.
24. From "Representative Men," which can be seen at www.emersoncentral.com/swedenborg.htm.
25. W. F. Thompson, *The Practical Philosophy of the Muhammadan People*, London: The Oriental Translation Fund, 1839. For Emerson's translation of title, see Robert D. Richardson Jr., *Emerson: The Mind on Fire*, Berkeley: University of California Press, 1995, p. 406.
26. Wai Chee Dimock, "Deep Time: American Literature and World History," *American Literary History*, Vol. 13, No. 4 (Winter 2001), p. 765.
27. *The Collected Works of Ralph Waldo Emerson* (historical introduction by Barbara L. Packer; notes by Joseph Slater), Cambridge, MA: Harvard University Press, 2003, p. 265.
28. Ibid., p. 128.
29. Ibid., p. 174.
30. Richardson, *Emerson: The Mind on Fire*, p, 407.
31. Henry David Thoreau, *Walden: A Fully Annotated Edition*, New Haven, CT: Yale University Press, p. 75.
32. Henry David Thoreau, *Journal* (Vol. V, 1852–1853), Princeton, NJ: Princeton University Press, 1981, pp. 289, 290.
33. Ibid.
34. John D. Yohannan, *Persian Poetry in England and America—A 200-Year History*, Delmar, NY: Caravan Books, 1977, pp. 135–136.
35. Henry David Thoreau, "Walking," available at www.transcendentalists.com/walking.htm.

36. "The Ottoman Porte: The Law of Succession—The Harem," *New York Times*, November 23, 1853, p. 2.
37. "The Holy Places Desolate," *New York Times*, November 13, 1851, p. 2.
38. "Highly Important from Washington: The President's Policy—New York, Ohio, Indiana, Illinois and the Cabinet Disposed of—Henry A. Wise and Judge Douglas—Rumors, Gossips and Small Talk About Things in General," *New York Times*, August 1, 1858, p. 1.
39. Noah Webster, *American Dictionary of the English Language*, Springfield, MA: Merriam, 1856, p. 663.
40. Irving, *Mahomet and His Successors*, Paris: A. and W. Galignani and Co., 1850, p. 142.
41. Ibid.
42. Thoreau's interest in *Mahomet and His Successors: The Essays of Henry D. Thoreau*, New York: North Point Press, 2002, p. 344.
43. The review can be found in: Henry A. Pochmann and E. N. Feltskog ed., *Mahomet and His Successors: The Complete Works of Washington Irving*, Madison: The University of Wisconsin Press, 1970, p. 533.
44. "An Arabian Tale," by Benjamin Franklin, 1779. See Arthur Stuart Pitt, "The Sources, Significance, and Date of Franklin's 'An Arabian Tale,'" *Publications of the Modern Language Association*, Vol. 57, No. 1 (March 1941), pp. 155–168. The story can be read in Rufus Wilmot Griswold, *The Prose Writers of America*, Philadelphia: Parry & McMillan, 1856, p. 69.
45. *The Algerine Captive: Or, the Life and Adventures of Doctor Updike Underhill: Six Years a Prisoner Among the Algerines*, originally published 1797; republished by Lanham, MD: Rowman & Littlefield, 1970. The quote is from the republished edition, p. 187.
46. For a description of the Barbary Wars and Americans' interpretation of it, see Chapter 1 of Timothy Marr, *The Cultural Roots of American Islamicism*, New York: Cambridge University Press, 2006. For notes on the numbers of hostages and ships taken by Algerian pirates, see Ibid., pp. 30–33.
47. To see the Marines' explanation of the Mameluke scimitar, go to www.marines.com/page/The-Sword.jsp. To see the Marines' hymn, go to www.usmc.mil/comrel/120day.nsf/marineshymn?OpenPage.
48. Extracts from *A Journal of Travels in North America, Consisting of an Account of Boston and Its Vicinity* by Samuel Lorenzo Knapp, Boston: Thomas Badger 1818, see pp. 59–61. See also Marr, *The Cultural Roots of American Islamicism*, p. 59.
49. Dimock, "Deep Time," p. 765.

50. Thompson, *Practical Philosophy of the Muhammadan People*, p. 69.
51. Ibid., p. 396.
52. Ibid., p. 406.
53. Ibid., p. 414.
54. Ibid., p. 452.
55. Ibid., p. 73.
56. Ibid., p. 92.
57. *Foreign Quarterly Review*, Volume XXIV (October 1839 and January 1840), pp. 174–186. Emerson is cited in an article about an address by W. E. Channing in Boston, 1838. The review is on pages 156–160.
58. Dimock, "Deep Time," p. 768.
59. The Hafiz line from Emerson can be found at www.rwe.org.
60. Defiant stanza from Gertrude Lowthian Bell, trans., *Teachings of Hafiz*, London: Octagon Press, 1979, XXXII, p. 136.
61. Richardson, *Emerson: The Mind on Fire*, p. 427.
62. Amos Bronson Alcott, *Table-Talk*, Boston: Roberts Brothers, 1877, p. 12.
63. Richardson, *Emerson: The Mind on Fire*, p. 568.
64. Ibid., pp. 349–350.

4 P. T. Barnum and the Taj Mahal

1. Philip B. Kunhardt Jr., Philip B. Kunhardt III, and Peter W. Kunhardt, *P. T. Barnum: America's Greatest Showman*, New York: Alfred A. Knopf, 1995, pp. 40–43.
2. Ibid., pp 48–69.
3. P. T. Barnum, *The Life of P. T. Barnum*, London: Sampson Low, Son, and Co., 1855. Quote is from p. 311 of the republished edition, titled *Struggles and Triumphs: Or, the Life of P. T. Barnum*, New York: Knopf, 1927.
4. William Knight Northall, *Before and Behind the Curtain*, New York:, W. F. Burgess, 1851, p. 165.
5. Andrew Jackson Downing, *The Architecture of Country Houses*, Mineola, NY: Dover Publications, 1969, p. 27.
6. *Struggles and Triumphs: Or, the Life of P. T. Barnum*, p. 311.
7. Ibid.
8. *Gleason's Pictorial Drawing Room Companion*, May 24, 1851, p. 57.
9. Seen during my tour of the Barnum Museum. Barnum referred to Arabic at least once during his career: In his 1855 memoir, Barnum recalled being with his grandfather, whose handwriting was so atrocious (Barnum called it "hieroglyphics") that, in 1820, the grandfa-

ther had to have three friends decipher it for a census project. "My grandfather walked up and down the room, being called every few minutes to explain some name or other word that was as unintelligible as if it had been written in Arabic." See p. 83 of *The Life of P. T. Barnum*.

10. *New York Times*, November 26, 1863, p. 7.
11. *New York Times*, November 15, 1872, p. 7.
12. Irving Wallace, *The Fabulous Showman*, New York: Alfred A. Knopf, 1967, p. 144.
13. Ibid., pp. 143–144.
14. Ibid., p. 147.
15. Calculation based on www.measuringworth.com/calculators/uscompare/result.php.
16. Barnum, *Struggles and Triumphs: Or, the Life of P. T. Barnum*, p. 349.
17. Wallace, *The Fabulous Showman*, p. 174.
18. Kunhardt et al., *P. T. Barnum*, p. 84.
19. Ibid.
20. Phineas Taylor Barnum, *Struggles and Triumphs, Or, Forty Years' Recollections of P. T. Barnum*, New York: American News Company, 1871, p. 262.
21. *Taj Mahal: Passion and Genius at the Heart of the Moghul Empire*, New York: Walker & Company, 2007, p. 186.
22. Henri Stierlin, *Islamic Art and Architecture: From Isfahan to the Taj Mahal*, London: Thames & Hudson, 2002, p. 180.
23. "The Indian Taste," Carl J. Weinhardt Jr., *Metropolitan Museum of Art Bulletin*, Vol. 16, No. 7 (March 1958), pp. 211–212.
24. Ibid.
25. John Dinkel, *The Royal Pavilion, Brighton*, London: Philip Wilson, 1983, pp. 39–40.
26. Barnum, *Struggles and Triumphs, Or, Forty Years' Recollections of P. T. Barnum*, p. 262.
27. P. T. Barnum, *The Life of P. T. Barnum, Written by Himself*, New York: Redfield, 1855, p. 403.
28. Ibid., p. 263.
29. P. T. Barnum, *Struggles and Triumphs, Or, Forty Years' Recollections of P. T. Barnum*, Buffalo, NY: Warren, Johnson & Co., 1873, p. 269.

5 Language and Names

1. James Peters and Habeeb Salloum, *Arabic Contributions to the English Vocabulary*, Librairie du Liban, Beirut, 1996, p. XII.

2. Garland Cannon, *The Arabic Contributions to the English Language: An Historical Dictionary*, Wiesbaden: Harrassowitz Verlag, 1994, p. 3.
3. Ibid., p. 43.
4. Peters and Salloum, *Arabic Contributions to the English Vocabulary*, p. XII.
5. Walt Taylor, *Arabic Words in English*, Oxford: Clarendon Press, 1933, p. 567.
6. Cannon, *The Arabic Contributions to the English Language*, p. 267.
7. Ibid., p. 265.
8. Ibid., p. 221.
9. George Henry Borrow, *The Zincali: Or, An Account of the Gypsies of Spain*, J.M. Philadelphia: Campbell & Co., 1843, p. 144.
10. Admiral: *Arabic Words in English*, p. 567. bazaar: *Arabic Contributions to the English Vocabulary*, pp. 21–22. cipher: *Arabic Words in English*, p. 568. drub: *Oxford English Dictionary*, online edition. endive: *The Arabic Contributions to the English Language*, p. 36. fanfare: Ibid., p. 37. giraffe: *Arabic Words in English*, p. 568. hazard: *Arabic Contributions to the English Vocabulary*, p. 56. imam: *The Arabic Contributions to the English Language*, p. 37. jasmine: *Arabic Words in English*, p. 568. kabob: *The Arabic Contributions to the English Language*, p. 38. lackey: *Arabic Contributions to the English Vocabulary*, p. 71. monsoon: *Arabic Words in English*, p. 568. nadir: Ibid. ogee: Ibid. pia mater: *The Arabic Contributions to the English Language*, p. 36. quran: Ibid., p. 40. racket: *Arabic Words in English*, p. 568. sequin: Ibid. tariff: Ibid. usnea: *Oxford English Dictionary*, online edition. vizier: *Arabic Words in English*, p. 568. wadi: *The Arabic Contributions to the English Language*, p. 40. xebec: *Arabic Words in English*, p. 581. yashmak: *Oxford English Dictionary*, online edition, plus a Nexis search of news reports from 2007. zero: *Arabic Words in English*, p. 568.
11. All words are from pp. 567–587 of *Arabic Words in English*, except for the following. From *The Arabic Contributions to the English Language:* alameda, p. 120; almanac, p. 131; amber, p. 135; arabesque, p. 137; artichoke, p. 140; barrio, pp. 150–151; caliber, p. 164; chemist, p. 170; chiffon, p. 171; soda, pp. 307–308. From *Arabic Contributions to the English Vocabulary:* ghoul, p. 50, hummus, p. 58; mecca, p. 80; mocha, p. 82; sherry, p. 111; tangerine, p. 118; tarot, p. 120; traffic, p. 122.
12. Alcatraz in Arabic: *The Arabic Contributions to the English Language*; Sir John Hawkins reference: *Oxford English Dictionary*, online edition, pp. 121–122.
13. Alcohol: *The Arabic Contributions to the English Language*, p. 123.
14. Alfalfa: Ibid., p. 124.

15. Algebra: Ibid., p. 126.
16. Alcove: Ibid., p. 123.
17. Alchemy: Ibid., p. 122.
18. Almanac: Ibid., p. 131.
19. Broker: Ibid., p. 158.
20. Checkmate: Ibid., p. 169, plus the *Oxford English Dictionary*, online edition.
21. Salloum and Peters, *Arabic Contributions to the English Vocabulary*, p. 33.
22. Sherry: Ibid., p. 111, and Jan Reed, *Wines of Spain*, New York: Sterling, 2005, p. 186.
23. Tangerine: *Arabic Contributions to the English Vocabulary*, p. 118.
24. Mocha: Ibid., p. 82, plus the *Oxford English Dictionary*, online edition.
25. Mecca: *Arabic Contributions to the English Vocabulary*, p. 80, plus the *Oxford English Dictionary*, online edition.
26. Caliber: *The Arabic Contributions to the English Language*, p. 164.
27. Candy: Ibid., p. 166.
28. *Arabic Words in English*, p. 567.
29. Salloum and Peters, *Arabic Contributions to the English Vocabulary*, p. XII.
30. Fred Bruemmer, "The Many Worlds of Tunisia," *The Gazette* (Montreal), September 30, 2006.
31. Tim Burt, "From Tunisian Desert to Hollywood Dealmaking," *Financial Times* (London), May 31, 2005.
32. Y. G. M. Lulat, *A History of African Higher Education From Antiquity to the Present*, Westport, CT: Praeger/Greenwood, 2005, pp. 69–70.
33. Fuad Baali, *Society, State, and Urbanism: Ibn Khaldun's Sociological Thought*, Albany: State University of New York Press, 1988, p. ix. See also pp. 2, 13–22.
34. Hans Daiber, *Bibliography of Islamic Philsophy*, Leiden, Netherlands, Brill, 1999, p. 712.
35. Richard Covington, "Rediscovering Arabic Science," *Saudi Aramco World*, May/June 2007.
36. Aziz al-Azmeh, *Ibn Khaldun: An Essay in Reinterpretation*, London: Frank Cass, 1982, pp. 26, 36, 45.
37. Islamic Crescents' Observation Project, www.icoproject.org/star.html.
38. See Jim Kaler, Adhara, at www.astro.uiuc.edu/~kaler/sow/adhara.html.
39. Adam Goldman, "Bagdads Across America Getting Attention Thanks to War in Iraq," Associated Press, April 4, 2003.

40. Lilian Linder Fitzpatrick, *Nebraska Place-Names*, Lincoln: University of Nebraska Press, 1960, pp. 43, 58, 59, 80, 91, 144.
41. Ibid., p. 36.
42. Ibid., p. 107.
43. William Henry Perrin, J.H. Battle, and Weston Arthur Goodspeed, *History of Medina County and Ohio*, Chicago: Baskin & Battey, 1881, p. 394.
44. The Illinois General Assembly says the town took the name Mahomet from a nearby Masonic Lodge called Mahomet Lodge #220 that was established in 1856. Dan McCollum, a former mayor of Champaign, Illinois, who has researched the town's history, says its name actually derives from the former town post office, which was named the Mahomet Post Office. McCollum told me the name change happened when the Illinois railroad extended its state tracks to the town and told townspeople that Illinois already had two Middletowns. The Illinois General Assembly legislation can be seen at http://12.43.67.2/legislation/94/HR/PDF/09400HR1519lv.pdf.
45. Giraffe: *Arabic Contributions to the English Vocabulary*, p. 51, plus *Oxford English Dictionary*, online edition.
46. Guitar: *Arabic Contributions to the English Vocabulary*, p. 51.
47. Lute: Ibid., p. 73.
48. Magazine: Ibid., p. 75.
49. Crimson: Ibid., p. 35.
50. Cotton: Ibid., p. 35.
51. Barrio: *The Arabic Contributions to the English Language*, pp. 150–151.
52. Rose Marie Beebe and Robert M. Senkewicz, *Lands of Promise and Despair: Chronicles of Early California, 1535–1846*, Berkeley, CA: Heyday Books, 2001, pp. 9–10.
53. As one example, see Patt Morrison, "Culture—125 Years—What Los Angeles Gave the World," *Los Angeles Times*, December 3, 2006. Morrison writes at the start of her article: "In 1510, a Spanish writer named Garci Ordonez de Montalvo published a fantasist novel called *Las Sergas de Esplandian*, about a golden island ruled by a dark-skinned Amazon queen called Califia. This book would end up giving California its name."

6 Arabs and the Ice-Cream Cone

1. *Official Guide to the Louisiana Purchase Exposition at the City of St. Louis*, St. Louis: Official Guide Co., 1904, p. 48.

2. Charles M. Kurtz, *The St. Louis World's Fair of 1904*, St. Louis: Gottschalk, 1903, p. 97.
3. *Official Guide*, p. 34.
4. See www.libertybellmuseum.com/Stereoviews/Panel4.htm; George Matthews and Sandy Marshall, *St. Louis Olympics, 1904*, Mount Pleasant, SC: Arcadia Publishing, 2003, p, 30.
5. *Official Guide*, p. 9.
6. Ibid., p. 7.
7. Ibid., p. 164.
8. Ibid., p. 136.
9. Ibid., p. 134.
10. Ibid., p. 5.
11. Author phone interview with Ray Doumar in September of 2007. See also Jack Marlowe, "Zalabia and the First Ice-Cream Cone," *Saudi Aramco World*, July–August 2003, pp. 4, 20; and Shannon Jackson Arnold, *Everybody Loves Ice Cream: The Whole Scoop on America's Favorite Treat*, Cincinnati, OH: Emmis Books, 2004, p. 20.
12. Edward Rice, *Captain Sir Richard Francis Burton: A Biography*, New York: Da Capo Press, 2001, p. 514.
13. Jack Marlowe, "Zalabia and the First Ice-Cream Cone," *Saudi Aramco World*, July/August 2003, pp. 2–5.
14. Renee Enna, "The Scoop on Cones; On the Centennial of a World's Fair Sensation, It's Time to Salute Ice Cream's Crunchy Sidekick," *Chicago Tribune*, July 7, 2004.
15. Author's phone interview with Thaddeus Doumar in September of 2007. Albert Doumar was 86 at that time, and a bit hard of hearing when I called Doumar's Cones & Barbecue, so I didn't speak with him after I interviewed Thaddeus.
16. Jackson, *Everybody Loves Ice Cream* pp. 19–20. The first cones were called "cornucopias." Other food items that owe their initial popularization to the Louisiana Purchase Exposition include the hamburger, the hot dog, and peanut butter, which was introduced there as a "health food" for the first time in a public way.
17. J. Spencer Trimingham, *The Sufi Orders in Islam*, New York: Oxford University Press, 1998, p. 199; Antony Wild, *Coffee: A Dark History*, New York: W.W. Norton, 2005, pp. 29, 98; Lloyd V.J. Ridgeon, *Aziz Nasafi*, London: Curzon Press, 1998, p. 133; Kenneth F. Kiple, *A Movable Feast: Ten Millennia of Food Globalization*, New York: Cambridge University Press, 2007, p. 86.
18. See William Harrison Ukers, *All About Coffee*, New York: Tea and Coffee Trade Journal Company, 1922, p. 26. Ukers relates an oft-

repeated story—perhaps apocryphal—about Pope Clement VIII, who is said to have blessed coffee as permissible for Christians. The pope, who was pontiff between 1592 and 1605, was asked by priests to condemn the drink. Ukers writes that "certain priests appealed to Pope Clement VII (1535–1605) to have its use forbidden among Christians, denouncing it as an invention of Satan. They claimed that the Evil One, having forbidden his followers, the infidel Moslems, the use of wine—no doubt because it was sanctified by Christ and used in the Holy Communion—had given them as a substitute this hellish black brew of his which they called coffee. For Christians to drink it was to risk falling into a trap set by Satan for their souls. It is further related that the pope, made curious, desired to inspect this devil's drink and had some brought to him. The aroma of it was so pleasant and inviting that the pope was tempted to try a cupful. After drinking it, he exclaimed, "Why this Satan's drink is so delicious that it would be a pity to let the infidels have exclusive use of it. We shall fool Satan by baptizing it, and making it a truly Christian beverage."

19. Jonathan P. Berkey, *The Formation of Islam*, New York: Cambridge University Press, 2002, p. 238.
20. Elmer H. Douglas and Ibrahim M. Abu-Rabi, *The Mystical Teachings of Al-Shadhili: Including His Life, Prayers, Letters, and Followers* (trans. by Elmer H. Douglas), Albany, NY: SUNY Press, 1993, p. 42.
21. Berkey, *The Formation of Islam*, p. 239.
22. Bennett Alan Weinberg and Bonnie K. Bealer, *The World of Caffeine: The Science and Culture of the World's Most Popular Drug*, New York: Routledge, 2001, p. 11.
23. Weinberg and Bealer, *The World of Caffeine*, p. 18; John Ayto, *The Glutton's Glossary: A Dictionary of Food and Drink Terms*, New York: Routledge, 1990, p. 74.
24. Daniel W. Brown, *A New Introduction to Islam*, Malden, MA: Blackwell, 2004, pp. 116–117.
25. Mark Pendergrast, *Uncommon Grounds: The History of Coffee and How It Transformed Our World*, New York: Basic Books, 1999, p. 6.
26. W. G. Clarence-Smith and Steven Topik, *The Global Coffee Economy in Africa, Asia and Latin America, 1500–1989*, New York: Cambridge University Press, 2003, p. 51.
27. Robert Nicol, *A Treatise on Coffee: Its Properties and the Best Mode of Keeping and Preparing It*, London: Baldwin and Cradock, 1831, pp. 11–12.
28. Weinberg and Bealer, *The World of Caffeine*, pp. 13, 18.
29. Wild, *Coffee: A Dark History*, p. 31.

30. Weinberg and Bealer, *The World of Caffeine*, p. 13.
31. Charles Dudley Warner, *Captain John Smith (1579–1631): Sometime Governor of Virginia, and Admiral of New England*, New York: Henry Holt, 1881, pp. 28–31.
32. Timothy Marr, *The Cultural Roots of American Islamicism*, New York: Cambridge University Press, 2006, p. 3.
33. Ukers, *All About Coffee*, p. 31.
34. Warner, *Captain John Smith*, p. 31.
35. Ukers, *All About Coffee*, p. 105; Weinberg and Bealer, *The World of Caffeine*, p. 181.
36. Marr, *The Cultural Roots of American Islamicism*, p. 3.
37. Ukers, *All About Coffee*, pp. 108–109.
38. Ibid.
39. Ibid., pp. 116–117.
40. Ibid.
41. By the turn of the 18th century, the United States was also a nation of sherbet drinkers—people who loved the beverage that was sweetened with fruit and stirred into a tempting concoction. This drink also originated in the Muslim world, which John Smith realized during his captivity by the Ottomans. Smith would write that, among Ottoman drinks, sherbet was as good as coffee. The Arabic drink *sharba* spawned the Turkish sherbet that Smith saw, but Europeans also encountered *sharba* because of Arab Spain, whose Muslim rulers brought the drink with them. They also brought fruit with them to plant in the Iberian Peninsula. Before the Arabs' arrival in 711, Spain had a limited range of fruits and vegetables. Among those the Moors introduced: sugar cane, lemons, oranges, bananas, strawberries, watermelon, apricots, dates, and pomegranates. The first pomegranate in Spain came from Syria, as did the date palm that now flourishes in Spain, and which was brought to America in Spain's colonization. During their rule in Spain and Sicily, Muslims also introduced durum wheat (from which pasta is made) and rice (which resulted in Spanish paella). All these items were exported to New Spain, including what is now Mexico and the United States.
42. Dana Knight, "If Joint Isn't Jumpin', Offer More Than Java," *Indianapolis Star*, April 9, 2008. Leia Baez, "Serving Up a Hot Cup of Success," *Omaha World-Herald*, November 7, 2006.
43. See "Beduoin camp" image at http://exhibits.slpl.org/lpe/IndexOf Images.asp.
44. See www.mohistory.org/Fair/WF/HTML/Artifacts/#, which describes Jetta in the section titled "Gerhard Sisters' Photographs." The

sisters, Emme and Mamie Gerhard, took studio photos of several fair attendees from overseas, including Jetta.

45. Ray Doumar's recollection during the author's interview with him in September of 2007.

7 The Height of Orientalism

1. Fred Van Deventer, *Parade to Glory: The Story of the Shriners and Their Hospitals for Crippled Children*, New York: William Morrow & Co., 1959, pp. 35, 37.
2. Ibid., p. 46.
3. Ibid., pp. 93, 268.
4. Ibid., pp. 72, 78, 83–90.
5. Ibid., p. 82.
6. Jasper Ridley, *The Freemasons*, New York: Arcade Publishing, 2002, p. 4.
7. Ibid., p. 3.
8. Ibid., pp. 17–19.
9. Ibid., pp. 90–109. Names listed pp. 105, 108–109.
10. William D. Moore, *Masonic Temples: Freemasonry, Ritual Architecture, and Masculine Archetypes*, Knoxville: University of Tennessee Press, 2006, pp. 4–5.
11. Lawrence Gardner, *The Shadow of Solomon: The Lost Secret of the Freemasons Revealed*, Newburyport: MA: Weiser, 2007, pp. 122–123.
12. Sydney Hayden, *Washington and His Masonic Compeers*, New York: Masonic Publishing & Manufacturing Co., 1866, p. 160. The edition I used was the online edition available through the University of Michigan's Humanities Text Initiative at http://quod.lib.umich.edu/m/moagrp.
13. Ibid., pp. 85, 160.
14. Ridley, *The Freemasons*, pp. 19–20. See also Moore, *Masonic Temples*, pp. 2–3.
15. Moore, *Masonic Temples*, pp. 94, 106, 107. See also p. 34 of Van Deventer, *Parade to Glory*.
16. Van Deventer, *Parade to Glory*, pp. 44, 60, 97.
17. On p. 2 of *Shriner Primer: The Ultimate Guide*, a 21-page history and explanation of the Shriners that was mailed to me by the Shriners organization.
18. Van Deventer, *Parade to Glory*, p. 19.
19. Ibid., pp. 83–84.
20. William B. Melish, *The History of the Imperial Council, Ancient Arabic*

Order, Noble Mystic Shrine, published by the the Imperial Council of the Ancient Arabic Order of the Noble Mystic Shrine, 1921, p. 11.

21. Van Deventer, *Parade to Glory*, pp. 37–38.
22. Moore, *Masonic Temples*, p. 94.
23. Van Deventer, *Parade to Glory*, pp. 121, 123.
24. Ibid., p. 124.
25. Ibid., p. 121.
26. Ibid.
27. Ibid., p. 124.
28. Ibid., p. 128.
29. "Harding Gives Salaam at Shriners' Parade: President Is Greeted Familiarly by Masonic Club Members in Washington," *New York Times*, May 10, 1921, p. 3.
30. Van Deventer, *Parade to Glory*, p. 214.
31. Ibid.
32. Ibid., pp. 211, 215. See also Paul E. Bierley, *Hallelujah Trombone!*, New York: Carl Fischer, 2003, p. 68.
33. Van Deventer, *Parade to Glory*, p. 212. See also Bierley, *Hallelujah Trombone!*, p. 67.
34. *New York Times*, June 6, 1923, p. 1: "Harding Rebukes Menacing Groups; Hit at Klan Seen; He Denounces to Shriners 'Secret Conspiracy' as Contrasted to Fraternity, Warns of Danger to Nation. President Defends Brotherhoods for Laudable Objects—Wears the Fez of His Order. Reviews Parade of 25,000."
35. Ibid.
36. Ibid.
37. Melish, *The History of the Imperial Council*, p. 245.
38. Moore, *Masonic Temples*, p. 173.
39. Edward W. Said, *Orientalism*, New York: Vintage Books, 2003 (25th anniversary edition), pp. 47–48.
40. Van Deventer, *Parade to Glory*, p. 150.
41. Moore, *Masonic Temples*, pp. 114–117.
42. Gulzar Haider, "Muslim Space and the Practice of Architecture—A Personal Odyssey," from Chapter 1 of Barbara Daly Metcalf, ed., *Making Muslim Space in North America and Europe*, Berkeley: University of California Press, 1996, pp. 31–33.
43. John T. Woolley and Gerhard Peters, *The American Presidency Project* [online], Santa Barbara, CA: University of California (hosted), Gerhard Peters (database). Go to www.presidency.ucsb.edu/ws/?pid=25756.
44. Go to www.presidency.ucsb.edu/ws/?pid=14314.

45. Laurence Leamer, *Make-Believe: The Story of Nancy and Ronald Reagan*, New York: Harper & Row, 1983, p. 139.
46. "Invitation to the Waltz," *Time*, April 30, 1945. Seen online at www.time.com/time/magazine/article/0,9171,797428,00.html.
47. Gary Reinmuth, "Medinah Mixes History, Friendship," *Chicago Tribune*, August 9, 1999.
48. In the 25th anniversary edition of this 1978 book, Said (who died soon after the republication) said that old and new orientalism was anything that produced "distorted knowledge of the other." In the most obscene cases, orientalists do not even speak the language of the lands they are involved with, nor do they with to. Instead, Said wrote, these lands have some kind of booty that draws them there—whether the attraction is material or geographical wealth (why Napoleon invaded Egypt); a mysterious and exotic culture that can be codified (why British scholar William Jones, the "founder" of orientalism, fixated on India in the 1700s); a history that can be cherry-picked for literary gain (why Dante used the prophet Muhammad to evince some of the worst aspects of Hell); or some other aspect. In *Orientalism*, Said uses terms like "cultural hegemony" and "positional superiority" and "reductive images" to explain how orientalists "dehumanize" lands such as Egypt and Syria. Traditionally, and throughout Said's book, "the Orient" included the Middle East, though the term now would apply (when it is applied at all) to Asia. A bestseller for 30 years, *Orientalism* has been translated into 36 languages.
49. Van Deventer, *Parade to Glory*, pp. 99, 105.
50. Ibid., p. 8.
51. Mattias Gardell, *In the Name of Elijah Muhammad: Louis Farrakhan and the Nation of Islam*, Durham, NC: Duke University Press, 1996, p. 72.
52. *Shriner Primer*, p. 3.
53. Ibid., p. 13.

8 The Lasting Appeal of *The Arabian Nights* and the Bearded Mullah from Turkey

1. John Charles Lounsbury Fish, *Engineering Economics*, New York: McGraw-Hill, 1939, p. 107.
2. Adam Parker, "Muslim Poet Rumi Speaks to All Religions," *Post and Courier*, October 7, 2007.
3. From the Rumi poem "Folly," translated by A.J. Arberry, in *The Rubaiyat of Jalal al-din Rumi*, London: Emery Walker, 1949. The version I saw was online at www.rumi.org.uk/therubaiyat.htm.

4. Coleman Barks, *The Essential Rumi*, HarperSan Francisco, 1995, p. 123. For his first book of Rumi poems, *Open Secret*, Barks worked with John Moyne, who gets a "with" credit in *The Essential Rumi*, along with Arberry and Reynold Nicholson.
5. From the Rumi poem "Beyond Reason," in Arberry, *The Rubaiyat of Jalal al-din Rumi*. Available at www.rumi.org.uk/therubai yat.htm.
6. Barks, *The Essential Rumi*, p. 243.
7. Coleman Barks and John Moyne, *Open Secret*, Putney, VT: Threshold Books, 1984.
8. Cameron McWhirter, "Rumi & Barks: Two Poets, One Voice," *Atlanta Journal-Constitution*, December 9, 2007.
9. I interviewed Barks for a story published in the *San Francisco Chronicle*, "Poet Follows His Own Muse in Translating Sufi Mystic," on April 4, 2002.
10. Barks, *The Essential Rumi*, p. 196.
11. Silke Tudor, "Night Crawler," *SF Weekly*, December 24, 1997.
12. Patricia King, "A Persian Love Machine," *Newsweek*, December 21, 1998.
13. Robin Givhan, "Donna Karan Forecasts a Dark and Gloomy Fall; but Armani and Wang Provide a Glitz Blitz," *Washington Post*, April 6, 1998.
14. Stephen Kinzer, "Konya Journal: Festival of Rumi, Poet of Life's Dance," *New York Times*, December 29, 1998.
15. Sefik Can, *Fundamentals of Rumi's Thought: A Mevlevi Sufi Perspective*, translated by Zeki Saritoprak, Somerset, NJ: The Light, 2005, p. 121.
16. William Dalrymple, "What Goes Around . . . The Popularity in the US of Rumi, a 13th-Century Turkish Poet, is a Tragic Irony, as the Order of Sufi Dervishes He Founded Is Banned at Home," *The Guardian* (London), November 5, 2005.
17. Can, *Fundamentals of Rumi's Thought*, p. 161.
18. Ibid., p. 151.
19. Ibid., p. 150.
20. My phone interview with Jelaluddin was for an article in the *San Francisco Chronicle*, "Islamic Verses," that was published on February 6, 2005. My in-person interview with Jelaluddin took place in September of 2007 in Sausalito, California.
21. Barks, *The Essential Rumi*, pp. 178–180.
22. The first reference to sexual intercourse is on page 5 of *The Essential Rumi*. As far as I can tell, the first reference to "Muslim" or "Islam" is on page 246.

23. In *Rumi and Islam* (SkyLight Paths, 2004), author Ibrahim Gamard explains the Muslim references in Rumi's poems and stories, and why even Rumi's name in the West is misleading: During Rumi's lifetime, the area now called Turkey was known as "Rum"—a variation of "Rome," since the Anatolian Peninsula was for centuries ruled not by Muslims but by Greeks; Rumi, then, was known not only as Jalal al-Din Muhammad Balkhi (a last name indicating that Rumi was born near Balkh, Afghanistan) but as Jalal al-Din Muhammad al-Rumi (a last name indicating that Rumi lived in "Rum"). "Rumi has always been known in the East by the respectful title of Mawlana, which means 'our Master' in Arabic," writes Gamard (p. xviii). "Only in the West has he been known by the less respectful and less accurate name Rumi ('the Greek')."
24. Dorie Turner, Associated Press, "He Brings Mystic's Works to the West," September 24, 2006, published in *Houston Chronicle.*
25. Majid M. Naini, *Mysteries of the Universe and Rumi's Discoveries on the Majestic Path of Love*, Delray, FL: Universal Vision and Research, 2002.
26. Timothy Marr, *The Cultural Roots of American Islamicism*, New York: Cambridge University Press, 2006, p. 13.
27. Husain Haddawy, trans., *The Arabian Nights II: Sinbad and Other Popular Stories*, New York: W. W. Norton & Co., 1995, p. 136.
28. Robert Irwin, *The Arabian Nights: A Companion*, London: Allen Lane, 1994. As one example, Irwin points out that Melville's 1851 novel *Moby-Dick* (cited here in the 2003 Dover edition) is "enriched by covert embedded references to the *Nights*." Among them: Captain Ahab's prime harpoonist is a turbaned man named Fedallah. As much as he works with and counts on Fedallah, Ahab has mixed feeling about the man with the Muslim-sounding name. Fedallah is old, dark in complexion, and the leader of a people who supposedly pray to the Devil himself, but Fedallah is also a master of seafaring—a prophet from a faraway land who, in the words of the narrator in *Moby-Dick*, is "such a creature as civilized, domestic people in the temperate zone only see in their dreams, and that but dimly; but the like of whom now and then glides among the unchanging Asiatic communities, especially the Oriental isles to the east of the continent" (p. 192).
29. Irwin, *The Arabian Nights: A Companion*, p. 48.
30. The different versions of *The Arabian Nights* have different spellings for King Shahrayar and Shahrazad, whose name is often spelled Scheherazade. For the spellings, I am using those from *The Arabian Nights*, translated by Husain Haddawy, New York: W. W. Norton & Co.,

1990, which is based on a Syrian manuscript of the *Nights* that was edited by Muhsin Mahdi.

31. Irwin, *The Arabian Nights: A Companion*, p. 46.
32. Ibid., p. 2.
33. Ibid.
34. Ibid., pp. 4, 81.
35. Ibid., p. 19.
36. Sir Richard F. Burton, trans., *The Arabian Nights: Tales from a Thousand and One Nights*, republished by New York: The Modern Library, 2001.
37. Haddawy, *The Arabian Nights*, p. ix.
38. Mina Marefat, "Wright's Baghdad," in Anthony Alofsin, ed., *Frank Lloyd Wright: Europe and Beyond*, Berkeley: University of California Press, 1999, p. 191.
39. Ibid., p. 192.
40. Ibid., p. 200.
41. Ibid., p. 201.
42. Ibid., p. 199.
43. Stephen Prickett, *Victorian Fantasy*, Waco, TX: Baylor University Press, 2005, p. 211.
44. "The Story of Taj-El-Mulook," in *The Thousand and One Nights*, reworked by Edward William Lane, Edward Stanley Poole, and William Harvey, London: Routledge, Warne, and Routledge, 1865), p. 470.
45. Sir Thomas Arnold and Alfred Guillaume, eds., *The Legacy of Islam*, Oxford: Clarendon Press, 1931, p. 186.
46. Ira Marvin Lapidus, *A History of Islamic Societies*, New York: Cambridge University Press, 2002, p. 127.
47. Arberry, *The Rubaiyat of Jalal al-din Rumi*, online at www.rumi.org.uk/therubaiyat.htm.
48. Barks, *The Essential Rumi*, p. 292.

9 The Trippy Sounds of the '60s

1. Deb Hopewell, "Powered into 'Pulp': Music Inspired a Movie," *San Jose Mercury*, November 24, 1995.
2. Steve Holgate, "Guitarist Dick Dale Brought Arabic Folk Song to Surf Music," *Washington File* (State Department), September 14, 2006. The story quotes Dale as saying he learned to play a drum called a "tarabaki," which is the journalist's mistranslation of *derbeki*, which is another name for the *doumbek* drum.

3. "Miserlou" means "The Egyptian": Ibid, plus author's interview with Dale. "Miserlou" is Turkish: Interview with Dwight Reynolds, professor of Arabic Learning and Literature, Univeristy of California at Santa Barbara.
4. George Baramki Azar, "The Sultan of Surf," *Saudi Aramco World*, March–April 1998. See also "Dick Dale and Yale Strom on 'Miserlou'," National Public Radio, January 8, 2006, Liane Hansen anchor.
5. "Dick Dale and Yale Strom on 'Miserlou'."
6. John Armstrong, "Dick Dale Rides New Wave," *Vancouver Sun*, July 20, 1993. See also www.dickdale.com/history.html.
7. "Dick Dale and Yale Strom on 'Miserlou'."
8. Mikel Toombs, "Surf Guitar King Dick Dale Is Still Proud to Be Loud," *San Diego Union-Tribune*, December 30, 1999. See also Beth Sager, "Dick Dale Surfs into the City," *Times-Picayune*, December 17, 1998.
9. Faisal as a fan of the Dead: see p. 9 of the liner notes of the 2006 Rhino Records re-release of *Blues for Allah*. For Hunter's description of Faisal: Ibid.
10. Roger Levesque, "African Virtuosos Create Musical Fusions: Ancient Music Blends with Western Influences," *Edmonton Journal*, January 22, 2004.
11. Plant was interviewed by Palmer for the 1990 Led Zeppelin CD retrospective *Led Zeppelin Boxed Set, Vol. 1.* See www.led-zeppelin.org/reference/discography/boxed_set_1_essay3.php.
12. For the Dylan interview, see www.playboy.com/blog/2006/09/me-and-bobby-d.html and www.interferenza.com/bcs/interw/play78.htm.
13. Dick Dale, The Doors, Led Zeppelin, The Rolling Stones, James Brown, the B-52s ("Rock Lobster" is drenched in Arabic influence), and Jefferson Airplane are the biggest examples of Arab music's timeless reach, but there are scores of smaller examples that have gone under the radar for decades. In 1966, a group called the Modern Folk Quartet released a song, "Nigh Time Girl," that starts out with a full-fledged Arabic edge before giving away to more traditional folk orchestration. Singer Jerry Yester says that the number "absolutely" borrows from Arabic music, telling me that the Modern Folk Quartet, "when it became a rock band in 1965 . . . we started experimenting with what we were calling 'Raga Rock,' but it was basically a Middle Eastern influence. During the folk days, and especially during the psychedelic period (of the 1960s), a lot of people were listening to Middle Eastern music. The Beatles used a sitar, but we wanted to take

it a lot further than that." Rhino Records preserved "Night Time Girl" on a collection of '60s folk music called *Folk Rock: Nuggets, Volume 10,* which has 14 songs, including The Byrds' "Mr. Tambourine Man," The Turtles' "It Ain't Me Babe," and Scott McKenzie's "San Francisco (Be Sure to Wear Flowers in Your Hair)." On the album is another song with Arabic influence: Jake Holmes's "Dazed and Confused," which uses Arabic-sounding instrumentation to accentuate lyrics describing a person in crisis. Yester says Arabic music is easily adaptable to folk, rock, and pop music. The Modern Folk Quartet used a Greek, lutelike bouzouki—and even a tambourine—to imitate Arabic sounds. "The bouzouki," Yester told me, "is so easily adapted to any kind of Middle Eastern music, and so is the banjo, actually, because of the way it's tuned, and when it's used with minor tunings, it really has a Middle Eastern sound."

14. Nicholas Cook and Anthony Pople, *The Cambridge History of Twentieth-Century Music,* Cambridge, UK: Cambridge University Press, 2004, p. 434.

10 East Meets West in Memphis

1. Patricia Jobe Pierce, *The Ultimate Elvis*, New York: Simon & Schuster, 1994, pp. 338–351.
2. June Juanico, *Elvis in the Twilight of Memory*, New York: Arcade, 1997, pp. 13–20.
3. Ibid., p. 105.
4. Ibid., p. 107.
5. Kahlil Gibran, *The Prophet*, New York: Alfred A. Knopf, 2003, p. 12.
6. Juanico, *Elvis in the Twilight of Memory*, p. 108.
7. Ibid., p. 250.
8. Ron Rosenbaum, "Among the Believers," *New York Times Magazine*, September 24, 1995.
9. Judith Colp, "Prophet and Loss," *Washington Times*, April 11, 1991. See also Rita Beamish, "Bush Dedicates Gibran Memorial, Pushes for Mideast Peace," Associated Press, May 24, 1991.
10. Colp, "Prophet and Loss."
11. Joan Acocella, "Prophet Motive," *The New Yorker*, January 7, 2008.
12. Chris Chrystal, "Maureen Reagan Weds Law Clerk," United Press International, April 25, 1981.
13. David Tarrant, "Reviews of Audio-Book Releases," *Dallas Morning News*, November 21, 1996.

14. Colp, "Prophet and Loss." See also Larry Luxner, "A Garden for Gibran," *Saudi Aramco World*, March–April 1990; and www.patriciam.com/OLD/Flip_Wilson_Kahlil_Gibran.htm.
15. Beamish, "Bush Dedicates Gibran Memorial."
16. Suheil Bushrui and Joe Jenkins, *Kahlil Gibran: Man and Poet*, Oxford, UK: Oneworld, 1998, p. 165.
17. Jean Gibran and Kahlil Gibran, *Kahlil Gibran: His Life and World*, New York: Interlink, 1991 (first published in 1974), p. 312.
18. Gibran, *The Prophet*, p. 6.
19. Bushrui and Jenkins, *Kahlil Gibran: Man and Poet*, p. 215.
20. Gibran, *The Prophet*, p. 75.
21. Bushrui and Jenkins, *Kahlil Gibran: Man and Poet*, p. 231.
22. Gibran, *The Prophet*, p. 44.
23. Bushrui and Jenkins, *Kahlil Gibran: Man and Poet*, p. 232.
24. Ibid., p. 231.
25. Ibid., p. 9.
26. Ibid., p. 191.
27. Ibid., p. 215.
28. Ibid., p. 231.
29. Gibran and Gibran, *Kahlil Gibran: His Life and World*, p. 22. See also Bushrui and Jenkins, *Kahlil Gibran: Man and Poet*, pp. 24, 37.
30. Charles L. Ponce de Leon, *Fortunate Son: The Life of Elvis Presley*, New York: Hill & Wang, 2006, p. 30.
31. Bushrui and Jenkins, *Kahlil Gibran: Man and Poet*, pp. 43, 62.
32. Ponce de Leon, *Fortunate Son*, p. 4.
33. Gibran and Gibran, *Kahlil Gibran: His Life and World*, pp. 388, 389.
34. Acocella, "Prophet Motive."
35. See the University of Memphis website, www.uc.memphis.edu/univ3581_S06.htm. The public schools are Kahlil Gibran International Academy in New York and the Kahlil Gibran School in Yonkers.
36. Elizabeth Kelleher, "Kahlil Gibran Day Celebrated in Boston," *Washington File* (State Department), October 27, 2004.
37. Alanna Nash, with Billy Smith, Marty Lacker, and Lamar Fike, *Elvis Aaron Presley: Revelations from the Memphis Mafia*, New York: HarperCollins, 1995, p. 338.
38. Jonathan Goldstein and Max Wallace, *Schmelvis: In Search of Elvis Presley's Jewish Roots*, Toronto: ECW Press, 2002, p. 15.
39. Larry Geller and Joel Spector, *If I Can Dream: Elvis' Own Story*, New York: Simon & Schuster, 1989, p. 158. The watch also flashed a Christian cross.

40. Bill Gladstone, "Trying to Put a Yarmulke on the King of Rock and Roll," *Forward*, April 19, 2002. See also John D. Spaulding, "The Kosher King: In Search of Elvis Presley's Jewish Roots," Beliefnet: www.beliefnet.com/story/107/story_10778.html.
41. Geller and Spector, *If I Can Dream*, p. 327. See also Connie Kirchberg and Marc Hendricks, *Elvis Presley, Richard Nixon, and the American Dream*, Jefferson, NC: McFarland, 1999, p. 85.
42. Geller and Spector, *If I Can Dream*, p. 326.
43. Ibid., p. 327.
44. Peter Guralnick, *Careless Love: The Unmasking of Elvis Presley*, Boston: Little Brown & Co., 1999, pp. 616–617. See also Pierce, *The Ultimate Elvis*, p. 287.
45. Pierce, *The Ultimate Elvis*, p. 287.
46. Ibid., p. 293.
47. Ibid., p. 295.
48. Ibid., p. 293.
49. Gibran, *The Prophet*, pp. 87–88.
50. Geller and Spector, *If I Can Dream*, p. 316.
51. Nash et al., *Elvis Aaron Presley*, pp. 333–344, 372–374, 414–415. On p. 340 is noted that Lacker "couldn't stomach" Presley's spiritual and religious interests. See also Guralnick, *Careless Love*, pp. 242–243.
52. Geller and Spector, *If I Can Dream*, p. 260.
53. Ibid., p. 83.
54. Ibid., p. 181.
55. Guralnick, *Careless Love*, p. 136.
56. Clyde Francis Lytle, ed., *Leaves of Gold*, Williamsport, PA: Coslett, 1948, p. 73.
57. Ibid., p. 30.
58. Ibid., p. 112.
59. Bobbie Ann Mason, *Elvis Presley*, New York: Viking, 2002, p. 97.
60. Geller and Spector, *If I Can Dream*, pp. 127, 180–181, 238–239.
61. Ibid., pp. 100, 125, 156. See also Geller and Spector, *If I Can Dream*, p. 29, and Pierce, *The Ultimate Elvis*, p. 64.
62. Michael Saba, "How Elvis Fought Racism, Ethnic Discrimination," *Arab News*, August 24, 2007. The article can be seen at www.arabnews.com/?page=7§ion=0&article=100362&d=24&m=8&y=2007.
63. During his life, Presley befriended several Arab Americans, including actor Danny Thomas, who (like Presley) lived in Memphis and loved Gibran's *The Prophet*. Presley's relationship with Thomas revolved around Thomas's involvement with St. Jude Children's Re-

search Hospital, the Memphis medical facility that Presley supported through years of donations and performances (for more information, see St. Jude's web site, www.stjude.org, especially the 2003 article "St. Jude's Remembers Elvis"). In a convergence of history and culture, Thomas's parents were from Bsharri, Lebanon—the same hilltop town where Gibran lived for years before coming to America. A Maronite Christian who (like Gibran) believed in religious bipartisanship, Thomas was proud of his Arab roots, even though he picked a stage name that distanced himself from his birth name of Amos Alphonsus Muzyad Yaqoob. "He who denies his heritage has no heritage," was a message—in Arabic and English—that Thomas chose to inscribe above an inner archway of St. Jude's Danny Thomas/ALSAC Pavilion. The pavilion, located on the grounds of the Memphis hospital, is a shimmering tribute to Arab culture—both Christian and Muslim. Its magnificent dome, for example, is modeled after the Dome of the Rock, the seventh-century Jerusalem shrine that is the oldest extant Islamic building in the world. Arabic calligraphy adorns multiple walls of the pavilion. A large map in a display case details the Arab cities from which the families of past St. Jude officials emanated. (The acronym for St. Jude's fundraising arm, ALSAC, stands for the American Lebanese Syrian Associated Charities.) Adjoining the pavilion, in a garden full of azaleas, junipers, and elms, is a crypt that is the final resting spot for Thomas and his wife. An excerpt from *The Prophet* overlooks the burial ground. Written in gold, and taken from the book's last chapter, in which Almustafa tells the Orphalese people that, after death, his spirit will live on and even be reborn, the excerpt reads:

> *Forget not that I shall come back to you.*
> *A little while, and my longing shall gather dust and foam for another body.*
> *A little while, a moment of rest upon the wind, and another woman shall bear me.*
> —Kahlil Gibran

The Danny Thomas/ALSAC Pavilion is just a short drive from Graceland, where Presley was also laid to rest in a garden. For more on Thomas and this pavilion, see Jerry Markon, "Entertainer to Be Buried at Pavilion," *The Commercial Appeal* (Memphis), February 7, 1991.

64. Juanico, *Elvis in the Twilight of Memory*, p. 196; Ponce de Leon, *Fortu-*

nate Son, p. 98; Geller and Spector, *If I Can Dream*, pp. 80, 82, 156, 171, 233.

65. Geller and Spector, *If I Can Dream*, p. 114.
66. Ibid., p. 282.
67. Ibid., p. 285.

11 Islam and the World Trade Center

1. The center was the McGregor Memorial Conference Center at Wayne State University, which in 1959 won the first honor award of the American Institute of Architects. See Vivian M. Baulch, "Minoru Yamasaki, World-Class Architect," *Detroit News*, August 14, 1998.
2. Minoru Yamasaki, *A Life in Architecture*, New York: Art Media Resources, 1979, pp. 59–63.
3. Yamasaki was interviewed in August of 1959 by Virginia Harriman. The interview has been archived by the Smithsonian and can be read at www.aaa.si.edu/collections/oralhistories/transcripts/yamasa59.htm.
4. Eric Darton, *Divided We Stand*, New York: Basic Books, 1999, p. 114.
5. Ada Louise Huxtable, "What's Your Favorite Building?" *New York Times*, May 21, 1961.
6. John Seabrook, "The Tower Builder; Why Did the World Trade Center Buildings Fall When They Did?" *The New Yorker*, November 19, 2001. See also Darton, *Divided We Stand*, p. 117.
7. Yamasaki, *A Life in Architecture*, p. 114.
8. Ibid., p. 115.
9. Architect Laurie Kerr wrote this in her article "The Mosque to Commerce: Bin Laden's Special Complaint with the World Trade Center," *Slate Magazine*, December 28, 2001. See www.slate.com/?id=2060207.
10. On p. 183 of his 2006 book *The Unavoidable Surgery* (Trafford Publishing), Mati Alon writes that the synagogue "is far from being modest and instead resembles a Taj Mahal or a Bahaist temple. The Jewish community in Glencoe, a northern suburb of Chicago, or elsewhere, should have been satisfied with a less fancy building, and the rest of the money should have been donated as charity to orphanages, schools, nursing homes, summer camps, Israel, and so on. A building like this can only cause jealousy, envy, and anti-Semitism."
11. "The Road to Xanadu," *Time*, January 18, 1963. See www.time.com/time/magazine/article/0,9171,874696-1,00.html
12. Ibid.

13. James Glanz and Eric Lipton, *City in the Sky: The Rise and Fall of the World Trade Center*, New York: Times Books, 2003, p. 90.
14. Philip Nobel, *Sixteen Acres: Architecture and the Outrageous Struggle for the Future of Ground Zero*, New York: Metropolitan Books, 2004, p. 23.
15. Glanz and Lipton, *City in the Sky*, p. 90.
16. "The Road to Xanadu."
17. Ibid.
18. Ibid.
19. Glanz and Lipton, *City in the Sky*, p. 91.
20. "The Road to Xanadu."
21. Baulch, "Minoru Yamasaki, World-Class Architect."
22. "The Road to Xanadu."
23. Ibid.
24. Ibid.
25. Ibid.
26. Ibid. The rival architect who was critical of Yamasaki and his McGregor Center was Gordon Bunshaft of Skidmore, Owings, and Merrill.
27. Glanz and Lipton, *City in the Sky*, p. 100.
28. Ibid, p. 101.
29. Ibid. p. 104.
30. Ibid., p. 115.
31. Ibid., p. 112.
32. Yamasaki, *A Life in Architecture*, p. 175.
33. "The Mosque to Commerce."
34. See www.sama.gov.sa/nc/en_fv.gif.
35. "Third Saudi Airport Fit for Kings," *Engineering News-Record*, December 19, 1985. See also "Saudi Arabia: Airport Signs," *MidEast Markets*, November 24, 1986.
36. "Third Saudi Airport Fit for Kings."
37. The pavilion can be seen online at www.the-saudi.net/kfia/kfia_king_pavilion.htm.
38. Yahya Aburadas Mohammed Sofian and Mohammed Al-Yami, "King Fahd International Airport: Link Between East and West," *Riyadh Daily*, May 14, 1999. The mosque can be seen online at www.the-saudi.net/kfia.
39. Yamasaki, *A Life in Architecture*, p. 175.
40. Dario Fernandez-Florez, *The Spanish Heritage in the United States*, Madrid: Publicaciones Espanolas, 1965, p. 287. Images of the old Madi-

son Square Garden's minaret-like tower can be seen online at www .nyc-archi tecture.com/GON/GON016.htm.

41. "St. Gaudens's Diana Homeless on May 1," *New York Times*, November 26, 1924.
42. "Diana and Her Tower Find a Home at Last with N.Y. University," *New York Times*, April 28, 1925.
43. Fernandez-Florez, *The Spanish Heritage in the United States*, p. 287.
44. The college boasts of its buildings having Moorish influence at its web site: www.citadel.edu/r3/about/tour/m/duckett.shtml.
45. Jean Bony, *French Gothic Architecture of the 12th and 13th Centuries*, Berkeley: University of California Press, 1983, pp. 17–19.
46. "The Road to Xanadu."
47. Yamasaki, *A Life in Architecture*, p. 114.
48. Angus Kress Gillespie, *Twin Towers: The Life of New York City's World Trade Center*, Brunswick, NJ: Rutgers University Press, 2001, p. 176.
49. William Armbruster, "Egyptian Apparel Makers Taking Aim at US Market," *Journal of Commerce*, September 26, 1989.
50. "Egypt Exporters Sound Alarm Bells over Textile Industry," Agence France-Press, published in *Arab-American Business*, December 2006/ January 2007, p. 24.
51. For corn as the biggest U.S. export to Egypt, see www.census.gov/ foreign-trade/statistics/product/enduse/exports/c7290.html.
52. Yamasaki, *A Life in Architecture*, p. 112.

12 Fashion, Tattoos, and Arabic Calligraphy

1. See www.murrysville.com/comm_dir_churches.html.
2. Mayor Somers' comments are taken from her "Welcome to Murrysville" greeting, posted on the community's web site at www.murrys ville.com/welcome.html.
3. "The Ultimate Hollywood Trivia Guide," *Daily Mail* (London), December 26, 2007. See also Michael Kane and Lindsay Powers, "Now, Tat's Hot! Jolie's Sexy Secrets Hidden in Body Art," *New York Post*, June 5, 2005.
4. Paula Brook, "More Skin, Less Ink: Tattoos Are Trendy but Permanence Is Passe, Thanks to Laser Removal," *Vancouver Sun*, October 16, 2006.
5. Jonathan Van Meter, "Learning to Fly: Angelina Jolie Has Become a Hollywood Powerhouse, Moved to England, Embraced Motherhood, and Won an Award for Her Tireless Work as a UN Goodwill Ambassador, Which Regularly Takes Her to Some of the Most Dangerous

Places in the World," *Vogue*, March 2004, which can be seen online at www.style.com/vogue/feature/022304. See also "Angelina's Tattoos," *UN Forum*, July 15, 2005, which can be seen online at www.unforum.com/UNinsiderJul05.htm, and Debbie Schlussel, "Mr. & Mrs. Smith, Please Don't Go to Washington—Angelina Jolie's and Brad Pitt's Nutty Politics," June 9, 2005, posted at www.debbieschlussel.com.

6. "Mr. & Mrs. Smith, Please Don't Go to Washington."
7. Maytha, "Arabina—Whoops! I mean 'Angelina'—Jolie Visits Iraqi Refugee Camps in Syria," www.kabobfest.com, September 15, 2007. See the blog entry online at www.kabobfest.com/2007/09/arabina-whoops-i-mean-angelina-jolie.html.
8. "Muslim Postage Stamp," *Arab American News*, September 15–17, 2007.
9. Raoul V. Mowatt, "Muslims Celebrate Stamp of Approval," *Chicago Tribune*, September 2, 2001.
10. Richard Carr, "Islam Joins 'Holiday Celebrations' Series," *Fort Lauderdale Sun-Sentinel*, August 26, 2001.
11. Sylvia Moreno, "Stamp Backlash Worries Muslims; Tribute to Islamic Holidays Scorned by Collectors' Newsletter, Conservative Group," *Washington Post*, November 24, 2001.
12. Clay Lambert, "Religious Stamps Spark Disapproval; Church and State Issues Surfaces in Debate," *Palm Beach Post*, November 27, 2001.
13. Betsy Wright, "Muslim Postage Stamp Gets Little Notice," *Virginia Pilot*, December 16, 2001.
14. Anchor tattoo: Toby Harnden, "Behind the Zarqawi Myth," *Daily Telegraph* (London), October 23, 2004. Bedouin tattoos: Dan Murphy, "Going After Iraq's Most Wanted Man," *Christian Science Monitor*, September 21, 2004.
15. Mary Anne Weaver, "The Short, Violent Life of Abu Musab al-Zaqarwi," *The Atlantic*, July 2006.
16. Taken from the lawsuit that Rasheed filed against Saddam Hussein in 2003. Part of the suit can be seen online at www.legalcasedocs.com/120/255/212.html.
17. "Democrats Criticize Bush's Tone," Times Wires, *St. Petersburg Times*, July 4, 2003.
18. David M. Brown, "Iraqis Here: Saddam's Death Is 'Justice,'" *Pittsburgh Tribune Review*, December 30, 2006.
19. Suzy Menkes, "The New Sobriety: Covering Up the Body," *International Herald Tribune*, February 28, 2006.

20. Ibid.
21. Renata Espinosa, "Dior Boards Marrakesh Express for Cruise Collection," Fashion Wire Daily, published in *San Francisco Examiner*, May 17, 2007. It's Espinosa who describes Galliano's collection as "an endless parade of *souk* looks."
22. At the opposite end of the fashion scale is the "burqini," a conservative beachware garment that has been purchased by many Americans. Created by Aheda Zanetti, a Lebanese-Australian who follows Islamic tenets of modesty, the swimsuit combines aspects of the *burqa* and the bikini. The result: a sleek, colorful, head-to-toe garment that contours to women's bodies, leaves the face, hands and feet exposed, and provides them with movement for activities or just lounging. Zanetti developed the Burqini in 2007, after which came sales around the world—and flattering mentions in *Time* magazine ("Modest beachware for Muslim women is taking off with secular swimmers too"), the *New York Times*, the *Chicago Tribune*, and Condé Nast's *Allure* magazine. An American woman who identified herself as "Katharina—United States," wrote on Zanetti's testimonial page (www.ahiida.com/index.php?a=testimonials) that, "As an Orthodox Christian, I was struggling with my need to exercise and enjoy the water at a lake, etc., but feel comfortable and modest. I had heard about suits that were modest, but they did not cover the legs and arms totally so I happened upon your website and am thrilled! The suit is fashionable, comfortable and I feel decent in it. I will recommend it to my female friends who also are looking for modest swimwear."
23. Saks Fifth Avenue catalog, spring of 2005, 162 pages, titled "Into the Mystic."
24. Ibid., p. 28.
25. Ibid., p. 90.
26. Ibid., pp. 42–43.
27. Ibid., p. 92.
28. Ibid., p. 3.
29. Ibid.
30. William Meade Stith Rasmussen and Robert S. Tilton, *George Washington*, Charlottesville: University of Virginia Press, 1999, p. 26.
31. "U.S. Accounts for 22 Percent of Iran's Persian Carpet Exports," *Asia Pulse*, July 19, 2006.
32. Carol Rosenberg, "A Kinder and Gentler Room to Question Terror Suspects?" *Miami Herald*, February 20, 2006.
33. Schuyler V.R. Cammann, "Religious Symbolism in Persian Art," *History of Religions*, Vol. 15, No. 3 (February 1976), p. 195.

34. Ibid., p. 197.
35. Ibid.
36. Ibid., p. 201.
37. Ibid.
38. P.R.J. Ford, *Oriental Carpet Design*, London: Thames & Hudson, 2002, p. 38.
39. Cammann, "Religious Symbolism in Persian Art," p. 195.
40. "The Pope Is Laid to Rest," CNN, Live coverage of the papal funeral, April 8, 2005.
41. "Iran Boasts That Pope's Coffin Rested on Persian Carpet," Agence France-Presse, April 10, 2005.
42. Front Page, *New York Times*, April 9, 2005. The photo was by Filippo Monteforte/Agence France-Presse—Getty Images.
43. Maria Rosa Menocal, *Ornament of the World: How Muslims, Jews, and Christians Created a Culture of Tolerance in Medieval Spain*, New York: Back Bay Books, 2002, p. 273.
44. Rosamond E. Mack, *Bazaar to Piazza: Islamic Trade and Italian Art, 1300–1600*, Berkeley: University of California Press, 2001, p. 2. See also Deborah Howard, *Venice and the East: The Impact of the Islamic World on Venetian Architecture 1100–1500*, Yale University Press, 2000, p. 174. As Howard notes, "In the early 14th century, the Venetians were walking an ideological tightrope, engaging in mutual exchanges of diplomatic flattery with the Mamluk sultans while struggling with the Papacy over the right to trade with the Islamic world, yet mourning the demise of the Crusader colonies."

13 Arabs and Muslims in the United States

1. Samuel P. Huntington, *The Clash of Civilizations and the Remaking of World Order*, New York: Touchstone, 1996, p. 318.
2. Joe Richi Dodge, at the corner of Lapham and Michigan Avenue in central Dearborn. Richi's Arabic welcome sign is a neon one that hangs prominently in the window of his dealership.
3. Exhibit featuring Anna Yousef is on the second floor of the Arab American National Museum.
4. Biographical information on Khalil Saad can be seen at www.encyclopedia-titanica.org/biography/1177. Biographical information on Ahmed can be seen at www.encyclopedia-titanica.org/biography/626.
5. For Yousef's account, go to www.authorhouse.com/BookStore/ItemDetail~bookid~36607.aspx.

6. Alejandro Bodipo-Memba, "Muslims Big Player in American Economy," *Detroit Free Press*. May 6, 2007. Reprinted in the *Houston Chronicle*, p. B6.
7. Jamie Farr explains his father's and grandfather's stories at www.lebanesemonthly.com/magazines/lebanese_monthly_volume-01_issue-06.pdf.
8. George N. Atiyeh, ed., *Arab and American Cultures*, Washington, DC: American Enterprise Institute for Public Policy Research, 1977. The conference took place at the Madison Hotel and the Library of Congress on September 22 and 23, 1976.
9. Atiyeh, *Arab and American Cultures*, pp. 171–172.
10. Ibid., p. 172.
11. Mona Megalli, "Arab Americans Seek Political Voice," United Press International, November 3, 1984.
12. David Lamb, "Loyalty Questioned; U.S. Arabs Close Ranks Over Bias," *Los Angeles Times*, March 13, 1987.
13. Paul Houston, "Civil Rights Group Says Anti-Arab Sentiment Is Increasing," *Los Angeles Times*, December 23, 1990.
14. Unbylined article, "Now We're Consumed With Managing Change and Decline," *Washington Post*, December 16, 1979. See "A Personal Look Back at the Iranian Hostage Crisis," *Weekend Edition*, National Public Radio, Scott Simon, host, November 3, 2007. William Morrissey, Associated Press, November 11, 1979. Dave Goldberg, Associated Press, January 14, 1982.
15. "As Americans Vent Anger at Iranians," *U. S. News & World Report*, December 10, 1979.
16. Ibid.
17. Ibid.
18. Charlotte Porter, Associated Press, November 12, 1979.
19. Ibid.
20. Charlotte Porter, Associated Press, November 19, 1979.
21. Edward M. Eveld and Lynn Franey, "Religious Group Wants KCMO 710-AM to Drop Michael Savage's Program," *Kansas City Star*, May 19, 2008.
22. Felicia R. Lee, "Black Migration, Both Slave and Free," *New York Times*, February 2, 2005. Elizabeth Grieco, "The African Foreign Born in the United States," Migration Policy Institute, September 2004; available online at www.migrationinformation.org. "African Immigration: The Numbers," *In Motion: The African-American Migration Experience;* see www.inmotionaame.org.
23. Grieco, "The African Foreign Born in the United States."

24. "African Immigration: Religious Communities," *In Motion: The African-American Migration Experience;* see www.inmotionaame.org.
25. Natalia Antelava, "A Different Kind of Islam in NYC," United Press International, July 30, 2002.
26. Ibid.
27. From the 2007 web site of the Amadou Diallo Foundation, which has since been changed to www.amadoudiallofoundationinc.com. The information from my 2007 research can be found online at http://web.archive.org/web/20070404092344/www.amadoudiallofoundation.org/lifehistory.html.
28. Ibid.
29. Mitra Kalita, "America's Ordeal: He Lived His Dreams Through His Children," *Newsday*, October 17, 2001.
30. Anthony DePalma, Aaron Donovan, Jan Hoffman, Tarannum Kamlani, Tina Kelley, N.R. Kleinfield, Melena Z. Ryzik, and Barbara Stewart, "Portraits of Grief: The Victims; Family Bike Rides, Wise Sayings, Snorkeling and a Red Roadster," *New York Times*, June 16, 2002.
31. Ibid.
32. "Family, Friends Remember Loved Ones," September 11, 2002. The story can be seen online at www.foxnews.com/story/0,2933,62663,00.html.
33. Posting found on www.september11victims.com, a web site that was active at the time of my research.
34. Ibid.
35. Ibid.
36. See www.9-11heroes.us/v/Taimour_Firaz_Khan.php.
37. Sherri Day, Anthony DePalma, Jonathan Fuerbringer, Kenneth N. Gilpin, Constance L. Hays, Lynette Holloway, Tina Kelley, and Melena Z. Ryzik, "A Loving Family, a Solid Best Friend, a Bride-to-Be, an Ardent Traveler," *New York Times,* February 10, 2002.
38. Aaron Donovan, Jan Hoffman, Tina Kelley, N.R. Kleinfield, and Barbara Stewart, "Portraits of Grief: The Victims; Literary Cook, Happy New Yorker, Quiet Helper, Proud Immigrant," *New York Times,* June 30, 2002.
39. Somini Sengupta, "A Nation Challenged: Immigrants; Lifelines to Home, Severed in an Instant," *New York Times*, September 23, 2001.
40. See p. 64 of www.co.rockland.ny.us/WTC/Remembers.pdf.
41. Atiyeh, *Arab and American Cultures*, pp. 71–72.

Index